THE HOME ENTERTAINER

Entertaining friends, making them feel at home, and making them want to come again is a gift—but a gift that can be acquired.

THE HOME ENTERTAINER

EDITED BY
SID G. HEDGES

ODHAMS PRESS LIMITED
LONG ACRE, LONDON, W.C.2

Copyright
G.1139

*Made and Printed in Great Britain
by Odhams (Watford) Ltd., Watford*

CONTENTS

A few conjuring tricks—even the simplest ones anybody can learn to do—are always a success at a party.

CHAPTER 1

THE ART OF
SUCCESSFUL ENTERTAINING

THERE are few sources of pleasure greater than entertaining friends. It does not much matter whether your home is large or small, whether you have a maid to help you or not; your hospitality can still be charming and in good taste, and need not involve you in any great expense. The success of all entertainment —dinners, suppers, parties and dances, depends not on elaborateness and heavy expenditure, but on imagination and careful planning.

The art of successful entertaining can be acquired only by practice. But a little friendly assistance at the start can do a great deal to help you. This is what this book sets out to do, starting in the first chapter with the basic essentials—inviting guests, food and drink and decoration.

The first thing to do before you start any entertaining is to settle what type of entertainment best suits your abilities, your home, your purse, and then to concentrate mainly on that. The best hostesses generally have a reputation among their friends for doing one particular thing unusually well. You may have a large polished floor—no common thing in these days—which is well adapted for dancing. Your garden may be picturesque and private. You may be a born games leader, with a genius for running indoor games. Or you may revel in preparing tasty suppers with dainty and original menus. Whichever way your talent and opportunity lie, exploit them fully. If you are conscious of no special ability try various types of party to find which your friends enjoy most.

WELL-PREPARED INFORMALITY

Remember that informality is the keynote of most modern entertaining. This does not, however, mean that lack of preparation and general slovenliness are any more permissible.

Consider carefully what guests to invite on any given occasion. Sometimes it is well to aim at similarity in their tastes, ages, and outlook; at others variety of interests is preferable. Be sure that they are likely to get on together in the circumstances in which they will meet. For a formal dinner party the placing of guests is of great importance, and every one should have congenial neighbours; but if food is taken from a buffet or the party is informal, less arrangement is necessary, and too much organization may easily spoil the party.

Take care that every one knows every one else as soon as possible. Don't just assume that they do; be sure. And watch out for shy

7

Fig. 1. Rolled sandwiches look attractive.

and nervous people, sparing no pains to make them feel at home.

There are two broad divisions of a hostess's responsibilities—before her guests arrive, and after. A good working maxim is: before the guests arrive, give all your attention to the arrangements; when the guests have arrived, give all your attention to *them*.

Too much trouble cannot be taken over the advance arrangements. If, for instance, you have maids to help you, rehearse them in every part of their duty. Let them actually try out the reception of guests; the taking of wraps and coats; the placing of chairs for the meal; the ushering of people in or out of a room; the handing round of dishes; the lighting of cigarettes; the serving of coffee, or whatever other needs you anticipate. For such rehearsals you can act as guest. Arrange cooking, serving, everything, in fullest detail. Leave nothing to chance, and your party will run smoothly.

HOW TO MAKE GUESTS FEEL AT HOME

Then when the guests arrive forget all these arrangements. It is too late, anyhow, to alter them now, or to make good things that may have been forgotten. Concentrate all your attention on your guests. Make them feel thoroughly at home, make them conscious of your concern in their personal comfort and enjoyment. This does not mean that you should fuss over them. But take care to keep an eye on them, and make them feel that you never neglect their comfort and pleasure.

It is very unpleasant for guests when their hostess is constantly distracted by anxiety about the food or the way the party is going. It makes them feel that they are giving her much trouble and worry.

Even the best laid plans may go astray, and if after all your care something does go wrong, don't worry overmuch. It is most depressing for your guests, and they often feel forced to condole with you and protest that they do not mind. But if you accept chance misfortunes philosophically, and refuse to be upset by them, your guests will appreciate your cheerfulness and enjoy the party all the more.

Do not attempt unnecessary display, especially when you expect them, or some of them, to entertain you in turn. Set a high standard of taste and originality, but not of extravagance. Ostentation and extravagance show the worst of taste, but on the other hand never apologize for, or boast of the cheapness of your party. This shows an equal amount of bad taste, for in either case it makes your guests ill at ease. Finally, never attempt more than you can conveniently manage. If you stick to these general principles you will seldom have a failure.

For women who are occupied with husbands and families during the weekends, a mid-week bridge tea is a convenient form of hospitality. A club, perhaps, may be formed, of four or eight members meeting at each house in turn. Arranging the food for a party of this sort is simple, for it is quite enough to offer your guests buttered scones, bridge rolls with a variety of fillings, sandwiches, cakes and tea, cigarettes, and a few home-made sweets. Fig. 1 shows an attractive way of serving sandwiches at a party.

FILLINGS FOR SANDWICHES

Fillings for bridge rolls and sandwiches can be creamed leftovers of chicken, pounded liver sausage, fish and meat pastes, cream cheese with chopped olives, or scrambled egg flavoured with curry paste or chutney. A good hostess will be ingenious enough to avoid the danger of the same cakes being provided at each tea, though this is not always easy if the number of local confectioners' shops is limited.

A popular cake for a bridge tea can be made from a tin of fruit (picnic size). Make a sponge mixture from three ounces of butter creamed with three ounces of sugar, three eggs and three ounces of flour. When baked and cold, split the cake and spread with thick cream. Strain the contents of a tin of raspberries, strawberries, oranges or pineapple, putting the liquid aside to be used in a fruit cup. Rub the pulp through a sieve, then mix it with icing sugar until it is of the right consistency for spreading over the top of the cake. Home-made eclairs are also general favourites.

GIVING AN "AT-HOME" PARTY

An at-home or afternoon reception is a useful type of party for it enables you to show hospitality to a large number of people with a minimum of cost and effort. It is the town equivalent of the country garden party. For an at-home, refreshments should be placed on a buffet and the guests invited to help themselves. There should be piles of plates in front of the table, with savoury and sweet sandwiches, cakes and biscuits evenly distributed behind. Sandwiches and bridge rolls should be labelled, preferably with the small decorative " flags " so popular today. Tea, hot coffee, iced coffee, fruit cup and Viennese chocolate (chocolate with a blob of thick cream on top) are the usual drinks offered.

In budgeting for a buffet supper of this sort for twenty-five guests, the hostess should allow five ounces of tea, a half-pound of sugar,

Fig. 2. The old-woman-who-lived-in-a-shoe cake.

three pints of milk, two quarts of ice cream and four quarts each of fruit cup and home-made lemonade or orangeade. Three bridge rolls or ordinary sandwiches, two patties or sausage rolls, three small cakes and one piece of sliced cake should be allowed for each person.

A foundation cake for a variety of small iced cakes can be made from half a pound of self-raising flour, three ounces each of butter and margarine, six ounces of sugar and four small eggs. Cream the butter and the sugar and add the eggs and flour. Flavour with vanilla and bake in a shallow tin in a moderate oven for half an hour. When cold cut into shapes and decorate with coloured flavoured icing, or put two together with jam and cream between and cover with marzipan. Use chopped nuts, crystallized flowers and glacé cherries for decorations.

HOW TO ARRANGE A GARDEN PARTY

A garden party would need much the same refreshments but with more soft drinks, and little garden tables are usually provided. Always supply plenty of paper napkins, and reserve one table for used crockery.

For an unmarried man or woman, probably the most convenient way of returning hospitality is to entertain your friends in a restaurant. It is always advisable to book a table in advance and for formal occasions it is probably better to arrange the menu and cost in advance with the head waiter.

When you give a children's party, remember to make the room

and table as bright and gay as possible, for children like colour and life and enjoy a party so much more in gay surroundings. These decorations need not be at all expensive: all you need are a few balloons and crêpe paper friezes, in bright animal and fairy-tale patterns. Remember also to have plenty of sweets around: these should be simple and digestible and very brightly coloured.

SOME IDEAS FOR CHILDREN'S PARTIES

A good way of overcoming shyness at the start of a party is to mark each child's place with a small cake or biscuit on which you have written the child's name in coloured icing. Children love this: it makes them feel so important.

Another good idea is to put a numbered card on their plates containing a " clue " to a hidden treasure. In the excitement of comparing numbers and deciphering the clues, the ice will be broken and the party well on the road to success.

After tea you can start the treasure hunt. Take one of the older children into the secret and, while the others are finishing their tea, dress him up as a pirate and hide him somewhere in the garden or house. A good pirate costume can be made from a pair of blue shorts, a white shirt, a gaily-coloured sash and a red handkerchief, completing the disguise with a burnt cork moustache and eyebrows.

Then set the children to decipher their clues and find the pirate and his treasure of cardboard money, dividing the " money " fairly equally round the party. With this money the children can buy themselves ice-cream and small toys.

WHAT FOOD WILL CHILDREN LIKE ?

Always have plenty of ice-cream for a children's party. If you cannot make it at home, a caterer will guarantee to deliver it at a stated time or send a man round with a barrow, so that the children can buy it direct for themselves.

Remember that in a summer party the children will not drink much milk, and will choose lemonade rather than tea. Sandwiches filled with honey and nut, banana and nut, tomato, paste or cucumber, brown and white bread and butter, cakes, jellies, fruit salad and trifle will provide both tea and supper.

Be sure always that an adequate supply of clean towels and warm water are ready in the bathroom, for children always get dirty and nowhere quicker than at a good party.

Children appreciate a cake made in an unusual form, such as the shoe in which the old woman lived with her children (Fig. 2). A plain madeira mixture baked in a large square tin is the best shape for making into the boot. It should then be covered with marzipan or chocolate icing, and the shoe lacings made of a contrasting icing in a forcing bag. The " children " are small china dolls, which can be bought at any cheap store, one for each guest when the cake is cut at the party.

Again, the cake might represent the witch's cottage with Hansel and Gretel at the door and the witch's face at the window or peering round the corner. A round or square house can be made, the chimney formed from cake iced with red glacé icing, the door section iced in blue or green with a silver ball as handle, a horseshoe as knocker, and windows outlined and latticed with icing the same colour as the door. To make a gabled roof, bake the cake in a square tin and cut off about one-third. This section can

Fig. 3. *How to make a Hansel and Gretel cake.*

then be split across diagonally lengthwise, and the two pointed wedges form the gables as shown in Fig. 3.

An Eskimo hut (Fig. 4) is another popular cake. This can be made from a large round cake covered with white icing, pulled up with a fork to represent snow. A " scene " can be made outside on a cardboard base with more snow and Eskimo figures, dogs, etc.

If the hostess is not a good cake maker a confectioner will make the cakes to order and possibly supply other ideas.

Jam sponge is always popular. A simple decoration, when icing is not desired, is to place a paper d'oyley on the sponge and sift fine icing sugar over it, as shown in Fig. 5. When the d'oyley is removed the sugar pattern remains.

Biscuits cut into shapes with animal cutters are easily made. Cream together four ounces of butter and three ounces of sugar.

Add one ounce of melted chocolate and beat together until the mixture is evenly coloured. Add a little vanilla essence, then six ounces of flour. Form into a stiff paste with a little beaten egg. Roll out, cut into shapes, and bake in a slow oven.

Shortbread biscuits for place names are made from four ounces

Fig. 4. An Eskimo hut cake.

of flour, two ounces of castor sugar, two ounces of butter and a pinch of salt. Rub the butter into the other ingredients until a stiff paste is formed. Roll it out very thinly and cut into shapes.

Small cardboard plates or soufflé cases bought in sixpenny packets can be used for jellies. The jellies should be set in basins, then be well broken with a fork and a few spoonfuls put in each case. Orange with added fruit juice, lemon, raspberry, greengage, cherry and blackcurrant are all favourites. Set one in each child's place. Orange jelly in particular is always popular. This can be made much more attractive to children by putting it in a gaily-decorated orange skin as shown in Fig. 6.

Possible additions for supper are trifle and a chocolate blanc-mange into which a generous quantity of coconut is mixed after the blancmange is removed from the fire.

For a formal luncheon a typical menu would be grape-fruit, lobster or salmon mayonnaise, cutlets (veal or lamb), a sweet, and a light savoury. More popular nowadays, however, is the informal " fork lunch," for which the food is placed on a buffet running the length of the room and chairs arranged along the opposite wall. There should be as little furniture in the room as possible.

Piles of plates, forks and spoons are placed along the front of the buffet, with plates of dry toast, biscuits or bread behind these.

Fig. 5. Sifting sugar through a d'oyley to decorate the top of a sponge cake.

The guests wait on themselves. Many of the things offered are on toast, such as for example, sliced mushrooms cooked in a little butter, mixed with some thick cream, sprinkled with gruyère and spread on small pieces of buttered toast.

Hot soup in cups is sometimes provided if the weather is cold. The main course can be steak or chicken pie, galantine—the pieces sliced and then cut across into large dice before being jellied. Potato or Russian salad—the latter a mixture of peas, diced beet, carrot, and potato flavoured slightly with onion and well mixed with salad cream or mayonnaise—are sometimes served. Individual jellies and blancmanges, charlotte russe (Fig. 7), jam tarts, apple puffs, and cakes can be given as the sweet course.

The supper or refreshments offered at a dance are very much the same as for a fork luncheon, but more ices, drinks and party sweets decorated with cream should be served.

HOW TO ORGANIZE A WEDDING RECEPTION

The arrangements for wedding receptions often cause some trouble but if you remember the main principles laid down here, the problem should be easier.

The bride's mother is the hostess at wedding receptions. She receives the guests at the entrance to the main room. They then pass on to greet the bride and bridegroom. If a wedding takes place in the morning, a luncheon follows for relations and close friends, the bride and bridegroom sitting together at the head of the table with the wedding cake in front of them. If the party is very large, arrange short tables running from the main table at right angles. At the end of the meal the bride cuts the cake and portions are passed round. At a smaller gathering the cake is placed on a small

Fig. 6. Orange jelly in a decorated orange skin basket.

table. The health of the bride and bridegroom is proposed by the most important person present, the bridegroom replying with a few words, and then proposing the health of the bridesmaids. The best man replies to this toast.

An afternoon wedding is followed by a reception, at which a buffet meal is served. A long trestle table, chairs, china and cutlery can be hired for this. If the room is large, or there is a garden or conservatory for the overflow of guests, it is more comfortable if a number of small tables are provided. In addition, there should be a table to receive used plates and another for drinks. These should include wine, preferably sparkling, orange-ade, lemonade, fruit cup and barley water. Remember to have plenty of good size paper napkins on the tables, as dresses are likely to be elaborate.

Fig. 7. Charlotte russe, a sponge casing filled with stiffened flavoured cream, garnished with chopped jelly.

If there are to be many guests at the reception, the labour of cutting the sandwiches will be considerable. If you can persuade your baker or caterer to supply bread ready sliced this will be reduced. Otherwise, bread should be cut and buttered at home on the previous day, wrapped in a damp cloth and left in a cold place. Bridge rolls, however, should not be prepared on the previous day as they dry up too much. Suitable sandwich fillings for a wedding are : sardine, *foie gras*, or cream cheese with chopped stuffed olives, but often on these occasions, lobsters, sardine or prawn patties or small sausage rolls are popular. These can be bought ready made at most large stores.

When the wedding is to take place in the morning, and the bride and groom wish to leave early for their honeymoon, a reception is now often held on the wedding eve. This enables a large number of people to be entertained when a luncheon party for them all would be impossible, and is becoming increasingly popular.

GIVING A DINNER PARTY

Giving a dinner party can be quite a simple matter if the menu is not too ambitious. The following menu is attractive and can be easily managed, for most of the food can be prepared early in the day.

Hors-d'œuvre

Soup

Jelly Chicken (Summer)

Hot Chicken Pie (Winter)

Potatoes

Other Vegetables in Season

Fruit Salad or Home-made Meringue

A pleasant hors-d'œuvre can be quite simply made up from tinned sardine, sliced cucumber, some potato and Russian salad and some sliced tomato.

For the soup, asparagus, celery and tomato are all suitable and can be easily prepared. To prepare chicken, steam a boiling fowl on the previous day with carrot and onion. Shred flesh from the bones and set in a jelly, made by boiling the liquid and adding a little powdered gelatine. Before adding the gelatine, mix it first with a small quantity of cold water. Decorate the dish with peas and diced carrot and flavour the jelly slightly with marmite. Instead of chicken a mushroom or cheese omelette is comparatively simple to make and is always popular. Other omelette fillings will doubtless occur to you, but it is as well to experiment with them for yourself before trying them on guests.

HOW TO MAKE MERINGUES

To make home-made meringues, whip the whites of three eggs stiffly, and pour in lightly six ounces of castor sugar, a few drops of lemon juice and half a teaspoonful of vanilla essence. Put into a forcing bag and squeeze into egg or steeple shape or on to a tin previously oiled with olive oil and dusted with flour. If the mixture is very stiff, it can be put on the tin in tablespoonfuls and the forcing bag dispensed with. Put the meringues in a very slow oven (Regulo ¼) for two hours, when they should be thoroughly dried. When cold, spread thickly with flavoured whipped cream and put two together. Another method is to remove the meringues after one and a half hours, push in the centres and return them to the oven for the remaining half-hour. This enables a larger amount of cream to be inserted. Home-made meringues are much softer than those bought from a confectioner and keep well in an airtight tin for a fortnight or more.

Chocolate trifle, jelly trifle, coffee trifle, decorated with ratafia biscuits, cream, and crystallized fruits, or orange jellies made with a pint jelly and a tin of mandarin oranges and ratafia biscuits, served with cream are alternative sweets.

Various suggestions for brightening up and decorating food for a dinner party are shown in Figs. 8, 9 and 10. Fig. 8 is a pleasant

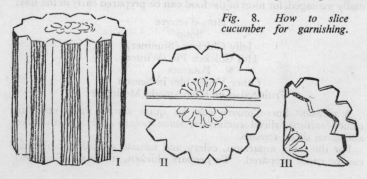

Fig. 8. How to slice cucumber for garnishing.

I   II   III

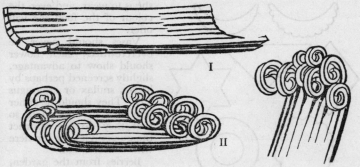

Fig. 9. How to curl celery for garnishing.

way of garnishing entrée dishes with pieces of cucumber. Cut off a piece of cucumber, score the skin lightly downwards in narrow strips and peel off alternate strips (I). Cut the cucumber in half lengthwise and then cut into thin slices (II). Pinch the slices slightly to make them stand round the dish (III). Fig. 9 shows how celery can be curled for garnishing. Cut the celery into short lengths, and cut the ends down in narrow strips to make a fringe (I); put them in water and they will curl in about half an hour (II). Fig. 10 shows some shapes for toast for the entrée dish. Little innovations like this will make your parties individual and memorable.

The juice of an equal quantity of oranges and lemons, sweetened with brown sugar and diluted with cold water, makes a delicious summer drink.

Do not offer a guest a choice of foods of which one has not been started upon or carved. Always begin to carve or serve one portion first to make a beginning, or your guest may refuse rather than have a dish specially started for his or her benefit.

SENDING THE INVITATIONS

Printed invitations are used only in the case of large luncheons or dinners, especially when the function is semi-public or the guests are members of a society.

Invitations to a formal dinner party should be sent out two or three weeks in advance. This gives the hostess time to fill the vacant place if a guest cannot accept. Last-minute dinner invitations can only be sent to very intimate friends who do not resent being used to fill a gap.

The hostess should think out a pleasant scheme of decoration, in harmony with the prevailing colour of the dining-room, the flowers in season, the vases and bowls at her disposal, the dress

Fig. 10. *Toast shapes for entrée dishes.*

she is to wear, and even the colour of the food she will offer.

Vases should never be overcrowded; each flower should show to advantage, slightly screened perhaps by leaves, smilax or asparagus fern. They should be either very low or very high, so that they do not obstruct the guests' view or interfere with conversation.

Berries from the garden, such as pyracantha, cotoneaster, rowan, japonica fruits, hips and haws, can be preserved and used for winter decoration by being brushed over with clear gum or artist's varnish, using a good camel-hair brush. The ends of the stems should be kept in jars of wet sand until summer flowers are over and the berries are needed. Even dried toadstools and pine cones, gilded and attached to gilded twigs, or globe artichokes with their large scales gilded and their stems left green, are now used by fashionable florists in their efforts to provide something new in decoration. Long sprays of hops with onion heads, persimmons or uncommon French fruits mounted on sticks, and South African fire berries remounted with their silver green foliage are also effective.

Never use artificial flowers on a dinner table. Alternatives to flowers and fresh fruits are crystallized fruits, glass fruits, etc. A few dishes of bon-bons or preserved fruits are also decorative.

Branches of trees provide good room decorations in spring and in autumn and winter. In May the lovely green of young beech and larch is effective in tall vases. For autumn and winter decoration the branches should be picked in their prime, and the stems put in crude glycerine and water for a month (using rather more than half as much glycerine as water).

Holly, if it is to retain its berries, should have the ends of the stems hammered. This should be done with any branches which have woody stems. Mimosa retains the fluffiness of its balls for as long as two weeks if the stems are plunged into boiling water for about half a minute.

Do not have strongly-scented flowers. Remember that women guests also contribute perfume, and the result may be overpowering.

If a large table-cloth is used instead of individual mats, a silence cloth should be laid underneath. This protects a polished table from hot plates and lessens the clatter of cutlery. Nowadays table napkins are not elaborately folded, but are laid flat on the plates on which hors-d'œuvre are to be served, unless the water-lily fold is used. This is decorative and very easy to do (Fig. 11).

A square and stiffened napkin is necessary. Find the centre by putting selvedge to selvedge and hem to hem, marking the folds well. Open out. Now fold the four corners, as exactly as possible, to the centre, pressing them down. Repeat this twice more so that the corners have been three times folded to the centre on the one side. Now turn the napkin carefully over, holding the points in position and fold the four points once to the centre on the other side. Then placing a cup or tumbler in the centre so as to keep the last four points firmly down, pull up the points carefully from underneath one at a time until twelve points have been curled round.

Name cards should be laid at the top of each plate. If menus are provided, do not write the date on them as is done in hotels.

HOW TO SET THE CUTLERY

On the left nearest the plate should be placed a large fork, then a fish fork; on the right of the plate should be the large knife, then a fish knife, a soup spoon and a hors-d'œuvre fork. If more knives and forks are required they should be supplied on plates with the courses. If butter is served with the hors-d'œuvre, a small bread plate is provided with a butter knife; otherwise a piece of bread or a roll is put on the table-cloth at the left of each person. Glasses should be brightly polished and placed on the right-hand side. Finger bowls and plates for dessert are put on later. Water jugs should always be on the table, and a cruet at each corner, with a salt cellar for every two guests.

Menus for dinner parties, however formal, are now much shorter than they used to be. Fifty years ago what was known as a full course dinner used to be served on special occasions, but these are now only served at banquets given by city corporations and other

Fig. 11. The water-lily fold for table napkins (see text).

public bodies. These menus were staggering in length consisting of nine courses. They were hors-d'œuvre, soup, fish, entrée, relevé (or remove), rôti, entremets—vegetable and sweet; dessert and coffee were not considered courses. In addition to the above they sometimes included a savoury entremet and a sorbet, i.e., a partly frozen semi-liquid fruit juice, thickened with sugar and stiffly whipped white of egg, which is eaten with a small spoon.

MODERN FULL DINNER MENUS

A modern full menu comprises hors-d'œuvre, soup, fish, a joint or poultry with vegetables, sweet, dessert and coffee.

The following would be quite a good choice for a menu of this sort: oysters, clear turtle soup, fried sole with piquant sauce, sweet-breads, lamb with haricots verts, sauté potatoes, roast chicken, asparagus or salad, charlotte russe, and perhaps cheese straws.

If the party is a large one (over twelve guests) both thick and thin soup should be offered; for a smaller party thin soup only, as this is the most generally acceptable. Second helpings are not offered at a formal dinner, though a guest may sometimes ask for a second helping of a sweet.

Everything that is offered should be taken to the left-hand side of the guest. When there is no choice of dishes, the plate with its contents is put down on the right side. Used plates are removed from the right-hand side, and clean empty plates are also taken to the right-hand side of the guest.

HOW THE COURSES ARE SERVED

Soup is carried round in plates or cups, beginning with the lady on the right of the host, and then passing straight round the table (not from lady to lady, omitting men guests). If the party is large dishes should be provided in duplicate, and serving proceed from the right and the left of the host, who is served last. When the party is small, the plates are left until all have finished the course. The plates of the host and hostess are collected last. At a large party each plate is removed a moment or two after it is empty. Plates should always be removed one at a time—never piled together.

When the fish is carried round the sauce boat is held in the left hand. Entrées must be garnished, as they are handed round, and not carved before serving, so that the whole dish is seen by the guests. Too much ornamentation, however, is in bad taste. Some suggestions for garnishing entrée dishes have been given on page 16. It is well thought out details of decoration like these that are effective, rather than attempts at ostentatious effects.

When the joint is carved at table the maid stands at the side of the carver and carries the plates to the guests. The vegetables are usually placed upon a sideboard and handed from there to the guests. After the roast (which is usually some form of game or poultry), the sweet and the savoury, the table is cleared of unused cutlery, glasses, and cruets, and the dessert plates and finger bowls placed upon it.

A good hostess will try to introduce some novelty of her own, with variety in food, especially in salads. Cubes of pineapple, tomato, bananas and orange, sharpened with lemon juice and served in a lettuce leaf, are sometimes offered with pheasant. Orange and lettuce salad with roast duck is now well established. Skinned and stoned white grapes each cut in half lengthwise, introduced into a thin gravy, are a good accompaniment to roast chicken.

While these pleasant little additions will never make badly-cooked food taste well cooked, they should succeed in making well-cooked food both look and taste even more interesting.

WHEN FRIENDS COME TO STAY

When you have guests to stay with you, it is best to try to keep to the ordinary meals and routine of the house as much as possible. Guests hate feeling they are a trouble and are upsetting the household. If you give them a comfortable bed and simple, well-cooked food, you are well on the way to becoming a successful host.

The hostess should ascertain overnight the guests' wishes for breakfast—early morning tea is now taken for granted. It is polite to ask what time the guests would like to be called, mentioning the usual breakfast hour. It is the hostess's duty to escort her guests to their rooms and ascertain that all their needs have been met. The wise hostess keeps a spare toothbrush and face glove in their cellophane wrappers ready for emergencies. Usually it is the hostess who suggests when to retire, though she tries to find out what are her guests' wishes.

Most people nowadays like a light breakfast. Grape-fruit, a cereal, one main dish, toast and marmalade, and tea or coffee are quite sufficient. Some hostesses make a point of offering their guests a choice of several main dishes but this is unnecessary.

For an hour or two in the morning, unless an expedition has been planned, the guests can well be left to their own devices, to walk in the garden, write letters or read the newspaper. Writing materials, a book of stamps, and a list of posting times should be kept on the writing table. In that hour or two household matters can be attended to and the hostess's mind freed for a time.

Never apologize for deficiencies in food or equipment. The guests will probably not notice anything amiss unless you point it out; the deficiencies of their own homes will probably be sufficiencies in yours, and it is these that they will notice. If you have honestly done your best in your circumstances, you can enjoy your guests' company with a clear conscience and untroubled mind.

CHAPTER 2

PLANNED PARTIES

Good parties don't just happen; they are planned. No matter what sort of occasion you are preparing for, you should know what is to happen and what equipment will be needed. One of the best ways to keep a party under control, to plan it properly and make it " good " is to have a common theme running through it. This is what this chapter tries to do—to suggest a few party themes that are nearly always successful. Invitations can be harmonized with the theme, and quite familiar games and amusements adapted, so as to fit in and seem fascinatingly new.

A NEW YEAR PARTY

For a New Year party, each guest on arrival is handed some small object, representing one of the months, to be pinned on jacket or frock. The guests are given slips of paper and pencils, and are made to guess what their labels mean. This is a good way of breaking the ice at the start of a party and fills in the time while late guests are arriving. Here are suggestions: January— page 1 of a book; February—St. Valentine's Day drawing of two hearts pierced by arrow; March—a picture of a lion coming in and a lamb going out; April—picture of a rainstorm; May—a bunch of appropriate flowers; June—a rose; July—picture of bather; August —seaside picture; September—" creeping like a snail " (Shakespeare's phrase about the schoolboy written on a slip); October— two clock faces, one with hand set an hour behind the other, to indicate end of summer time; November—paper with " Bang! " written on it; December—a Christmas greeting.

Following this " New Year " games can be played, one for each month; and each can be announced and explained, or led, by the person wearing the emblem of that month. For this you will have to give a written description of the game to each such person. Such games might be:—

Resolutions (January). Play this like consequences. Each player has a slip of paper. First, all write down their names; then papers are folded over, collected, shuffled, and redistributed. Next is written a New Year resolution. Again papers are taken up, mixed, and given out again. In the same fashion two more things are written: own name once more, and another resolution.

Finally the papers are read out by the play leader, in this manner: " I (first name), resolve to (first resolution), providing that (second name) will (second resolution)."

Catch Your Mate (February). At one end of the room is a table on which are small curtain rings. By this table stand the girls who are taking part. At the opposite end of the room are the men. When the starting signal is given the girls dash to the men, each seizing one by the wrist and dragging him back to the table. Here she fits a ring over his and her thumbs and races back up the room with him. The first girl to arrive goes out of the game, and is allowed to " sit with her mate " throughout the rest of the play. Those left in go to their original places and begin afresh. So it continues until all are out.

Blow Wind (March). The players are divided into two teams and line up on opposite sides of the table. A matchbox is placed between them, and a " goal " is scored each time this is blown over the opponents' edge.

Farmyard Story (April). Every player is given the name of some animal or bird occupant of the farmyard. Then the leader begins to narrate a story, bringing in the various names at intervals. Whenever a name is mentioned the person who bears it must immediately make the appropriate noise. If he fails to do the right thing, or makes any sound when he should not, a penalty follows— a forfeit, a point scored against him, or he may have to drop out of the game, whichever you decide at the beginning.

Naturally the game depends largely on the skill of the narrator, who aims at making the tale so enthralling that players miss their cues.

It must be remembered that when the word " farmyard " is spoken all the animals and birds unite in one big chorus.

Hay Wagon (May). Chairs are placed in the middle of the room, in the form of a square, to make the " wagon." The number of chairs must be one less than the number of players. While music is being played the players, from the sides of the room, pretend to toss hay to the middle. When the music breaks off all dash to the wagon. One, of course, will fail to get " on the wagon " and so will drop out. A chair is removed, and the game restarts.

Gardening (June). To each player is handed a pencil and a paper slip, on which is written the name of some flower, fruit, or vegetable. Each is required to write a sentence the words of which begin, in proper order, with the letters of the name. The sentence must give advice on how to grow the thing in question. For instance, for " pea " someone might write " Plant early August."

Surface Dives (July). This is a " bathing game," like that of diving from the surface of water to recover objects from the bottom. A magazine is stood up on the floor, and each person in turn stands on one leg and tries to pick it up with his teeth, while keeping the other three limbs clear of the floor (Fig. 1).

Holiday Trunk (August). One player starts off by saying: " I have packed in the trunk——" adding anything appropriate, such as " shoes." The next player then says the same thing, but

Fig. 1. How to play the game of " Surface Dives."

adds some new article to the first—perhaps " shoes and blazer." So each player in turn repeats the list and adds to it. Any one who blunders drops out of the game.

Back at School (September). The teacher sits in the middle and tosses a handkerchief to any player, saying the name of some school subject, and a letter of the alphabet. That player must immediately respond with a word or name connected with the subject and beginning with that letter. For example: literature, D —Dickens; arithmetic, M—multiplication; history, C—Cæsar.

Ducking for Apples (October). For this favourite Hallowe'en game, put a large basin of water with apples floating in it in the centre of the floor. Then stand an upright chair beside the basin with its back to it. The apples should now be stirred round fairly fast and each member of the party in turn should kneel on the chair and try to spear an apple by dropping a fork from his mouth over the back of the chair into the water. As soon as each player has secured an apple, he can fall out of the game.

An alternative version of this game is for each player to kneel on the floor beside the basin and try and catch an apple in his mouth.

Guy Fawkes (November). All the players but one stand round the room, facing the wall. One is " Guy Fawkes," and his task is to carry " explosives " to the " vault "—which is a ring in the middle of the floor. The " explosives " are a bunch of keys, or something equally difficult to move without noise. "Guy Fawkes" tries, but if any one hears a sound he must point backwards towards the sound. Any one locating "Guy Fawkes" changes places with him.

Snowball Fight (December). Have " snowballs " made of cotton-wool, and let two teams pelt each other.

At some interval in the evening you may stage a shadow drama, behind a sheet, of Father Time hustling off the Old Year and welcoming the little New Year in.

GIVING A BIRTHDAY PARTY

For a birthday party remember above all, the cakes and the candles, and if you do not put candles on the cake put " surprises " into the cake for the children; but remember to warn them before-hand so that they do not swallow them by accident and are not frightened when they find them. Cheerful rhymes can be folded in tinfoil and spaced round the outer edge of the cake, so that every one is likely to find one in his or her slice. Here are samples of wishing rhymes—you will readily invent more for yourself :—

> May this year bring lots of joy
> To you and every girl and boy.

> Love and joy will be your treasure,
> Happiness in growing measure.

> May each year for you be bright,
> Pleasures many, sorrows light.

> Your life serviceably spend,
> And you'll never lack a friend.

> Gladness ever on you smile,
> Bless your lifetime all the while.

If there are many guests, find out the birthday month of each on arrival, and then call them into groups without divulging to what months they belong. Each group can then act some tableau or charade typical of their month, and the rest may guess what it is.

Congratulations can be played. Each person writes down the word " birthday," and is then allowed a short time to compose a congratulation or greeting, the words of which must begin with the letters of " birthday " in their proper order.

Happy Returns. In this game one player is blindfolded. He shakes hands with one person after another, while he says " Many happy returns," and afterwards each time tries to guess whose hand he has held. When he is successful the two change places.

Other games having to do with months of the year, as described for the New Year party, will also be appropriate, as will number games based on age or the day of the month. For instance, if the person with a birthday is eighteen, then you may see who can make most words with eighteen letters picked at random from a pile; who can repeat eighteen three- or four-syllable words in a single breath, or make such words into a single sentence; who can first score eighteen points in any other games you may wish to play.

An unusual kind of party, but one which will always be popular is the **Country Dance Party**. There are plenty of simple folk and group dances which require very little space, and can be enjoyed even by people who have never danced before. If you have a friend who is knowledgeable in such matters, or if you happen to be experienced, then plan a full programme of such dances and invite your friends to come and do them.

As each dance is introduced, let one or two first demonstrate and explain it, then let each dancer partner a novice so that all can join in.

Some of the more popular English and Scottish country dances are the following: " Haymakers," " Petronella," " Dashing White Sergeant," " Strip the Willow " and " Rufty Tufty." If desired introduce other simple group dances, such as " Lancers," " Palais Glide," " Lambeth Walk," and " The Chestnut Tree." These are too well known to need any description, and music or gramophone records for them, and for country dances, are quite easy to obtain.

Fig. 2. The Walking Relay. Players must walk heel to toe fashion.

An **April the First Party** is often highly amusing, for all the world loves a fool. You must be careful, however, that the guests are congenial and chosen carefully.

You can hang misleading placards about the house, wrongly directing guests, and inappropriate greetings hung up—" Happy Christmas," and so on.

Fix a squeaker or motor-horn under the front door mat, to startle every one who steps on it, and any other similar surprises you can plan—rubber pegs which collapse when clothes are hung on them; fake chocolates or fruit; a dark passage in which guests blunder into unseen balloons or dangling bells; books with pages glued together; hot drinks which are cold and cold which are hot.

Displays of simple magic will fit in well, and games like these :—

Dunderheads. Each person is given the following list, and allowed five minutes in which to write it out correctly:—

1. Madame Curie—Comedienne.
2. Dombey and Son—Universal providers.
3. Longfellow—Another of those soldiers.
4. Grace Darling—Had knives on her wheels.
5. Edison—Pirate adventurer.
6. Vickers—Name of a book.
7. Drake—Invented things.
8. Napoleon—Great poet.
9. Gracie Fields—Dared the sea.
10. Boadicea—Scientist.

Hat Dance. Fit two players with dunces' hats, and let them see who first can knock off the other's.

Have also a **Quartet.** They stand up, apparently quite seriously. The pianist begins an impressive introduction, and continues with the announced song. The four singers open and shut their mouths for the words, but make no sound whatever. This game is particularly suitable for children.

Another good party theme is an **Indoor Athletic Party.** Here the programme should consist of mock-serious events, in which either teams or individuals may compete. Here are items :—

1. RUNNING HIGH SQUEAL. Each competitor runs from the starting line to the middle of the room, then sings a very low and a very high note. Biggest " jump " wins.

2. LONG BUZZ. Two at a time dash up to " jumping " line, then begin to buzz. That one whose breath holds out longest wins.

3. PUTTING THE WEIGHT. Throwing balloons. Farthest wins.

4. YARD MEASURE. Each tries to chalk a line just one yard long on a blackboard.

5. PENNY PUSH. Two compete at a time, pushing pennies the length of a table, with a pin.

6. WALKING RELAY. Team contest, each person walking heel

to toe fashion along a set course. This is made clear in Fig. 2.

7. LIFTING WEIGHT. Lifting dried peas with matches; two at a time take part, each with a saucer containing the same number of peas.

8. SWIM TEST. Each competitor receives marks for reciting the following tongue twister :—

> Swan swam over the sea—
> Swim, swan, swim !
> Swan swam back again—
> Well swum, swan !

9. LIGHT-WEIGHT BOXING CHAMPIONSHIP. Two at a time take part, in " knock-out " bouts. Each has a matchbox balanced on the back of his left hand. Boxing is done with the right hand. First to drop his matches loses.

For a **Progressive Games Party** arrange suitably small tables, with two couples sitting at each, in the manner of a whist drive. On each table have some different game or contest, and allow perhaps ten minutes for every playing period. At the end of each period the winning pair of each table takes two points each, writing them on their separate cards and having them initialled by their opponents. Then, all the girls move up one table and all the men down a table. At the new tables each man who has just been a winner sits by the girl who has been a loser.

Here are suggestions for the game:—

1. Lifting dried peas with pencils, from one saucer to another.
2. Ludo.
3. Snakes and Ladders.
4. Tiddley winks.
5. Jig-saw puzzles. Two sets of each puzzle must be provided, one for each couple. That couple wins which fits most pieces.
6. Making words out of one long word.
7. Dominoes.
8. Noughts and Crosses.
9. Building castles of cards—the winners being the couple who get up most stories.
10. Bouncing a ping-pong ball into a basin, from beyond a marked line.

If you have friends who would be likely to enjoy it, try giving **A Hikers' Party.** Guests are asked to come in hiking garb, with food, knives and forks, harmonicas and other requirements in their rucksacks. A " camp fire " is provided—an electric lamp covered with red and yellow muslin serves well (Fig. 3)—and all squat round this for the supper. Food is put on to common dishes in the centre, and all help themselves. A singsong and yarning may follow the meal, and impromptu stunts on a " sing, say, or pay " basis.

Fig. 3. A hikers' party round a Camp Fire.

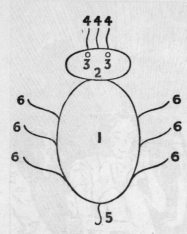

Fig. 4.   *A completed Beetle.*

A Beetle Drive Party should be arranged much like a whist drive, with four players to a table. Partners sit opposite each other, and should be man and girl if possible. Dice are provided at each table, and a pencil and paper for each player. All four in turn take one throw with the die. Players always keep the scores of their partners. The object of the game is to draw a beetle. No one can begin until a one has been thrown. The player who throws this, and his partner, each draw the body of the beetle on their papers. When a two is thrown the head can be added. For the eyes two separate threes are needed, and a four must be gained for each of the three feelers. Everything, of course, must be taken in proper turn; the feelers, for example, cannot be drawn until both eyes have been put in. With a five the tail can be drawn. Then six separate sixes are needed for the full set of legs. A beetle with the throws necessary to draw each part is shown in Fig. 4.

As soon as any player has completed the beetle he calls out "Beetle!" and all play stops. Those at each table examine their drawings, and the pair from each four whose beetle is farthest advanced becomes the winner.

The winning men move down one table, to partner the loser girls they find there; the winning girls go up one table, and partner the loser men. New papers are used for the restart. At the end of the evening the scorekeeper will be able to determine who is the winner. The winning couple of each " round " get five points each, and the winning couple at each other table two points.

A Hopscotch Party is quite simple to organize, and can be great fun. Your invitations might include a rhymed indication of the party's object, such as :—

> Say what you think's the nicest game;
> We'll see if others think the same.

Each guest is expected to introduce and take charge of one game. After all have been played, distribute paper slips so that every player may write down which he would like to have again, finding which is most popular by comparing the slips. The guest who introduced the most popular game might win a small prize.

CHAPTER 3

PARTY GAMES

I N arranging a party, always try to make the games varied. Mix quiet games with lively ones, musical games with brain teasers. This will ensure that all your guests have some games to suit their own particular tastes and talents. First of all some lively games; these help to break the ice and get all the guests properly mixed.

Hello Circle is excellent for this, especially if the guests do not know each other very well to begin with.

Everybody should stand in a large ring, facing inwards, the play leader among the rest. Turning to the right, the leader shakes hands with her neighbour, saying " Hello," and the neighbour responds cheerfully. Then the leader passes on and greets the next person in the same way, continuing round the whole ring. But close behind her follows the second person, who originally stood on her right hand. This second player likewise shakes hands with each in turn and says " Hello." Behind the second follows the third player, and so on.

In this way the ring slowly turns in on itself, and every one shakes hands with and greets every one else. Those who were nearest the leader at the outset will have the farthest walk to pass round the ring, and the last player of all—who was originally the left-hand neighbour of the leader—does not have to move at all, for every other person in turn passes in front of him.

Another good game is **Found Animals.** Here everybody sits in a ring. The leader should explain the game carefully at first, and even try over a little " preliminary run." For this she had better use only a " dog " (say a piece of india-rubber).

The leader passes the rubber to her right-hand neighbour saying :—
" I found this dog."
" This what? " her neighbour must ask.
" This dog," repeats the leader.

Then the second player passes the rubber on to her other neighbour, saying :—
" I found this dog."
" This what? " questions the third player.

The second turns back to the leader and asks :—
" This what? "
" This dog," says the leader.
" This dog," declares the second to the third player.

Then the third turns to the fourth player, and the thing goes on in similar fashion. Each time a new player, on receiving the rubber, asks " This what? " The informant must send the question back along the line to the leader and the answer must be passed

Fig. 1. *Orange Battle. An energetic game for any number of players.*

up by every intermediate person. A minute or two of rehearsal like this, and all in the ring will understand what has to be done.

Then the leader will recall the dog, and announce that a real start is to be made, and that she has also been fortunate enough to find a " cat " as well. A match will serve for the cat.

So both objects are started off simultaneously, the dog to the left, the cat to the right—and the fun begins. The really lively stage comes when the two animals have passed each other half-way round the circle, so that players are called on to answer queries from both directions, about the dog and the cat.

Peanut Prowl. Prepare a good supply of shelled peanuts, and hand ten to each person as he or she arrives—this too is a game for a fairly large party. It has the advantage that new-comers can begin to join in at any moment without there being any formal start.

The object of the game is to secure as many nuts as possible. Any player can challenge any other player by guessing " odd " or " even," and the one challenged must then open his hand and show how many nuts are in it. The challenger takes one nut from the other person if his challenge was correct, but if the guess was wrong he must give one of his own nuts to the second.

When a player has lost all his nuts he may still take part in the play, the empty fist reckoning as "even"—though any one who happens to guess it correctly will not be able to receive any reward.

No one may refuse a challenge, and the same player may be

challenged any number of times, though never twice consecutively.

Any number of players from two upwards can take part in the **Orange Battle** game (Fig. 1). It can be played either with oranges or tennis balls.

Each player has two dessert spoons—one in each hand. On the left spoon is balanced the orange. The right spoon is used as a weapon, to upset the oranges of others and to defend one's own.

Whenever an orange falls to the floor, its owner is out of the contest, so that eventually only one, the winner, remains.

This can also be played as a team game.

Army Orders. One person is chosen as the " colonel." His job is to stay at the rear of the " army " and give orders. Every order he shouts must be promptly obeyed by the rest, but by their doing just the opposite of what he says. If he says " stand " they must sit, and so on.

It is worth while preparing the orders beforehand, for it is not always easy to invent them impromptu, and much depends on the possibilities of the room. Here are suggestions for orders :—

> One pace forward, march.
> Salute with the right hand.
> Nod the head, signifying " Yes."
> Cease marking time.
> Stop.
> Raise the left arm above the head.
> Keep the right arm down.
> Close the arms together.
> Raise both arms upwards.
> Heads, to the right, bend.
> Head forward bend.
> Trunk backward bend.
> Right about turn.
> Say " No " in a whisper.

If you like you may have forfeits for defaulters, or marks can be scored against them and appropriate penalties awarded afterwards.

Lemon Golf (Fig. 2) is played with walking sticks and lemons. Even high golfing skill will not be found of much avail; the novice is just as likely to do well.

Chalk rings on the floor to serve as " holes " or use four-inch circular pieces of paper or cardboard. Distribute your holes as widely as possible, and see which player can get round all of them in the fewest strokes. Alternatively, each hole may be played for separately by all the players, before any one goes on to the next hole. The winner will then be the person who has won most holes. Few things can roll more unexpectedly than a lemon !

Circular Skipping is a really strenuous game. A cord several yards long is needed, with some small weight attached to one end

Fig. 2. Lemon Golf is not always won by the expert golfer!

which will keep it out straight when it is being swung. The other end is held by the leader, who crouches in the middle of the room.

All the players stand round in a circle, whose radius is rather less than the length of the cord, though at the start they will need to be farther out, just until the rope is moving.

The leader swings the rope round, so that it describes a circle, about six or nine inches above the floor. Each player in turn jumps into the air so that the rope passes freely beneath him. Any person whose legs or feet are touched by the cord drops promptly out of the game, and at last only the winner remains.

The leader will need to change the cord from hand to hand as it passes behind and in front of him. If the last players are difficult to get out, raising the cord a little higher will soon remove them.

To play **Hands on Knees** a ring of players should be formed, this time sitting on chairs, with one player, the " it," standing in the middle. The circle keep their hands flat on their knees in front of them, palms down and the player in the centre has to try and slap the exposed hands. To avoid this the others may slide their hands down the sides of their knees into safety, but immediately the danger is past they must be slid up again. When the " it " succeeds in slapping another player's hands, the two change places.

The fun of the game depends on the agility and unexpectedness of the player in the middle, who is free to move in any direction.

As the same chair formation is used, **Vacant Chair** is a good game to follow " hands on knees." This time, however, you have a vacant chair in the ring, which the person in the middle must try and secure.

To prevent the seat being taken, all the other players should move round continually—one chair at a time, so that the vacant place is always changing, and it is no easy matter to drop into it. When the standing player does manage to sit down, the player at his side, who failed to move quickly enough to get the vacant place, must go to the middle.

Poison Spot is another vigorous game, but strength is really of less importance than agility. All the players stand in a circle, hands clasped, round a " poison spot." For the " poison spot," you can use either a three-feet chalk circle marked on the floor, or a rug about the same size.

The players must move round the whole time, each trying to push his neighbour on to the spot. Nobody must release his partner's hands, but you may jump backwards and forwards to avoid the spot as much as you like. When a player's foot touches the spot, he is out.

Hot Potato. The " hot potato " may be a rolled up handkerchief, or anything convenient for holding. It is passed round a ring of seated players, or tossed across from one to another. All the while there is one free player at the middle trying to capture it. When he succeeds he changes places with the person who last touched the potato. When the potato falls on the floor it must promptly be snatched up by the nearest player.

Winking is an old favourite, but somehow it never seems to lose its freshness.

A ring of chairs is arranged, and the girls sit in them, facing inwards, and leaving one empty seat. A man stands behind each girl, behind the empty chair stands another man, and it is he who starts the play. He winks at any girl he chooses, and she must immediately try to leave her chair and come across to his. The man who stands behind her must try to seize her shoulders before she can get clear, and so hold her back in her seat. The man must *not* keep his hands on the girl's shoulders the whole time. Except when actually preventing an " escape," they must be kept on the back of the chair. If he fails, he must wink in his turn, until some girl manages to get across to him. After some time, the players behind the chair should change with the ones sitting to see how they do in their turn.

Half a dozen players are sufficient for **Hunt the Feather**, though more may take part if desired. All except one are seated, and between them they hold a sheet, stretched out flat. On the sheet is a feather (Fig. 3).

The odd player stands outside the others, and dodges round trying to snatch off the feather. But the others, whilst keeping the sheet taut, try to blow the feather out of his reach. As soon as it is grabbed, however, the player nearest to the one who is standing gives up his seat, and himself pursues the feather in his turn.

Sardines is a magnificent game if it can be played over a whole house or a number of rooms, but it *does* need plenty of space. Sardines must be played in the dark. Before you start playing, put everything away that can be easily broken. Then turn out the lights and send one person away to hide.

After, say, a minute, start to look for him. As each finder discovers the sardine he hides with him, until finally the whole party is crammed into one small hiding place.

The person who arrives last at the hiding place is the next sardine.

QUIET GAMES THAT PLEASE EVERYBODY

The best number of players for **Numbered Seats** is ten. They all sit in horseshoe formation, and number round. It is important to remember that the numbers belong to the seats, and not to the players, and the seats retain the same numbers all through, irrespective of who is sitting on them.

The game is started by one player calling out any seat number. The occupier of that seat must immediately respond by calling another number. The holder of the seat mentioned calls a third number, and so the game goes on.

This, you say, sounds all rather simple, and even dull. But the interesting feature is that certain numbers are always barred. No player may call (1) his own number; (2) the number of either of his neighbours; (3) the number which was last called. It is a " fault " to do any of these things; to reply when one's number is not called; or not to reply when it is called.

Any person committing a fault goes either to seat *ten* or seat *one*— these two places are used alternately—and the other players are compelled to move round one place to accommodate the defaulter. This means that those who are thus forced to change their seats change their numbers too. The more faults that are made, the more often seats are changed, and the more players are likely to be confused.

The advantage of sending defaulters to *one* and to *ten* alternately is that it prevents players remaining at one end with small chance of being dislodged, as would be the case if all were sent to one end and the other left undisturbed.

The game of **Conversation** calls for a good deal of ingenuity, and you should make sure that everybody understands what is to happen.

Two people are sent out of the room, and the rest choose two sentences on widely differing subjects—for example, " I have always thought cyclists should be compelled to carry fire-extinguishers," and " How do you spell ' Transjordania ' anyway? " The two

Fig. 3. Hunt the Feather needs a sheet, a feather, and some chairs.

sentences are written on pieces of paper, and the two players are called in. Each is given one piece of paper, which he reads to himself. They must then engage in conversation with each other, each trying to guess the other's sentence. A time limit may be set.

The Oracle Game can only be played when a radio " talk " is in progress. The players all sit round a radio set. The leader tunes it in to the talk, then switches it off or turns it too low to be audible.

Each player then, in turn, asks the " oracle " some question— the more ridiculous the better—and the leader switches on the wireless so that the ensuing words of the broadcaster give the reply. It may—or may not—be appropriate.

Some preparation beforehand is necessary for **Sounds.** The players sit quietly, while behind some sort of screen, various sounds and noises are made. The first player to guess correctly what the sound is scores one point.

Possible sounds are : striking a match, dropping a pencil on the floor, gargling, drawing a cork, folding a newspaper, cutting finger nails, squirting from a syphon of soda water, stirring a cup of tea, tearing a piece of paper, cutting cloth with scissors, brushing shoes, hitting a table-tennis ball, sharpening a pencil.

Each time that a sound is to be produced the one in charge should warn the listeners. If desired those listening may write down their solutions, and at the end all can be marked together.

In **Lost Identity,** one player goes out of the room, and in his absence the others decide who he or she shall be.   Any fairly well-known character, living or dead, may be chosen : Grace Darling, Nansen, Shakespeare, Confucius, Sappho, George Lansbury.

The player outside is then recalled, and told to discover his identity.   This he may do by asking any questions he likes.   The questions may be put to anybody, and the answers given must be truthful, but must consist simply of the words " Yes " and " No."

When the questioning player at last succeeds, whoever gave him the clue that led to his final correct guess goes out of the room, and play begins afresh.

Chit-Chat.   The name of a particular trade or occupation is given to each player, and then the leader begins to tell or read a " gossip paragraph," in burlesque imitation of the ordinary newspaper account.   At each suitable point she stops, and points to one of the players, who must at once add some word connected with his or her occupation.   The following example will make things clear:—

Leader—The wedding, which attracted much attention, took place at the

Farmer—Dairy.

Leader—It was attended by many guests, most of whom arrived on the

Fireman—Fire engine.

Leader—The bride was dressed in

Decorator—Panelled wall-paper,

Leader—Trimmed with

Gardener—Lettuce leaves.

Leader—After the ceremony the happy couple left in a

Carpenter—Packing case,

Leader—Accompanied to the station by friends riding

House Furnisher—Clothes horses.

And so on.   The game can continue indefinitely.

Gossip is an amusing game for it shows how news changes when it is retailed from mouth to mouth.   First you must have a piece of gossip written down, with or without a local colouring.   It is best for it to be quite absurd, and should be about the following length :—

" It is rumoured that Miss Jane Honoria Figglebat, ward of the well-known boxing promoter Jem Shambles, will next week try to break the underwater swimming record for girls of English extraction. Her fiancé Mr. Wallaby, the animal dentist, recently fitted seven new teeth to a Zoo leopard which had broken its jaw in a fight with a lion and two llamas."

This piece of gossip is then read over quietly by the leader into the ear of the first player in the seated ring.   The player immediately whispers it to his neighbour, who in turn passes it on, until it has finally travelled all round the circle from player to player.

The last player repeats aloud what he has heard, and finally the

leader, who has retained her piece of paper, reads out the original
" paragraph." The fun consists in the changes which the gossiping
will have brought by degrees into the first player's version.

For **Back Stage Effects,** a story is told by the play leader, and into
it he introduces as many references to sounds and noises as possible.
Each time such a reference is made the player, whose next turn it
is, imitates the sound referred to.

Any one who makes the wrong sound, or fails to make the right
one, drops out of the game, or has a point scored against him.

The aim of the leader is, naturally, to make her tale so enthralling
that players miss their cues.

Here are suggestions that can readily be introduced into a
narrative—applause, hisses, animal noises—barking, roaring, mooing,
miauing and so on, bird noises, door slamming, screech, laugh,
moan, explosion, tapping, splash, thud, yell, whispering, snoring,
howling of wind, weeping, baby prattle, starting of railway engine,
sigh, ticking of clock, sneeze.

Public Speaking. The players sit in horseshoe formation, with
the " speaker " standing in the open end.

He begins to harangue the rest, talking seriously or nonsensically
as he chooses, and gesturing a good deal. Each time he raises his
right hand every one must clap; when his left hand goes up all
must hiss; when both arms are raised together his audience must
shout " Throw him out."

A player failing to do the right thing, or doing the wrong, has
to change places with the speaker, and begin a new speech.

Intense solemnity must prevail throughout **Mother Magee.**
—even the slightest smile being enough to disqualify a player.

The leader starts off by turning to her neighbour and saying :—

" Mother Magee is dead."

" How did she die? " inquires the second player.

" Like this," says the leader—and closes one eye.

The second player now turns to her other neighbour and passes
on the same information, in the same little dialogue, finishing up
by closing one eye, as did the leader. So the thing goes round,
until every player has one eye shut. The leader then begins the
next round, and tells how Mother Magee died with her mouth open
also. So at the end of this round each person has one eye closed
and mouth open. With each new round some new peculiarity is
added, such as : holding the left ear; right leg straight out; head
on one side; one shoulder raised; nose wrinkled up.

It is unlikely that many players will last even so long, but if they
do plenty of additional trials can be added.

Serial Story is a particularly good game for it taxes the invention
and ingenuity of every player. One person starts off a stirring tale
of incident and thrill, continuing until he reaches a dramatic crisis.

Fig. 4. For Long Distance Flights you need a map and some cardboard aeroplanes. The player making the flight is blindfolded.

Then he breaks off abruptly—like a serial story. His neighbour must immediately carry on with the narrative, doing her instalment in the same fashion and breaking off at an exciting stage.

So every player takes his or her turn, and the story continues for as long as you like.

Can't You Smile? Men and girls sit in two straight rows, facing each other and about two yards apart. There must also be a time-keeper, whose job it is to allow fifteen seconds to each side in turn.

During the first period the men must try to make the girls smile—it is understood that " partners " must look squarely into each other's faces all the while. Any girls who succumb and do smile are out of the game and must for the rest of the time stand behind their chairs. When the first fifteen seconds are up the girls, irrespective of whether they are standing or sitting, have their chance for a similar period, and try to make their men partners smile in the same way.

The game continues until none is left sitting.

Long Distance Flights. Fasten up on the wall a large map of the world; one roughly drawn on a sheet of brown paper will serve. But clearly mark your home town—where the game is being played —on it. You will need also a number of tiny aeroplanes, cut out of cardboard or paper, each with a pin stuck through it. If there are several planes, it is best to have them of different colours, so as to be easily distinguishable; if you use only two and run the game off with competing pairs of players the colouring will not matter.

Each player in turn is blindfolded and made to walk across the room to the map. On arriving, with outstretched hand in which his aeroplane is held, he sticks the pin into any part of the map he likes, though he is not allowed to feel for the edge of the paper. The pin must be pressed in at the point where it first touches the map.

The length of the flight is the distance measured in a straight line from the home town to the plane. But if the plane has been pinned on to any ocean or lake, it is said to have crashed and does not count at all.

The winner of the game is the one who makes the longest flight.

GAMES PLAYED TO MUSIC

Here are a few musical games. These are always popular, and you should always try to include one or two in your programme. First we have **Musical Basket,** a variant of Musical Chairs. The players sit in a large ring and pass a basket round from one to another while music is being played. At intervals the music breaks off without warning, and whoever chances to be holding the basket drops out of the game. The players spread themselves out evenly again and play restarts, minus one player each time the music starts. So player after player drops out, until only the winner is left.

As fewer players are in play, the basket will probably have to be tossed from one to the next. Should it fall to the floor the one who last touched it must recover it, and it is he who pays the penalty, if the music is interrupted before the basket has been recovered. This game is also suitable for children.

Musical Balloons. A game similar to the preceding one can be played with a ring of players and two or three balloons. The players stand facing outwards, and each balloon is kept poised on a tin plate. Patted and controlled by the plate each balloon is thus made to travel round the ring.

In this case, when the music stops, two or three players will be out simultaneously.

In all games of this very common and popular " interrupted music " type, the one in charge of the music must adjust the frequency of his breaks to the number of players. If there are thirty folk in play at the beginning, you obviously must not have long spells of play, if all are to be got out one at a time. Otherwise those who have been put out early will quickly weary of their inaction.

A-Hiking We Will Go is a very popular musical dance game, for it requires no knowledge of dance steps, but merely walking and sliding steps in time with the music, while the song is being sung. Any number of players not less than ten can take part, providing the room is large enough for every one to dance around in comfort.

To begin, two straight lines are formed down the middle of the room, men in one, girls in the other. They face inwards so that every man is opposite his partner, and about two yards from her.

All begin to sing the following song, and continue, repeating it as long as the game lasts—which is usually until every couple has been once down the middle. The music here given is of the simplest kind, so that any novice can play it; more experienced musicians will naturally amplify the harmony.

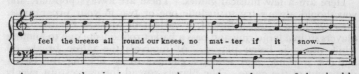

As soon as the singing starts, the couple at the top of the double file join hands and go down the avenue between the two rows, taking sideways, skipping or sliding steps. They go right to the bottom of the line, then without pause return to the top. Again they go down, and this time they stop at the bottom, and, each stepping back, they raise their arms high in the air so as to form a wide arch, big enough to allow other couples to pass beneath. This is the signal for the two lines to turn up towards the top end of the room and to begin to march in single file. Each line, led by the top player, turns outward; marches down the side of the room : turns in at the bottom. So the leading couple meet each other at the middle of the bottom end of the room, and taking hands continue up the middle of the room side by side, passing under the arch formed by the stationary pair, and going on until they come to the top of the room. Here they drop hands, turn inwards, and step back into their original positions once more. All the other players follow behind, in the same way. When the original double line is formed again the two who have been making the arch under which every one else has passed, step back and go to the bottom ends of the lines. Then the new top couple join hands and come down the middle, and the whole thing begins again.

The Hidden Treasure requires interrupted music, but the players retain their seats all through—there is no defaulting by which they are compelled to drop out of the game.

All sit in a ring, and pass a parcel round from hand to hand while the music is played. When it stops the player happening to have the parcel begins to unfasten it, but has to desist and pass it on again as soon as the music restarts. Finally one lucky player uncovers the " hidden treasure," which may be a box of chocolates, and so retains it as a reward.

Everything depends on the proper preparation of the treasure. Take your packet of chocolate and wrap it into an ordinary parcel, with paper and string. Wrap this into another parcel, with more string and paper. So continue, adding covering after covering, until you have perhaps a dozen wrappings, each tied separately with string. Thus any player, during a break in the music, will be unlikely to take off even a single wrapping, and the complete uncovering will keep the game going for a considerable time, with excitement increasing as the last stages are reached.

The Statue Dance. Partners are taken and any ordinary dance is performed to music. But when the music breaks off each couple must suddenly become "petrified" in whatever position they happen to be. Any couple that moves during the " freeze-up " drops out of the dance. This " freeze-up " lasts until the music recommences, when all come to life again and the dance continues until the music stops again and more couples drop out—and so on until only the winning couple remains.

To play **Alibis,** a murder is assumed to have been committed at a certain time; two " conspirators " are sent out of the room, and they decide on an alibi—making up any story they like of what they were doing together from an hour before the crime until an hour after. One of them then comes in and tells his story. The others ask him questions, and then call in his fellow conspirator, who in turn tells his story and is asked questions. The first conspirator is not allowed to speak or make any signs during the examination of the second.

The object of the rest of the party is of course to make the second conspirator contradict the first. When the questioning is finished, the party decide whether or not the conspirators have established a convincing alibi.

Two Dogs and a Bone is an enthralling, exciting game for twelve to sixteen energetic players. They are divided into two equal teams, which line up and number across opposite ends of the room. There must in addition be a play leader, who will call out numbers, and a scorer, who will occasionally announce how the score stands and whose verdict on all questionable points must always be accepted. In the centre of the room stands a skittle, indian club, or something similar—this should be on a marked point, perhaps a chalked cross, so that it can always be replaced at the same spot half-way between the teams.

The leader calls out any number, and the two players of that number, one from each end, dash to the centre, each hoping to grab the skittle and return with it to his team. The one who gets it back safely scores a point for his side; but should a player be touched by the opponent while holding or carrying the skittle, the point goes to the opponent.

After this first point has been gained by one of them, the player with the skittle replaces it at the centre, and the two teams are ready for a new number to be called.

The game goes on until one side has scored nine points.

One rule that must be enforced is that each player, during the feinting at the middle, must stay on his own team's side of the skittle.

PASSING THE NUT

In **Back and Front,** teams stand in straight rows down the middle of the room, facing inwards. At the top end of each row is a plate on a chair, containing a dozen peanuts, or other small objects. It is better fun still if the objects are all different, for their unexpectedness lends additional confusion to the game.

When the starting signal is given, the end player of each line picks up a nut and passes it to his companion. As soon as it is gone he passes on another, and so on until all are taken from the plate. The nuts must be passed all the way one at a time. They go down the front of the line, round the bottom player, and come up again behind the backs of the team. When they reach the first player again they are replaced on the plate—and that team wins which first gets all its nuts back.

The fun of the game lies in the confusion which can easily result when players are being called upon to pass nuts in front of them and behind them at the same time. Any one who lets a nut drop must himself recover it, and his team is kept at a standstill until he is back in his place.

Table-cloth Who's Who is more uproarious than strenuous. Two teams of any size take part. Each stays at one end of the room, hidden behind screen, door, curtain, or anything convenient. Throughout the game they must be invisible to each other.

Each team has a sheet or table-cloth, and each chooses one of its number to walk out into the middle of the room. The chosen two drape themselves, head and all, in the sheets and walk into the middle until they meet. Neither, of course, can see the other, and they do not speak. But when they meet they may, through their sheets, touch each other's head and shoulders. The first to discover and call out the identity of the other scores a point for his team. If either should make two wrong guesses the point goes to the opponents.

Then both players return, and new people are chosen to go out.

The Spelling Bee is one of the oldest party games and it has been brought back into popularity by the radio. The teams should sit facing each other with the " spelling master " placed at the end, between the lines, holding the previously prepared list of words.

The first word is given to the No. 1 member of the first team. If he spells it a point is scored for the team; if he fails the word passes to the No. 1 of the second team. Thirty seconds should be allowed for each word.

Each player, having spelt his word, should repeat it, to prove that he knows the word he has spelt. And the spelling master will give a brief dictionary definition of each word as he announces it. The thing will go like this :—

" Hurricane," says the spelling master, " a violent storm characterized by sudden changes."

And the speller proceeds : " H-u-r-r-i-c-a-n-e. Hurricane."

Rhubarb Charades. The team producing the charade choose the name of a character, living, dead, or fictitious. They then act in turn each letter of his name, by playing a little scene portraying another character whose name begins with that letter. For instance, if a team had chosen the name HITLER, they might act Henry VIII, Isaiah, Trotsky, Lawrence of Arabia, Epstein, and Roosevelt. Finally the character himself is portrayed.

The only rule is that the entire dialogue must consist of the one word " Rhubarb "—repeated again and again and spoken with appropriate feeling ! The audience has to guess the name of the character himself, and of each of the characters representing the initial letters of the main character's name.

A TEAM GAME WITH SKITTLES

Two or more teams take part in **Bob Skittles**.

To begin, the competing teams stand in single file at the bottom end of the room, the first player of each toeing a starting line. At the top end of the room, opposite each team, stands a skittle, close to the wall, with a " bowling line " three yards in front of it.

When the starting word is given each first player, carrying a ball, dashes up the room and halts at his bowling line. From this point the ball has to be rolled at the skittle. If the skittle is not knocked down, the ball must be recovered and bowled afresh. Only when the skittle falls, can the player run back to his team and touch off the next player by handing over the ball. No player must return down the room, until he has replaced the overturned skittle.

So each team member in turn has his chance, and the game continues until one team finishes. No one must pick up a ball except the player to whom it belongs for the time being.

To play **String Relay**, each team needs a length of string which will reach from one end of the room to the other. The string must be rolled into a ball.

To start, the first player in each team, holding his end of string, runs up the room; the ball is held by the second team member, who allows it to unwind in his hand. When the first player reaches the far end he immediately turns and begins to make his way back, winding up the string which he holds into a new ball. As soon as he reaches his team again he hands the fresh ball to the third team member, while the second, gripping the end which he is already holding, runs up the room and returns, just as did the first player.

That team wins which first gets each of its members up the room and back again, with the string properly rewound each time.

Take care that the full course is covered at each lap. It is a good plan to compel each runner to touch the wall at the top end of the room, and to make the one who holds the string with his team stand with both feet touching the wall at the starting end.

BRAIN TEST GAMES

To play **Alphabet Dinner** everybody sits in a circle, facing inwards, and the leader starts off by saying :—

" I had for dinner today some ——" here she puts in the name of some food beginning with *a*, perhaps *apples*.

The second player repeats this, adding something beginning with *b*. She might say :—

" I had for dinner today some apples and beef."

So each in turn repeats what has already been said, adding a word beginning with the next letter of the alphabet. Thus before long someone may be saying :

" I had for dinner today some apples, beef, carrots, dumplings, eggs, fried fish, grape-fruit, ham, ice-cream, jelly, ketchup, liver, marrow, nuts, orange pudding, pancakes."

Any one who fails to add some new thing beginning with the appropriate letter, or blunders in repeating the complete list, either drops out of the game or has a point scored against her.

The next game **Buzz** is one for quick thinkers only. Again the players sit in a ring, and each in turn takes his or her part, those who default dropping out.

The first player starts to count by saying " one," and each in turn follows on—two, three, four, five, six, and so on. But " seven " must not be said; instead the word " buzz " must be substituted. Similarly, buzz must be substituted for every later number which contains a seven or into which seven will divide—like this :—

" One, two, three, four, five, six, buzz, eight, nine, ten, eleven, twelve, thirteen, buzz, fifteen, sixteen, buzz, eighteen, nineteen, twenty, buzz." Buzz is also said for seventy, and the succeeding numbers are given as follows : " buzz one, buzz two, buzz three, buzz four, buzz five, buzz six, buzz buzz, buzz eight, buzz nine, eighty, eighty-one, eighty-two, eighty-three, buzz."

To make the game still more difficult you may play **Fizz Buzz,**

substituting " fizz " for all fives or multiples of five, in addition to
the buzz for sevens. Counting then would run :—

" One, two, three, four, fizz, six, buzz, eight, nine, fizz, eleven,
twelve, thirteen, buzz, fizz." For thirty-five, fifty-seven, seventy,
seventy-five you will say " fizz buzz," or " buzz fizz," as is
appropriate.

In **One Awkward Albatross,** all the players sit round in a circle,
and each player in turn adds to the spoken list as it reaches him
two new words beginning with the next letter of the alphabet—an
adjective or a descriptive word and the name of some living creature.
Thus the first starts by saying :—

" One awkward albatross."

The next might follow with :—

" One awkward albatross; two bulging bullfinches."

The numbers follow automatically each time. When the game
is well advanced some such result might be reached as :—

" One awkward albatross, two bulging bullfinches, three charming
canaries, four dumpy ducks, five electric eels, six flying fish, seven
gawky gorillas, eight horrible hamadryads, nine introspective iguanas,
ten jumping jaguars, eleven kicking kangaroos, twelve lolling
lambs."

What's Wrong? is another very interesting game, for in reality
it is a genuine and most interesting test of observation. All are
sent out of the room, to be recalled later. In the meantime the
leader has moved something in the room—turned a chair, changed
a picture, moved a rug or something of the sort. The first player
who discovers " what is wrong " with the room scores a point, and
is allowed to stay in and make a new change when all the rest have
been sent out.

Tailed Quotations is a literary game and demands a good knowledge of familiar prose and poetry.

The game consists of following one quotation with another, the
second beginning with the letter that finished the first. Thus, if
the first player starts off by quoting " The proper study of mankind
is man " another player might " tail " it with "Never did sun
more beautifully steep in his first splendour, valley, rock and hill."

Any player may follow on. Here is a sample of what might come
after the two quotations already given:—

" Let me not to the marriage of true minds admit impediment."

" To be or not to be? that is the question."

" Necessity, the mother of invention."

" Noble by birth, yet nobler by great deeds."

" Sleep that knits up the ravelled sleeve of care."

" Enter ye in at the strait gate."

" Evil events from evil causes spring."

Tailed Towns is a simpler version and easier to play. Here the names of towns are used instead of literary quotations. Each player may be compelled to follow on in turn (this is the best plan); or any player may be permitted to call out as soon as he thinks of a name: the disadvantage of this is that one or two people will probably monopolize the play. If each person round the ring in turn is allowed to try his hand, those who fail within a reasonable time may be passed over, but they will later have another chance and their interest will thus be maintained.

Each town must begin with the last letter of the previous word. Thus, if the leader starts the game off with " London " the others might follow with :

" Nantwich, Harrow, Wendover, Rheims, San Francisco, Omsk, Khartoum, Mulhouse, Elgin, Newcastle, Erzerum, Madrid."

Earth, Air, Water, is another old favourite, but is always amusing. The players sit in a ring, and one tosses a handkerchief to any other, at the same time calling " earth " or " air " or " water." The one who receives the handkerchief must immediately respond with the name of some creature living in that element. He might say " lion " or " nightingale " or " shark." To set a time limit the one who throws the handkerchief may count twelve, as quickly as he likes, and if a correct reply has not been made within that time he takes the handkerchief again and tosses it to someone else. But if the recipient gives a right name in time he takes over the next throw.

Probably counting will not be necessary, the game proceeding briskly enough without it.

Another version of the same game is Animal, Vegetable or Mineral. Here the nature of the thing is substituted, i.e., Mineral—water, iron, etc.; Vegetable—rose, bulrush, etc.

A GAME FOR PSYCHOLOGISTS

Likenesses is a good game for testing people's ingenuity. Explain that you wish to make an experiment in telepathy, and ask all the players to sit silent and intent for a moment and to try to visualize what is in your mind. You will, you may explain to them, be thinking of some common object.

Then ask each to say what he or she has thought of. It is almost certain that there will be a big variety of objects. You yourself may have had in mind a telegraph pole, while others may have thought of—bottle of ink, dog, pencil, motor car, apple, chair, ship.

That, however, is only the beginning of the game. You should now ask each person to explain how he came to receive such an impression in his or her mind, by showing the similarity or connexion between the object thought of and your telegraph pole. There is scope for much ingenuity here.

CHAPTER 4

PUZZLES AND PAPER GAMES

Puzzles aren't merely a waste of time, they are an excellent way of making sure that the daily round hasn't blunted your mental alertness, and their solution is, for most of us, that complete change of occupation which is the best kind of rest. It is important to remember that what may be a " real teaser " to one person is obvious at first sight to another : so if you, or your guests, solve the first of these that you attempt, in five seconds, try another—and you will probably find, before long, something you think worthy of your steel. The following problems are not arranged in order of difficulty : most of them are simple, if only you can see the solution, but here and there a really difficult one is included, that only an alert mind will tackle quickly with success. You will find solutions, if you need them, on page 58. And even when you've solved one there's no harm in looking to make quite sure.

1. Spelling Bee. Here are four words, one of which is mis-spelt. Can you say, without looking in the dictionary, which one it is?

HARASS   PEDLAR

FUSCHIA   STICH

Yes, it's very simple—but are you SURE?

2. All you need for this one is a knowledge of the alphabet. Start with the single letter E and build up the word

PRESENTS

by adding one letter at a time. At each stage the resulting letters must form a word out of the dictionary, though you may shuffle about the order of the letters as much as you like.

3. The Learner's Puzzle. This is a very simple test. Take a pencil and tick the following statements if they are right, putting a cross against them if they are wrong :—

(a) Cloepatra was an Egyptian,
(b) Milton wrote *Love's Labour's Lost.*
(c) Australia's smallest city is Brindisi.
(d) King Alfred was the first King of England.
(e) The pyramids of Egypt have four sides.

There's a time limit of ten seconds for each statement. You pass if you finish the lot correctly in under one minute.

4. Euclid's Ice. If the last one made you warmish, here's an ice-cream cone to reduce the temperature. It's designed by a French artist, very modern. The problem is this. How many different triangles are there in Fig. 1? You only have to count!

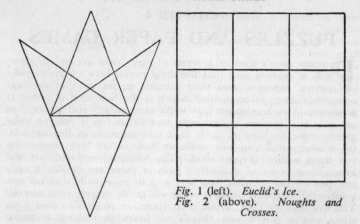

Fig. 1 (left).   *Euclid's Ice.*
Fig. 2 (above).   *Noughts and Crosses.*

5. Noughts and Crosses. And if you were wrong that time, and want an easier one, how many rectangles are there in Fig. 2? And how many of those rectangles are squares?

6. F-F-Final Sight Test. As a change from geometry, how many times does the letter " f," appear in the following sentence?

The Federal Fuses are the result of scientific investigation combined with the fruits of long experience.

Too simple? Well, never mind. But look up the answer before you ask any one else.

7. Keeps the Doctor Away. Leslie went raiding Mr. Rinck's orchard. Now Leslie is twice as many years old as there are apple trees in the orchard, and twice as tall in inches as the number of apples he stole, of which he ate half, thus eating twice as many apples as he is years old. Mr. Rinck keeps as many dogs as his wife grows vegetable marrows (and she only grows half as many vegetable marrows as he grows apple trees). If Leslie is almost as tall as his brother George, who is twelve, then how tall is Leslie?

Don't give it up too quickly. There's no need to start working it out with a complicated system of algebraic equations. All you need is the ability to multiply by two—and a little common sense. Now, how tall is Leslie?

8. Corporation Houses. My house has as many rooms up as down, and if I start from the kitchen garden and go first into the scullery, passing from there in turn into every other room in the house, never entering any room twice, and using each door once and once only (there are seven doors in all) it is possible to complete the tour and return once more to the kitchen garden. Obviously, in order that this should be possible, if the trip includes upstairs as

well as down, I must be
allowed to enter the hall
more than once, unless I
have two staircases! You
can assume that I have, if
you like: I am not saying
I haven't. When you've
settled this point, go on and
see whether, as a prospective
owner-occupier, you can
find out if any door leads
from kitchen to garage.

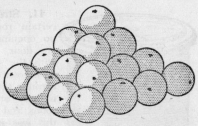

Fig. 3. Oranges and Lemons.

9. Oranges and Lemons. " Horanges," said Mr. Plummett the
greengrocer, " didn't hought to be such a hawkward shape for
arrangin'. When I was a boy, the Boss put me on ter winder
dressin', I 'ad to pile oranges in the winder, and I 'ad to pile 'em
in pyramids. Square pyramids, too. Yer know, sixteen oranges
in the bottom layer, nine in the second layer, then four and then a
bright 'un at the top (a pyramid with four sides, as shown in Fig. 3).
But when the Boss comes round and says as in future each square
pyramid must consist of a square number of oranges (1, 4, 9, 16, 25, 36
and so on), well . . . ! An' wot ah wants to know," he added,
" is 'ow in Brixton we makes a square pyramid wiv a square
number of oranges ? " How can it be done ? In other words, how
many oranges will there be in the square pyramids ?

10. Athene, Babbette and Katrina were not their real names.
What could you expect when one was a film star, one an actress,
and the third a circus rider ? But not
in that order. Yet Athene, who kept
a flat in Lynden Gardens, London, W.,
had whiter teeth than any circus rider,
and the film star had brighter eyes than
Katrina, and travelled south to London
every morning. The crux of the matter
was, however, that Babbette had longer
lashes than the actress, and finally their
friendship was severed because of jealousy.

The little circle drifted
apart, and each of them
for the time devoted herself
to her respective art or
business. Which brings us
to the problem. What were
the professions of the three
friends ? Look at Fig. 4 and
then decide for yourself.

Fig. 4. Three stars—which is which ?

Fig. 5. Scottish Reel.

11. Strong Room Mystery. A certain room is steel lined, and has no openings or exits apart from the one door, which fits flush when closed with the walls and floor. Indeed, it is impossible to leave the room except through the unlocked door. Now there is only one key to the lock of this room, and at the time of which I speak this was in the possession of Arthur. Now Bernard was locked in the room by Arthur, who went away, having first made sure that Bernard was really inside the room, that the door was really locked, and that the only key to the lock was safely tucked in his pocket (Arthur's pocket, that is). Now when Arthur returned in an hour he found the door still locked, but was surprised upon opening it to find that Bernard had vanished. Bernard could not have picked the lock, since there was *no keyhole on the inside of the door* and nothing in the room had been damaged or disturbed. How had Bernard escaped?

12. Scottish Reel. You know the nice bobbins of cotton which mother buys?(Fig. 5). Well, one of these reels or bobbins was an inch in diameter, the cotton was one-hundredth of an inch in thickness, the depth of cotton was a quarter of an inch from the outside, and the colour was deep rose. What is the simplest method of finding out the length of cotton wound on the bobbin?

13. For Mathematicians. Here is a simple long division sum. What are the missing figures?

```
    ....)869015(...
          .0..
          ——
          ..96.
          .....
          ——
          ...3.
          .....
```

There is no remainder, so the sum should be quite simple.

14. Colonel Bogey. Why is it impossible to construct golf links within twenty miles of Manchester?

Perhaps we'd better warn you that it isn't merely a matter of rainfall !

15. Get Home Safe, Mother ! At a certain bank the staff, consisting of a manager, senior clerk, and junior, are named Smith,

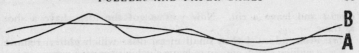

Fig. 6. Which of these two bicycle tracks is on top?

Jones, and Robinson, though not necessarily in that order. Whilst the manager can grow better wallflowers than Robinson, there is no doubt that Smith can run faster than the junior. If the manager's mother had previously married a Welshman, what is the name of the senior clerk?

16. For the Hendon College Boys. The tracks shown in Fig. 6 have been left by a bicycle, and the police are very anxious to know which of the two lines lies on top of the other—A or B. I wonder if you can assist them? Here is the chance for all amateur detectives!

17. **THE CURTAIN FALLS**
A problem play in three acts.
Cast:

ARNOLD........*A young man.*   BLANCHE.......*A housewife.*
AMANDA.....*A young woman.*   BERTRAM.......*A dramatist.*
CLAUDE........*An actor.*
CELIA........*An actress.*

The scene is an asylum throughout.
First produced in Agony, 1935.

Our local dramatic society asked me to review their production last year. At the end of the evening I found my pad covered with these notes.

Claude has twice as many entrances as Arnold, and twice as many exits as Celia; Arnold goes out as often as Celia, who has only half the exits allotted to Claude. Blanche, with twice as many entrances as Amanda (who was very good in the first two acts, though she was on only twice altogether), has as many exits as Celia has entrances, for Celia makes one appearance more than Amanda. The play brightened a little when the love interest started to move, and in the end the lovers fought their way to a passionate and protracted love-agony when all the other characters, probably feeling very fed up, had apparently gone home. This wasn't much good as a review, but as I'd lost my programme and forgotten who was who, it seemed to make a good problem. What are the names of the hero and the heroine, if the curtain rises on a blank stage in each act and falls on an empty scene in the first two? You have all the facts you need.

18. Subtraction. You think, perhaps, you don't need a dictionary for mathematics. Well, can you remove a stitched border from a purveyor of drugs and leave a prehistoric tomb? Which, after a little simplification, means just this. Remove a *hem* from a

chemist and leave a *cist*. Now you've got the idea, have a shot
at these :—

(a) From adorned with small metal disks which glitter, remove
a sudden spasm of pain to leave a vehicle for use on snow or ice.

(b) From transparent or perspicuous, remove a mischievous child
leaving a hinged or detachable cover.

(c) From a hare in its first year take away at all times or at any
time to leave an obstacle.

(d) Cure a scoundrel by taking away what ails him, yet the result
will be useless !

(e) From a customary procedure remove some deed or procedure
to leave what the cynic says every man has already !

(f) From what is figuratively the scene of an action, especially
of a dramatic one, remove a preposition denoting nearness
to some position, leaving a preposition meaning precisely the
same as that which you removed.

19. Eggsiting. Mr. Firth eats two eggs for breakfast every
morning, yet he neither buys, begs, borrows, steals nor finds the eggs.
He doesn't keep hens and the eggs are not given to him, nor does he
barter for them. No strange hen comes into his garden every morning
to lay them for him, since that would necessitate finding them,
which, you'll remember, he doesn't do. He doesn't hire them,
and no pun is intended on the word " lay," since he doesn't merely
lay them on the table. The problem is this. How does he get
those two eggs each morning? It's an old one, and it caught your
grandfather. See that it doesn't catch you !

20. This Month in the Garden. First of all plant four poplars
in the positions shown by the dots in Fig. 7.

Now purchase six more poplars, but not until the previous four
have grown to a reasonable height. Then plant the other six you
bought (that makes ten in all), so that the poplars form five lines of
four poplars in each line. By this means, showing visitors five
lines in a row, you will give the impression that you have twenty
poplars when actually you have only
ten. This is one way of getting your
poplars half price. By the way, how
would you plant the remaining six to
achieve this result, supposing that the
four shown are planted in the corners
of your garden? You must *not* go
planting poplars in Mr. Middleton's
next door, or anything like that.

21. Lap Record. A certain high-
light in the speedway world found that
he could obtain a remarkable spirit for
his bike if he mixed certain grades of

Fig. 7. Problem for a
gardener.

petrol. These were four in number, and priced at 16s., 17s., 21s. and 25s. a gallon. The whole secret, naturally, lay in the proportions used, and he refused to make these known. However, he let slip that the resulting special blend, which broke the lap record every week, cost him exactly 20s. a gallon. What proportions did he use?

22. Siberian Garrison. Some friends of mine were in Russia when the Tsarist regime ended abruptly. One of them, John Redwood, was captured by

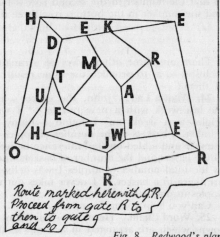

Route marked herewith G.R. Proceed from gate R to then to gate g and so

Fig. 8. *Redwood's plan for escape.*

the rebels and carried off to a Siberian garrison. Surrounded by high walls, it was a solid structure, honeycombed with passages, from some of which ran off the cells. But every few yards along these tunnels a stout iron grille barred the way, and at each grille hung a key. But the key hanging at any one grille was the key for some other grille, and if you knew the order in which to visit them you could go along all the passages, unlocking one gate and finding hung there the key to the next one. In all there were twenty gates and the same number of keys. Redwood's friends tried hard to find the right room, since any rescue must depend upon their doing this, and the prisoner himself attempted to smuggle out a letter explaining it. But the guards, with a sense of irony, allowed the letter and plan to go through, but kept back the key to the route, which he had written underneath. The plan and the scrap of paper he used is shown in Fig. 8. Can you solve the problem of the Siberian Garrison? It is obviously necessary to start at one of the outer gates, and since we do not know where the prisoner is, to visit every gate once before we return to our starting point. But since we dare not run unnecessary risks, no gate must be visited twice. There may be several ways of doing this, but only one route will ensure that at each gate we find the key to the next gate. Which is the right route for John Redwood to follow?

23. On the Square. If you look at this diagram you will see that the nine digits have been arranged in the form of a square, so that the number in the second row is twice that in the first row, and the number in the bottom row three times that in the top row.

$$1 \quad 9 \quad 2$$
$$3 \quad 8 \quad 4$$
$$5 \quad 7 \quad 6$$

There are three other ways of arranging the numbers 1 to 9 inclusive so as to produce the same result. Can you find all three of them?

24. What a Lad! John, the grocer's assistant, came round to me last week with a new puzzle. " I were deliverin' baskets of apples larst week, an' I found a funny thing. If I added the number of baskets to the number of apples in a basket, reversed this number and added on the difference between the number of apples in the basket and the number of baskets, then I got the same number as the total number of apples I was deliverin'. 'Ow many apples, are there in a basket, if I never takes out more baskets than I 'ave apples in one basket? "

Can you help young John?

25. Word Chain. Here are definitions or descriptions of six towns which are arranged in a chain so that the last three letters of the first one are the first three letters of the next, and so on down the chain. When you have found the words, reshuffle the initial letters to form a word which means *HARANGUED*.

(*a*) In Palestine and famous for a witch.

(*b*) Hardy wrote of it, though it sounds like the entrance to a Roman camp.

(*c*) In Victoria, is granite when I am there.

(*d*) Hirsute rodent in Asia Minor.

(*e*) The beginning of what may turn out either a fruit or an ape, and may be in Algeria or Argentina.

(*f*) The start of the Road to Mandalay. When you've found the beginning you just go on.

Now reshuffle those initial letters and make the word which means " harangued."

26. For Amateur 'Tecs. Here is a little problem of the kind they use to test the strength of candidates for jobs in private detective agencies. If you can solve it you might ask one of them to give you a job!

The other week I found a most unusual point, where a certain case depended entirely upon the means which had been used to effect the death of the victim. Now as soon as I entered the room where the crime had been committed, I realized that either the fire or the gas jet (which lit the room) was responsible for the death, which had been by coal gas asphyxiation. Both the tap of the light jet and the switch of the fire were turned off, but I realized that whoever had found the body would have taken that precaution and I determined to find out more about this point later. But I knew instantly which of the two, the light jet and the fire, had caused the victim's death. Can you tell me how?

27. For Sleuths. Here is a detective story without the trimmings. No red herrings, no clock alibis, not a single journey on the train, and no mention of Scotland Yard. A problem in deduction. The Mallern Mansion Murder Mystery! The party consisted of Henry Mallern the jeweller, his daughter Freda, her fiancé, John Lester, and Myrna Velie, Freda's friend. V. C. Brooks discovered, as soon as he took up the investigation, that the servants could be absolved from any responsibility, since their alibis were perfect. Only five minutes before our story opens, V. C. Brooks had been called to the mansion by an urgent phone message. Now he sat questioning the jeweller himself. Said that great man, "I'd invited Flecker with the intention that he should give us an exhibition of his diving. As you know, he's the biggest expert in the country. He's Myrna's younger brother, of course, and as she says, every member of their family for generations has been an aquatic expert. Velie is the name of her husband; she married young. Well, since Flecker came three days ago, he's steadily avoided that bathing pool—been determined too. Of course, he seemed nervous, and kept away from Myrna, but I suppose its some sort of family quarrel. Anyhow, half an hour ago I tackled him directly, and asked him how about a little diving. He flatly refused, walked away from me, and since then he's vanished entirely. We've searched the grounds, but there's not a trace of him. And now I'm scared. I'm afraid perhaps that maybe, he is in that pool after all . . . drowned. And I want your advice. Do we drag that pool right now?"

HOW DID FLECKER GET THERE?

The telephone bell broke into his speech, and V. C. lifted the receiver. After a few tense moments he replaced it.

"Mallern," he said slowly, "the body of Flecker the famous diver has just been found, terribly mutilated, at Mainbreck. What's more," he added, "they are positive about its identity."

"Mainbreck! But that's two hundred miles away!"

"Precisely," said V. C. "He vanished from here at two o'clock or thereabouts, and he is found dead two hundred miles away at two-fifteen." He paused. "Mallern, are you confident that it really was Flecker who was here the last three days?"

"Why, I've known Flecker for years," replied Mallern, "How could I be mistaken?"

"Then," said V. C. slowly, "I'd like to have a word with . . ."

PROBLEM. With whom did V. C. Brooks wish to speak? Why did Flecker avoid the pool? If Mallern could be relied upon, how had the crime been committed? The clues are shouting at you!

SOLUTIONS TO PUZZLES

1. FUSCHIA should be FUCHSIA; STICH is in your dictionary—or should be.

2. TE (tonic solfa) — TEN — RENT — ENTER — RESENT — PRESENT — PRESENTS.

3. (a) No : Cl*e*opatra was an Egyptian.
   (b) No : Shakespeare.
   (c) No : Brindisi is in Italy.
   (d) No : King Alfred was the first King of the English.
   (e) Yes.

4. There are seventeen different triangles.

5. There are thirty-six rectangles of which fourteen are squares.

6. Six times. Did you count the two " of's " ?

7. Write down the unknown items:—

Leslie's age	A
Number of apple trees	B
Leslie's height	C
Number of apples stolen ..	D
Number of dogs kept	E
Number of vegetable marrows	F

And at once you will see the following statements are true: A equals 2B; C equals 2D; D equals 4A; B equals 2F.

Combining these it is obvious that C equals 32F. In other words Leslie's height in inches is thirty-two times the number of dogs kept. Now you can't keep half dogs—it must be a whole number, and it says " dogs " and not dog, so that Leslie's height, in inches, is sixty-four inches if they have two dogs, ninety-six inches with three dogs, and one hundred and twenty-eight inches with four dogs. Your only other information says that Leslie is almost as tall as his brother George, who is twelve. Obviously then sixty-four inches or five feet four inches is the answer.

8. If there is such a door, then the garage must be considered part of the house; if no such door exists, then the garage is separate. Now since we start outside and finish outside, there must be an even number of doors outside the house. That would leave us only three doors. Also it would mean three rooms downstairs, since we enter each room once, and thus three rooms upstairs. That is, we should need FOUR doors upstairs. Therefore, no door can connect the kitchen with the garage.

9. The smallest number of oranges, barring " one " which can't be " oranges," is 4,900.

10. Athene must be the actress, Babbette the film star and Katrina the circus rider.

11. This is easy if you remember that there is no keyhole on the inside of the door. The answer is that the lock was of the Yale

type. Yale locks have no keyhole in the inside. All you have to do is to turn the knob. You probably leave your own house by this very same method.

12. The simplest method is to read the label stuck on the end.

13. This problem arises from the division of 869,015 by 3,547 to give the answer 245.

14. A golf " links " is the name given to a course by the sea. A golf *course* is all that can be constructed inland.

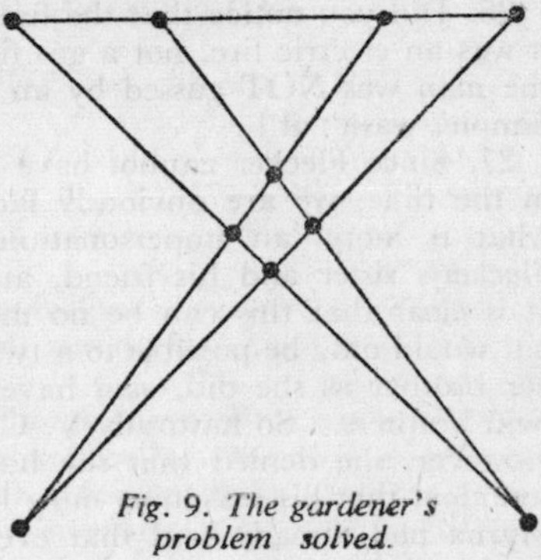

15. Smith.

16. B, because of the sharper

Fig. 9. The gardener's problem solved.

turns, must be the track of the front wheel, so that A must lie on top of B.

17. Since the curtain rises on a blank stage in each act, falls on a blank stage in the first two, and on the hero and heroine in the last, it follows that each character apart from the hero and the heroine must have a number of exits equal to the number of his or her entrances. Claude is out of it, since both exits and entrances are even numbers and there cannot be a difference of two. Arnold and Celia fall under the same reasoning. Therefore, Bertram must be the hero, and a little thought will prove Blanche the heroine.

18. (*a*) Spangled   -   pang   -   sled.
    (*b*) Limpid   -   imp   -   lid.
    (*c*) Leveret   -   ever   -   let.
    (*d*) Villain   -   ill   -   vain.
    (*e*) Practice   -   act   -   price.
    (*f*) Theatre   -   at   -   there.

19. Mr. Firth keeps ducks.

20. Fig. 9 shows planting directions for the ten poplars.

21. One gallon at 16s.
    One gallon at 17s.
    One gallon at 25s.
    Two gallons at 21s.

22. If you go round the diagram in the direction indicated by the letters " Route marked herewith J. R." you'll find you've solved it.

23. The top row must be one of the four following numbers : 192, 219, 273, 327. The first was the example given.

24. John must have had nine apples in a basket. This satisfies the equation however many baskets he had.

25. Endor—Dorchester—Terang—Angora—Oran—Rangoon.

26. Did you notice that the fire had a switch, not a tap? Then it was an electric fire, not a gas fire. Therefore, my dear Watson, the man was NOT gassed by an electric fire but by the light jet. Simple, wasn't it !

27. Since Flecker cannot have traversed the two hundred miles in the time, we are obviously faced with an impersonation, and, what is more, an impersonation carried out under the eyes of Flecker's sister and his friend, and over a period of three days ! It is clear that this can be no mere matter of theatrical disguise, but would only be possible to a twin. Now surely Myrna, knowing her brother as she did, *must* have known of the fact that she had twin brothers. So naturally V. C. wanted to speak to Myrna first. However, she denied that she had twin brothers, but V. C. was confident that his reasoning must be correct. He carried it further. Myrna had already said that every member of the family was a good swimmer. In that case why should the twin avoid the swimming pool, since a good display would not have shown up his deception? The reason *must* be either a birth or tattoo mark, visible when wearing a bathing costume. Now since the impersonation was an essential part of the plot, it follows that the twin brother must be deeply in the plot. V. C. issued a description of the wanted man which tallied in every way with the description of the victim—surely an unprecedented situation in criminal history— and added to his description the fact of the tattoo or birth mark. The twin was arrested and the reconstruction proved accurate.

PENCIL AND PAPER GAMES

Give a pencil and slip of paper to each person, and a multitude of games and diversions are possible. Some are genuine tests of knowledge, skill, ingenuity; others are sheer fun. But be sure that each player is near enough to a table to write comfortably, or is provided with a firm book or magazine which can be placed on the knees. Have a plentiful supply of papers and pencils.

First try **Squared Words.** Each player marks on his paper a large square, and divides it up into twenty-five small squares— five rows across and five down. If you happen to have printed crossword paper with squares ready made, this can be used.

In turn, every player calls out any letter he may choose, and that letter is written down, in any square. A specimen layout is shown in Fig. 10. Naturally, the player calling chooses the letter that suits him best. When all twenty-five squares have been filled, players count up the completed words which are spelt in their squares, reckoning them vertically, horizontally, and diagonally. Words may contain two to five letters.

To decide on the winner the total number of letters in all com- pleted words is reckoned, and the player with the biggest total wins.

Transformations is another ingenious game. The leader announces two words, containing the same number of letters. All the players set off to change one word into the other, by altering a single letter at a time and still retaining a word in the dictionary at each change.

For instance, to transform *man* into *boy* is easy—man, ban, bay, boy. *Five* can be turned into *four* as follows—five, fire, fore, fort, foot, fool, foul, four.

The more letters you have in the word the more difficult the transformation becomes. To alter *black* to *white*—black, slack, shack, shark, share, shire, shine, whine, white. Proper names are even more trouble—*Pat* into *Tom*. Pat, Pam, Sam, Sim, Tim, Tom.

There are two ways of planning the game. The winner may be he who first gets a solution, or he who gets the transformation in fewest words. If you are using the first method the round will be over as soon as someone completes his list; if the second, a certain time limit, say five minutes, should be allowed.

Questions and Answers is an amusing nonsense game.

Every player has two slips of paper. On the first each person writes a question—any sort of question will do; and on the second the answer to that question.

The questions are then collected into one pile, and well shuffled; and a second pile is made of the answers. Finally the leader draws questions and answers out of the pile at random and reads them.

Knowledge test games are always popular, and one of the best of these is **Knowledge List.**

Each player writes a list of general headings down the left-hand side of his paper, such as : fish, flower, fruit, vegetable, mineral, animal, reptile, colour, tool, weapon, great man, great woman, musical instrument, book, poem, liquid, mountain, river, insect, country, town, game, god or goddess. The list can be varied to taste.

Then a letter of the alphabet is chosen, and all players begin to write down all the names they can think of beginning with that letter, against the various sections of their list.

After five or ten minutes the game is halted, and the leader reads out any list. Players can mark their own lists, or each can mark his neighbour's. Two points are reckoned for each name that no other player has written; one for a name that one or more other players have; none when every player has put down the same name.

Fig. 10. *How to play Squared Words.*

A variety of this game is **Subjects.** Here a five-letter word, say " hardy," is chosen in which no two letters are duplicated. Then five subjects are chosen, say painters, rivers, historians, British birds and politicians; each player must write down a name to each letter in each of these subjects. That is to say, twenty-five names in all.

Endings is another good knowledge game. One player is invited to name a subject, another to choose a letter. Then every one writes down as many names as they can, fitting the subject and ending with the chosen letter. Suppose, for example, the subject is foreign towns and the letter N, then a player's list might run— Mukden, Baden, Rouen, etc. Score as for Knowledge List.

A GOOD GAME FOR ARTISTS

Art School is quite a different type of paper game, for this time artistic skill is more important than general knowledge.

Two teams are needed. They sit in straight rows, each with the " artist " at the end. The artist has pencil and paper. At the end of the room is the leader. When she calls the two artists run to her, and to each of them she whispers the name of some object. The artists then settle down and draw the object. As soon as they have finished they dash back to their teams, passing the papers down their respective lines. Not a word must be spoken, just as no word must be written on the papers.

As soon as any player guesses what the drawing represents he runs to the leader and whispers his guess to her. The first team to get the thing right wins. A fresh artist is chosen by each team, and the game begins anew.

The same object should always be whispered to the two artists, so that both teams are simultaneously guessing at the same thing. There is thus a genuine contest between the artists in making their pictures intelligible to their teams. The leader may use any amount of ingenuity in deciding on the objects to be drawn. Scope is unlimited. For example, any of the following might be chosen: onion, dome of St. Paul's, fire engine, buffalo, water-polo ball, Cinderella, flute, shilling.

Journalism is a game that requires quite a lot of ingenuity to play well. Before starting every one must have three slips of paper.

On the first slip everybody must write a question; then these slips are collected and mixed in a pile. On the second slip each person writes a single word—any word in the dictionary can be used. These slips are also collected separately, and jumbled.

Each person is then served out with two slips, taken at random from the piles—one question and one word—and must answer the question, including in the answer the word on the second slip.

This is not always easy. You may be faced with such a question as, " How are internal combustion engines best lubricated? " and compelled to include the word " sonnet " in your reply.

Proverb Delve is a good game for conundrum enthusiasts. Here a proverb is announced, and written down by all the players. Then an agreed time is allowed during which all try to find as many hidden words as possible in it.

The most interesting form of the game is to allow letters to be taken only in the order in which they occur. The finding of these takes a comparatively short time. Here is an example : " A stitch in time saves nine "—as, tit, it, itch, chin, hint, times, me, save, ave." But to get a longer hunt for words you can allow any of the letters to be used in any order.

Partner Poetry is a very similar game to Consequences, except that the papers are passed between partners. The players should be seated in two straight rows, each person facing his partner.

After pencils and papers have been issued, everybody writes down a line of poetry, passes it to his partner, hiding the line already written so that neither knows what the other has written. When four lines have been completed, the " poems " are read aloud.

Before starting the game, decide upon the metre of the poem, taking a well-known poem, such as " Twinkle, twinkle, little star," as a model of rhythm and line length.

When the player hides the line he has written, tell him to write the last word again, so that the second player knows the rhyming word that he has to match.

Poets All is a variation of Partner Poetry. Here everybody sits in a ring and numbers round up to ten.

Each poem consists of four lines and must conform strictly to rule, each player using his name to end the first line and his number to end the second. The third and fourth lines should rhyme with the first and second, for example :—

> My name you know is Mary,
> My number it is three,
> I'm not a bit contrary,
> But nice as nice as can be.

Everybody should read his own rhyme.

Another good Consequence game is **Drawing Consequences.** Everybody is given a slip of paper on which each draws a head, folding it over to leave only the two lines of the neck visible. Then the slips of paper are passed round, the second person drawing the body to the waist, the next down to the legs, the next the legs to the ankles and the last the feet. Finally a name is given to this composite masterpiece and all of them are thrown into a hat and taken out and displayed one by one.

Book Consequences is also played like Consequences, but with books as the subject. First everybody writes down a real or imaginary book title at the top of his slip of paper, folds it back, and passes it on. Next, everybody writes down a sub-title or alternative title, folds it down again, and passes it on. In the next round the name of the author is written; then a few lines from the book itself; then an extract from a review; then the name of the journal which published the review; then an extract from another review; then the name of the second journal. At the end, the slips of paper are collected and read out.

I Fear is still another variety of Consequences. Seat everybody in a ring and give them all a piece of paper. On the first piece must be written " what I fear," this may either be serious or not but probably will not be. As soon as all have finished, the papers are folded over so that the writing is hidden, and passed round and round until all trace of the owners is lost.

Then they are halted, and each person writes on the slip which has come to hand, " the steps I propose to take to overcome my fear." The paper is folded over again.

Once more papers are passed round until no one knows which is which. Then each person opens and reads the slip he has.

" I'm afraid of babies swallowing pins," someone may read, with the " cure "—" Keep a trap baited with cheese under the bed."

Dotty Designing is a game that gives everybody scope to exercise their skill and ingenuity. Give everybody a fair-sized piece of paper—perhaps a page from an exercise book, telling them to put five dots on the paper, scattered anywhere, and pass the paper round one place.

Then the contest begins. Every player must make a drawing based on the five dots, and in which the dots are an essential part of the design. As soon as all have finished, the papers should be passed round again, one place at a time. Each player can thus judge the merits of every drawing, and write on it how many points out of ten he considers it deserves. Finally the points are totalled and the winning artists discovered.

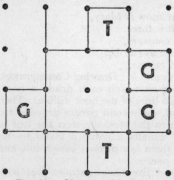

Fig. 11. *How to play Boxes.*

Constellations is very similar to the last game, except that the dots are stars in a newly found constellation. Each player therefore, joins up the dots and then christens the resulting design —just as Orion can be drawn on the group of stars which form that constellation.

Where there are plenty of

ingenious people in the party, **Limericks** is always a successful game. A first line is chosen, such as " There was a young lady of Clapham," and everybody has to write a Limerick beginning with that line, and after a reasonable time they are collected and read out. A small prize might be given to the writer of the Limerick voted to be the best.

The next game **Sixteen Spot** has two variations. Either all the players compete at once, or each can try in turn with the others looking on. Plenty of paper is needed for there are sure to be many spoiled attempts.

First you must put sixteen numbers, or dots, down in a square formation, like this :—

$$\begin{array}{cccc} 1 & 2 & 3 & 4 \\ 5 & 6 & 7 & 8 \\ 9 & 10 & 11 & 12 \\ 13 & 14 & 15 & 16 \end{array}$$

Then draw a pencil line from 1 to any other number, returning again to 1. Continue to some other number, going back to 1 again. Go on similarly until you have linked up every number with 1, always returning before you set out for the next number. Numbers can be taken in any order. No line must cross another line, nor must lines touch.

If you find a square of sixteen points too troublesome then try one of nine first.

Sentence Building is an amusing exercise in ingenuity. First announce any word of three letters, and tell everybody to write it down. Then see who can first make a sentence composed of three words, whose initial letters are the letters of the original word in proper order. For instance :—

See—Spectacles ease eyes.

You may award the first person to get a sentence one point, or wait until all have succeeded, and then have them read out. If possible, sentences should have some bearing on the original word.

Go on to a four-letter word, then words of five, six, seven letters, and so on. Here are a few more examples :—

Game—Gives adventure, makes excitement.

Award—A winner accepts rightful due.

Rabbit—Run away bunny before it thunders.

Only two players at a time can play **Boxes,** so that it is better to confine it to small parties. Choose your two players, and put a piece of paper between them with a square of twenty-five dots marked on it—five rows each way. The dots should be at least a quarter of an inch apart, as shown in the partly completed square in Fig. 11.

Each player then takes it in turn to add a single line joining two neighbouring dots. The aim of each is to finish off small squares.

H.E.—C

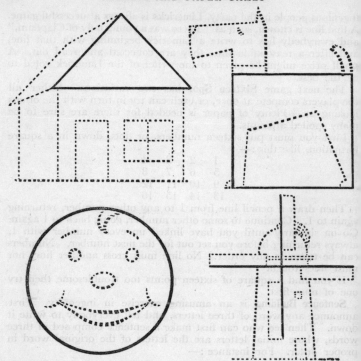

Fig. 12. In the game of Academy, every triangle must be made a house, every square an animal, every circle a face; a cross can be made anything.

Every time either player adds the fourth side to a square he writes his initials inside it. When every square has been completed, the player who has initialled the largest number of squares wins the game.

Academy is a drawing game giving scope for much invention and skill.

Number the players round in fours. Then instruct the *ones* each to draw a circle on their papers; the *twos* to draw a square; the *threes* a triangle and the *fours* a cross. All these figures should measure about three inches across.

The drawing contest now begins.

Every circle must be made into a human face; every square an animal; every triangle into a house; every cross into anything the artist chooses. Allow perhaps five minutes, and then have an

" exhibition " of signed pictures. Some examples of circles, squares, etc., transformed into drawings are shown in Fig. 12, and the game will produce numberless others.

If you like to have a second round, variation can be obtained as follows :—

Ones—letter Z, to be made into a tree.

Twos—oval, to be made into a bird.

Threes—rectangle, to be made into a motor.

Fours—letter S, to be made into anything.

To play **Instalment Picture** properly, it is best to use a black-board and chalk, but a piece of brown paper pinned on the wall or to a table, will suffice.

The game is similar to Drawing Consequences, except that only four artists take part, and they have to draw animals. None of course may see the others' work, so that while one is working, the other three should be sent out of the room. The first artist draws the head which is covered over with a piece of paper, only exposing two lines of the neck. The next draws the body, the third the legs and feet, and the fourth the tail.

The final animal is unlikely to be one known to any zoo !

Who's Who is a game with an unexpected ending, but it is important to say nothing of this at the start. Give each player a strip of paper, telling him to number it 1 to 20 down the left-hand side and giving instructions as to what must be written against each number, for example :—

(1) Some year, after 1800; (2) any town; (3) another town. Neither of the towns need be in England; (4) *yes* or *no*; (5) *none*, *a few*, or *a lot*; (6) occupation or profession; (7) a sum of money; (8) another sum of money; (9) any descriptive adjective; (10) a number; (11) a colour; (12) another colour; (13) some part of the face or head; (14) a bad habit; (15) a recreation or sport; (16) a flower; (17) a vegetable; (18) an exclamation or expletive; (19) a number; (20) a sum of money.

Only you will know what all these details really mean. They are to be descriptions of the persons who are writing them down. Thus :—

(1) Year of birth; (2) place of birth; (3) where educated; (4) whether married; (5) number of children; (6) occupation; (7) total annual income; (8) annual expenditure; (9) personal appearance; (10) size of shoes; (11) colour of hair; (12) colour of eyes; (13) most handsome feature; (14) worst fault; (15) favourite sport; (16) favourite flower; (17) favourite vegetable; (18) favourite expression; (19) anticipated length of life; (20) probable amount of estate at death.

When all players have completed their writing you will ask each to put his or her name at the top, and then collect them in for

reading aloud. Each paper will be read in the manner of a
Who's Who entry. For example :—

" John William was born in 1814, at Oxford, and educated in
Chicago. He is married and has a lot of children. By occupation
he is a sausage sorter. His annual income is £19 0s. 4d., and his
annual expenditure £943 3s. 11d. His personal appearance is
triangular. His size in shoes is 22, his hair is mauve, his eyes pink
and his ears are his most handsome feature. Breaking people's
windows is his worst fault, and his favourite sport is hopscotch. The
flower he likes best is the nasturtium, and his favourite vegetable is
the swede. His commonest exclamation is " Just fancy that now ! '
He anticipates living to the age of 218, and leaving an estate to the
value of 3s. 4d.

A GAME TO RUIN FRIENDSHIPS

Life Stories is another, but very different, biographical game.
Players should be seated in two rows, facing each other—if possible
with girls opposite men. Incidentally, it is essential that each
player shall know the person opposite fairly intimately.

The men are provided with paper, and each is informed that the
girl opposite has been recently appointed principal of a famous
women's prison. The man must, for " newspaper purposes," write
a brief biography of his partner, telling the outstanding facts of
her life, and showing how each had its influence in fitting her for
the present appointment.

Meanwhile, each girl similarly sets out to write the life sketch of
her male partner, who has just been made a cardinal, and she tries
to explain in the same way how his whole life has led up to this
eminent post.

When all have finished, the papers should be read out. Each
biography must be prefixed by the name of its subject, and the name
of the biographer. For instance : " The life story of James Brown,
new Cardinal Archbishop, told by Peggy Potts. James Brown was
virtuous even as a baby. He once . . ."

There are plenty of other choices for the subjects. If desired, a
number of slips may be passed along and each biographer can draw
one, and then write about his or her partner with this slip in view.

On the men's separate slips might be : convicted thief; Prime
Minister; channel swimmer, etc.

For the girls' papers you might have : latest darling of the screen.

Only one person at a time can try **Mirror Writing**. A mirror is
propped up on a table and two sheets of paper laid flat in front of
it, so that they are reflected in the glass. One sheet has some
writing on it, the other is blank. The player's task is to copy the
writing on to the blank sheet, looking all the time at the reflections
in the mirror, and never at the actual paper (Fig. 13). Thus he

Fig. 13. *Mirror Writing
is more difficult than it
appears.*

will see inverted writing, and will be writing upside down himself.

This is not at all easy.

In order that the writer shall not be able to see his own hand or the real papers, a piece of card or paper should be held just above the writing hand by a second person.

Some preparation is needed for **Syllables.** First a number of long words must be written out in large, plain letters; then these words must be cut up into single syllables—it is well in writing them that their syllables shall be divided to allow for the cutting, for example : num-ber; rel-at-ive; wit-ness-ing. All these single syllables on separate bits of paper are then mixed in a large heap.

The players sit round, and each in turn draws three slips, trying to arrange them into words on the table in front of him. A single syllable may, of course, be a word in itself.

Players draw their trios of syllables until no more are left, or until every player for three successive rounds has not been able to make any new words. Then the game is finished, and the person with most words is the winner.

But when each player after drawing his slips has used what syllables he can, he must pass back the others into the general pile. Thus no player ever has any waste syllables on hand.

CHAPTER 5

INDOOR PASTIMES

THERE are countless sports and pastimes that can be played at home in a fairly confined space. Some of them have become world-famous sports with an organized code like table tennis; others are more humble, but all have this in common—they are sufficiently simple to be enjoyed by all.

The first, **Table Tennis,** is a development of the old ping-pong, in which a ball was patted backwards and forwards on a table by hollow parchment-covered bats. The game today, however, is very different, demanding energy, skill and hard practice.

The ball must be perfectly round, and not less than 4½ inches or more than 4¾ inches in circumference. It must weigh not less than 2.40 grammes or more than 2.53 grammes. The net, running across the middle of the table, must be 6¾ inches high and 6 feet long, projecting 6 inches over each side of the table. The table must measure 9 feet by 5 feet and its surface must be 2½ feet from the floor.

A game consists of 21 points. Each player is allowed five serves, after which the service goes to his opponent. Should the score reach 20–20 two successive points must be taken by one of the players to win, and service is changed for every point.

Singles or doubles can be played. For service the ball must first be played into the server's half of the table so that it bounces over the net into the opponent's half. In doubles the serve is made to the opponent diagonally opposite. Should a server miss the ball in serving, he loses a point. A *let* is allowed when a service ball touches the top of the net in going over, and the receiver may claim another service. At other times it is permissible for the ball to touch the net. A ball can be returned round the net posts. If a player has hit the ball off the table, the opponent may forfeit a point, if he touches the ball with his racket and so " plays " it. A

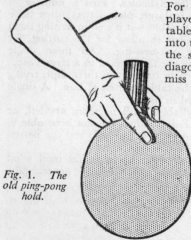

Fig. 1. *The old ping-pong hold.*

player moving the table in making a stroke forfeits the point, and does likewise if he puts a hand on the table for support; his body may touch the table subject to the first condition. Volleying—i.e., hitting a ball before it bounces —is not allowed. In doubles, partners must hit the ball alternately

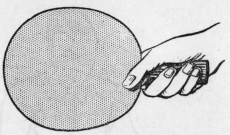

Fig. 2. The hold for a forehand stroke.

—a point is lost by going out of turn. Service is always taken by the right-hand player. After five serves the partners change places, and the opponent who was previously receiving becomes the server.

If the full-size table is not available at home, one of smaller dimensions will do just as well.

The best rackets are sturdy, with surface of rough rubber on each side. Be sure that your racket grip is correct. The old ping-pong bat was held in the manner of a pen (Fig. 1), pointing always downwards, with the forefinger at the front pointing also to the table. As a result, only forehand strokes were possible. Now backhand is used as much as forehand, so a different, firmer grip is necessary. The handle of the racket should pass naturally across the palm, with the little finger and the next fingers curling round the wood, close to the racket's flat surface. Your thumb must be across on the rubber itself, lying rather on its edge, and on the front of the racket. Slant your forefinger similarly across the back rubber surface of the racket. Thus, when you make a forehand stroke your thumb is towards the ball, but for a backhand the first finger is at the front. Figs. 2 and 3 show this quite clearly.

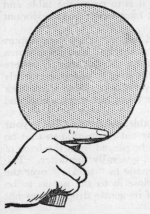

Fig. 3. The backhand hold.

Never stand too near the table. It is best to be several feet out from the end, so that you may have complete freedom of movement. For the same reason, always try to play the ball when it is well out from the body. A good action for serving is shown in Fig. 4.

For service you must toss the ball up and then hit it on to your half of the table. Generally, you should serve low,

Fig. 4. A player ready to serve.

fast shots which just clear the net and glance off your opponent's side of the table very swiftly. You will soon develop the ability to make your ball arrive on any spot of your opponent's half that you desire, so until you get that ability, be content to drive plain, hard shots. Imparting *spin* or *side* to a ball is something which must come after, not before simple competence.

To get effects of this sort the racket is sliced across the ball as the stroke is made. Spin can also be got into a service by twisting the ball sharply with the fingers when it is tossed into the air.

But the straight, hard drive, though the most important stroke in the game, is not the only one. Besides it, there is the smooth lofting shot, which lobs the ball to the back of the opponent's court, with the object of tempting or deceiving him.

This stroke needs careful handling if it is to reach the table end without reaching the floor beyond. It may tempt your opponent to a *smash* if it is too high.

There is a lot of satisfaction in a good *smash*. When your opportunity to make one comes, get well over the ball and drive down with fullest power. But don't hit wildly. Know exactly where you intend to place the ball, or it may rise so high and conveniently that the other player may *kill* it by an unplayable slam back into your own half. The smash may be taken either on a forehand or backhand.

The little *dropshot* is also most valuable, when you have your opponent off his guard for an instant, or out of position so that he cannot get across to it in time. It may be played from the back of the table or from close up at the middle, generally the latter. The essential thing is that the ball shall be made to " trickle " over the net, with tantalizing slowness, and so close in to the net as to be unplayable. And, of course, because of its gentle drop it does not bounce.

Often you may put sting into a shot by a final flick of the wrist, and you may soften down the stroke, even though the arm movement has been much the same as before, by a corresponding slackening of the wrist at the moment of impact.

Backhand play is shirked by some players, who run across to the left side of the table when the backhand seems necessary, in order to be able to take the ball on the forehand. This is a thoroughly bad policy, for it is not difficult to imagine the advantage yielded to an opponent when such a player gets right across out of position in this way—a fast shot down the right-hand side of his court will almost certainly find him helpless.

Your backhand (Figs. 5 and 6) should be developed from the outset,

Fig. 5. Another backhand hold.

so that you can take shots on either side of the court with equal ease and without moving from your normal position at the middle of the table end.

Always be " on your toes," ready to retreat several yards if necessary, so that the force of a fierce drive has lessened before you attempt

Fig. 6. A player making a backhand stroke.

to return it. Springing forward is always easier than leaping back, so as a general rule it is safer to be too far back than too far forward. The better your opponent the harder will be his drives.

However much you are compelled to move about, try always to get back into position after every stroke. This necessitates smooth, easy footwork. If you are playing doubles, good footwork is even more necessary, for as strokes are taken alternately by partners, each must keep clear of the other. You must step up for your hit, then drop back quickly so that your fellow may take your place. Keeping the eye on the ball is a vital rule in *all* table tennis. It

is less easy than in most games, for the ball is travelling at such a high speed and over such comparatively short distances. You *must* concentrate the whole time.

When receiving balls that have *spin*, remember that you must not play a plain stroke, or the ball will shoot away out of play. You must counteract the spin by slicing your racket across in the opposite direction. You may neutralize top spin, for instance, by slicing under the ball with your racket face upwards. A good position to hold the racket for this stroke is shown in Fig. 7. Practise this matter of spin assiduously. The best way is to have a companion who will serve across just the sort of balls you want. Failing this, push your table up against a wall and use the wall for an opponent. If you slam hard enough at it, with a top spin, the ball will come back to you.

Fig. 7. A hold for receiving spin shots.

It is important to become as expert in defensive as in offensive play, but whenever possible it is better to take the initiative and attack against an aggressive opponent; although to " stonewall " is often a way of making him play less cautiously. Tactics matter a great deal, particularly against unfamiliar adversaries. Having found an opponent's weakness, you can concentrate on the shots that give him most trouble or spring one on him unexpectedly now and again.

The more proficient you become the more energy you will be able to put into your game, and the more entertainment you will get.

LUDO AND OTHER BOARD GAMES

Ludo is played on a special board by two, three, or four players. Each player chooses a different colour and has four counters. The four colours are generally red, yellow, blue, and green. A die is the only other requirement.

At the beginning of the game the die is thrown to settle the order of play, the player throwing the highest number starting. Each player puts his counters in his corner of the board, ready to play, and the first throws the die.

No counter can start off until a six has been thrown. When a player gets six, he moves a single counter out on to the coloured square in the " round the board track "; this square is just by his corner and is of his colour. Whenever a six is thrown at any later stage of the game it is followed by a second throw; a fortunate player may even get a series of sixes, but for the first move of the game the six merely brings one counter into play.

The object of the game is to get all four counters round the board and into their " home " at the centre.

A player throwing a six can please himself whether he uses it on a counter already travelling round, or brings a new counter out with it; and he is always at liberty to use his throws on any counter he likes. One throw, however, cannot be divided between two counters, and when the " home line " is reached the exact number must be thrown to allow a counter to reach home.

Should a counter, while travelling round, overtake and fall on the same square as an opponent, the overtaken counter is sent back to its starting corner and has to begin all over again. A player is allowed to get two or more of his own counters on top of one another, and they can then be moved round like a single counter—all of them, for instance, going forward three places when a three is thrown. But if an opposing counter overtakes and drops on them they are naturally all sent back.

ALTERNATIVE RULES OF LUDO

There is an alternative rule about double counters. Where double counters occupy the same square, they are held to form a " block " and no enemy counter can pass or harm them. On the whole, however, this rule is not advisable, as it tends to hold up the game and take some of the excitement out of it.

In ordinary play the aim of each person is to get his counters round as quickly as possible into the safety of the coloured home line which leads up to the centre, for not until then are they secure from being overtaken. No counters can enter a home line that is not of their own colour.

When four are taking part in the game, those sitting opposite each other may be partners, and so two can oppose two. Partners can then help each other round just as if their counters were of the same colour, but they must each go to their proper homes. Similarly, when there are but two players, each can have two colours and so play eight counters simultaneously. Throws of the die will not, however, be transferable, but should always be taken by colours in their usual order.

Snakes and Ladders is played on a board divided up like a draughtboard, except that it contains more squares; usually a hundred. Each square is numbered. Two, three, or four players take part, with one coloured counter each. The counters are moved so many squares according to the number thrown by the die, and

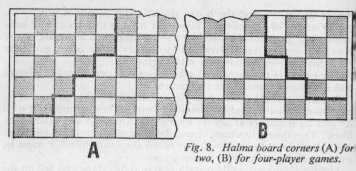

Fig. 8. Halma board corners (A) *for two,* (B) *for four-player games.*

they travel according to the numbering of the board—from the bottom left-hand corner along the bottom row to the right; back across the board to the left on the second row of squares; to the right again in the third row, and so on. The first player to get his counter to the top square, which is marked with the highest number, wins the game.

But scattered over the board are many ladders and snakes, of various lengths. The heads of the snakes are always nearer the top of the board than the tails, and the head of each ladder higher than the foot. When a counter arrives on a square in which is the foot of a ladder it slides up to the top of the ladder, and when a counter comes on the head of a snake it slides down to the tail.

No extra throw is allowed when the die turns up a six, and it does not matter if two counters fall on the same square.

Play is occasionally varied, to shorten a game, by allowing an extra throw for a six and also to a counter which has just ascended a ladder.

The board used for the game of **Halma** has 256 small squares, sixteen each way. Two or four players take part in the game, each with a set of small " men " of distinctive colours—yellow, blue, red, green. The men are rather like small chess pawns. When two take part they have nineteen men each; when there are four players each has thirteen men.

A player starts with his men filling the squares of the enclosure or " yard " marked on his corner of the board. The aim of the game is to get the complete set of men across to the enclosure in the diagonally opposite corner, before the opponent achieves the same end. Thus the two players simply exchange corners.

A corner used when two are playing (nineteen squares) is shown in Fig. 8, A. Fig. 8, B shows the corner used for the four-player game.

Every square of the board may be used. Players take one move each in turn. A man can be moved only one square at a time, unless jumps over other men are available. A man in an adjoining square can be jumped providing the square on the farther side of him is vacant. Jumps may be made both squarely and diagonally. And the halma man can continue jumping, in any direction, over friends or opponents indiscriminately, so long as the men and the empty squares are available. Men jumped over remain untouched; none are taken off the board at any part of the game.

Fig. 9. *The possible Halma moves.*

Play thus consists largely in building up a " ladder " or " bridge " along which one's men travel across quickly and conveniently into the far corner. To build up this bridge is the first object of play. With the succeeding move a new man comes along, moves similarly to the head, and so on.

Figs. 9 and 10 will make clear the methods of moving.

In Fig. 9 a man is shown on the centre square. With a single move he can go into any of the adjacent eight squares, numbered one to eight, providing they are unoccupied.

Or if an adjacent square has a man in it and the square beyond it is empty, he can jump over. The numbers nine to sixteen show all the possible jumps from the square at the middle. Of course, jumps can be made over men of any colour.

A player accustomed to draughts does not find it easy to realize that in halma one can jump backwards or forwards in any direction, squarely as well as diagonally, and also over one's own men.

Fig. 10. *A typical continuous move in Halma.*

In Fig. 10, a section of a halma board is shown with various men scattered over it. If a man were to start at the square marked A he could jump continuously on to all the squares numbered from 1 to 13.

It will be noticed that in plain moves a man may go on to a square of either colour, but in jumping he remains always on the same colour, as the jump is always made into the second and not the adjacent square. The men jumped over are not removed in halma —here again is a point which is a little confusing for a draughts player.

The game is finished when one player has all his men across in their new yard or enclosure. The board can then be turned round for a new game, for the winner's men will thus be all in position.

TWO WAYS OF PLAYING " DOUBLES "

Four players can either form two groups of partners, or each can play singly. Every player, of course, is quite free to jump over all four colours, and there is naturally more opportunity of zigzagging right across the board.

Partners can sit side by side, assisting each other, and each playing to occupy the yard of the opponent opposite. Or the partners may sit facing each other, the purpose of play being that they shall occupy each other's yards as quickly as possible.

Skill in halma is shown by keeping one's lines of communication clear and stealing runs over those of the opponent. Attention should particularly be given to planning jumps right into the new enclosure and not merely up to it. Similarly, men should be brought out of their original places by jumps rather than single-square moves whenever possible. Another thing to watch is that there are no stragglers left when the last men are being brought up towards their new yard.

Roughly, there are three main parts of a halma game, and the best methods of dealing with each can be learned only by practice.

HOW TO OPEN A GAME

First there is the opening, in which you begin to open up your enclosure so that men can pass out freely. This involves the building up of a ladder from each side and the rear part of your enclosure, leading directly across the board towards your opponent's corner. Incidentally, it is important at this stage to remember that your enclosure line is a mere convenience for the preliminary marshalling of your men, and in no way makes the enclosure section any different from the rest of the board. Your ladders and communication lines must therefore begin right in the enclosure.

The second part of the game comes when the opposing bodies of men meet at the middle of the board; there is probably a confused mêlée here as numbers increase and passage becomes more

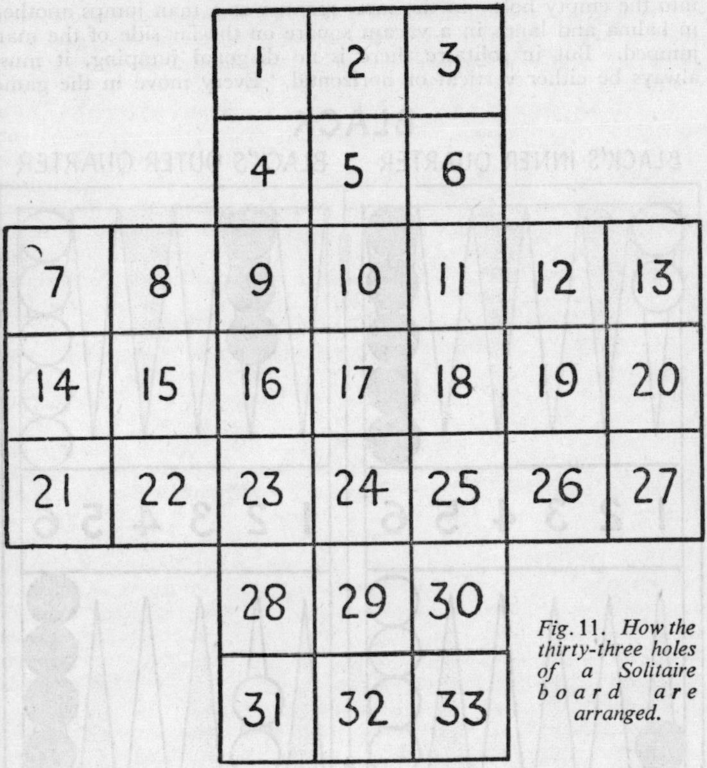

| 1 | 2 | 3 |
| 4 | 5 | 6 |

7	8	9	10	11	12	13
14	15	16	17	18	19	20
21	22	23	24	25	26	27

| 28 | 29 | 30 |
| 31 | 32 | 33 |

Fig. 11. How the thirty-three holes of a Solitaire board are arranged.

difficult. Every stratagem must now be tried to enable you to use the enemy's lines for your own ends, and to prevent him using yours. Sometimes it will be quicker to make a big detour near the middle than to try to struggle through.

The third stage comes when the enemy is passed and you have to bring your men into their new yard. Remember now that the enclosure is just a part of the board, and run your ladders into every part of it. Good planning will pay.

Solitaire is an interesting game for one player. A board containing thirty-three holes, laid out as in Fig. 11, is used. In each hole a marble or small coloured ball is placed.

To begin play a single ball is removed. It then becomes possible for some other ball to " jump " a ball adjoining the vacated place into the empty hole—in the same manner as a man jumps another in halma and lands in a vacant square on the far side of the man jumped. But in solitaire there is no diagonal jumping, it must always be either vertical or horizontal. Every move in the game

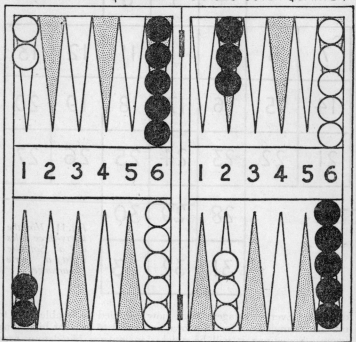

BLACK

BLACK'S INNER QUARTER   BLACK'S OUTER QUARTER

WHITE'S INNER QUARTER   WHITE'S OUTER QUARTER

WHITE

Fig. 12.   A Backgammon board with men ready for play.

must be a jump. Just as in draughts, any ball that is jumped is removed from the board.

In early games you continue until no more balls can be jumped, and will then possibly find several balls left, scattered about the board. But it will not need very much practice to enable you to get through with only a single ball left on the board at the end.

When more proficiency is gained go on to the real game. This consists in various problems, which you can devise for yourself in endless variety. It is necessary to start by taking off some particular ball and to finish by leaving the remaining single ball in that same, or some other, hole.

The commonest and most popular game is played by removing the centre ball from hole seventeen, and leaving the last ball in this same hole. Once you have mastered this game you will readily be able to set yourself other problems. Here is one solution set out, according to the numbered diagram :—

Remove 17.

Move	1.	Jump	5 into 17, removing 10.
,,	2.	,,	12 ,, 10, ,, 11.
,,	3.	,,	3 ,, 11, ,, 6.
,,	4.	,,	18 ,, 6, ,, 11.
,,	5.	,,	1 ,, 3, and on into 11, removing 2 and 6.
,,	6.	,,	30 ,, 18, removing 25.
,,	7.	,,	27 ,, 25, ,, 26.
,,	8.	,,	24 ,, 26, ,, 25.
,,	9.	,,	13 ,, 27, and on into 25, removing 20 and 26.
,,	10.	,,	22 ,, 24, removing 23.
,,	11.	,,	31 ,, 23, ,, 28.
,,	12.	,,	16 ,, 28, ,, 23.
,,	13.	,,	35 ,, 31, and on into 23, removing 32 and 28.
,,	14.	,,	4 ,, 16, removing 9.
,,	15.	,,	7 ,, 9, ,, 8.
,,	16.	,,	10 ,, 8, ,, 9.
,,	17.	,,	21 ,, 7, and on into 9, removing 14 and 8.
,,	18.	,,	24 ,, 10, and on into 8, 22, 24, 26, removing 17, 9, 15, 23, 25.
,,	19.	,,	19 ,, 17, removing 18.
,,	20.	,,	16 ,, 18, ,, 17.
,,	21.	,,	11 ,, 25, ,, 18.
,,	22.	,,	26 ,, 24, ,, 25.
,,	23.	,,	29 ,, 17, ,, 24.

Backgammon is one of the oldest " table games." It was played by the Greeks and Romans, and has had periodic spells of popularity ever since. It is played between two players, on a special board, which is divided into four " tables " or " quarters." In each quarter six spear-shaped points are marked; these are of two distinctive and alternate colours—often red and black. The colours have no significance in actual play.

Each player has fifteen checkers or men, which at the beginning of play are placed on the board as shown in Fig. 12.

The aim of the player is to get all his men round into his own

" inner quarter," and from there off the board, before his opponent can do the same. Each player, it will be seen, already has five men within his inner quarter.

Two dice are used simultaneously for every throw, and men are moved round accordingly from point to point. If a four and a three are thrown by a player he may move one man four points and another three places, or he may move a single man seven places. This choice is always allowed. If he likes he can ignore one die altogether and use only the number of the other. But he cannot divide the total number thrown, in any other way than that shown by the dice : if he has thrown a four and a three, for instance, he cannot put one man on six places and one a single place—it must be a four and a three.

Players sit facing each other on opposite sides of the board, so that each has the points in front of him pointing at his opponent. In diagram 12 the white player will have his inner quarter on his left, while the black player will have his inner quarter on his right.

HOW TO MOVE YOUR MEN

You move your men round the board as follows—from your opponent's inner quarter to his outer quarter, then to your own outer quarter, and so on into your own inner quarter. It will be seen that players move their men in opposite directions to each other. Each set of men travels always in the same direction.

A man can be put down on any point that is unoccupied by the enemy. If there is one opponent's man there, you can still put your man down, but the opposing man is then taken from the point and put into the division running across the middle of the board called the " bar." If two or more enemy pieces are already on a point you cannot put your own man down there.

If you have a man sent into the bar, you cannot move any other piece until this man is taken out and put back into play. It goes back into play in the inner quarter of the opponent, and, as usual, can only be put down on a point which is not already occupied by two or more enemy men. To get out from the bar you must throw a suitable number with one of your dice, or with the numbers of both of them added together. The points of the opponent's inner quarter are numbered from the edge of the board, so that if the third point is unoccupied, or has only one enemy man on it, and you chance to throw a three, then you may go on that point.

You may have as many as five of your own men on any point. At the beginning of the game, as the diagram shows, each player has five men on the sixth point of his own inner quarter.

In all your play you will aim at capturing, and putting into the bar, as many of the opponent's men as possible, while moving so as to escape capture yourself. Also you will aim at getting two men on each point, for this blocks the point to the opponent.

When a double—that is the same number on each dice—is thrown, double that number of moves is allowed. Thus, if each dice shows three, the throw will count as twelve instead of six, and one man can be moved twelve places or each of two men can be moved six places.

If it should happen that you have a man on the bar, which therefore must be got back into play before you can move any other man, and yet each point in your opponent's " home " or inner quarter has two or more men of the opponent on it, then you are completely held up until such time as the opponent has cleared one of the points. He thus goes on taking throw after throw of the dice until you are able to take your turn again.

When a player has got all his men home, to his inner quarter—not before—he proceeds to remove or " bear them off."

The points are numbered from the side of the board, as has already been said. Therefore if you throw a three and a two with the dice, you may take a man from the third and one from the second point, or a single man from the fifth point. So play goes on until one of the inner quarters is completely emptied, and the player to whom it belongs has won the game.

THE " END GAME " IN BACKGAMMON

During this removing or bearing off process, a throw of the dice may be used to remove a man, or to move any man within the home quarter. If, for example, you have five men on the sixth point, and none on any of the others, you will obviously stand more chance of clearing quickly, if you scatter the men over the other points, than if you depend on getting five separate sixes. Thus, if you throw a two you might move one man on to the fourth point, so that a later throw of four will be able to bear it off—and so on with the other men.

Doubles have a special value also in this final stage of the game, the double number being counted or used as already described.

The winning of a game may have a single, double or treble value—called a *hit*, a *gammon* or a *backgammon*, according to the position of the opponent when the winner completes his bearing off.

If the opponent has begun to bear off his men, the winner has made a single, or hit. If the opponent has not begun to bear off his men, the winner has made a double, or gammon. If the opponent has not begun to bear off his men and has one or more on the bar or in the winner's home quarter, then the winner has made a triple, or backgammon.

The dice are thrown to see who shall start the first game. For the second game the previous loser starts—if the game finished as a hit.

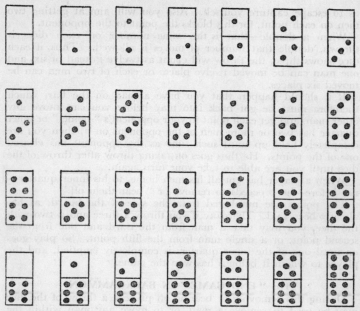

Fig. 13.   *A complete set of Domino " cards."*

If it was a gammon or backgammon, the dice are thrown afresh.
The player throwing the higher number, of course, begins.

The popular game of **Dominoes** is played with twenty-eight
brick-shaped pieces, or " cards," made of ivory, wood or some such
substance.   The face of a domino may be white with black indented
spots or " pips," or black with white pips; the back is usually black.
The face is divided into two halves, each of which may be blank or
may have from one to six pips.   Fig. 13 shows the complete range
of cards.

Their customary names are : double-blank, one-blank, double-one,
two-blank, two-one, double-two, three-blank, three-one, three-two,
double-three, four-blank, four-one, four-two, four-three, double-four,
five-blank, five-one, five-two, five-three, five-four, double-five,
six-blank, six-one, six-two, six-three, six-four, six-five, double-six.

There are many domino games, for two, three or four players.
Some of the most popular of them are here described.   The same
method of beginning is common to most of them.

The cards are placed face downwards on the table and shuffled.
Then each of the players draws one, and the person getting the

lowest number of pips, or lowest card, is entitled to begin play. Double-blank, naturally, is the lowest possible. The drawn cards are replaced on the table and all are shuffled afresh. Finally, whatever cards are needed for the game are drawn out by each player. A pencil and paper, or a cribbage board, can be used for scoring.

OTHER DOMINO GAMES

All Threes is very popular. The first player begins by placing a card, face upwards, in the middle of the table—this is generally termed " posing " a card. If the total number of pips on the card he poses can be divided by three, he scores a number of points corresponding to the number of threes it contains.

The second player must then " match " one end of the first domino. Thus, if the first card was a six-blank, scoring two points, then the second must have either a six or a blank on it and that particular end must be placed by the corresponding end of the first card. Thus, the second player might put down a six-three, with the six placed against the previous six. The two free ends of the posed cards would therefore be blank and three—and the second player would, as a consequence, score one point, as that total is divisible once by three.

The third player might have nothing better than a two-blank, but would be compelled to put this down, blank against blank. The two ends would now be a two and a three, making five, which will not divide by three without a remainder and so does not score any points.

The first seven cards which might be played are shown in Fig. 14. Below the cards are the order in which they are played, and above the scores which their owners gain.

Continuing, the fourth player might put down six-two, matching the two. There would thus be a six at one end and a three at the other, totalling nine, which gives three points.

The fifth move—with the first player taking another turn—might be a double-six. Any " doublet " or " double " is put down crossways—*à cheval*—so that all its pips count. Thus the double-six reckons as twelve, and added to the three at the other

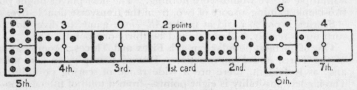

Fig. 14. *A typical game of All Threes after seven cards have been played.*

end of the row gives fifteen. Divided by three, this scores five points.

Continuing, at the sixth play, the second player's turn, three-blank is put down, as in the diagram. This gets a score of four.

So play goes on.

Each of the players at the outset will have drawn six or seven cards—six if four are playing, seven if there are only two or three. Thus, some cards have been left untouched, to form a pool or "stock." There must never be fewer than two of these, thus ensuring that no player can know for certain what cards his opponent or opponents hold.

When a player cannot follow on because none of his cards will match the two ends exposed on the table, he calls "go," or raps the table, and the next person takes his turn. When any player puts down his last card he calls "domino," and the game is over; it likewise comes to an end when no player is able to "go." This latter situation is termed a "block."

SCORING FOR ALL THREES

When one player is "out" he reckons as his score a figure equal to the number of times that three will go into the total number of the pips his opponent still holds, neglecting any remainder. Supposing all the pips of all the remaining cards held by the one or more other players total twenty-two, then the winner will reckon seven. The cards are then re-shuffled and a new round played. Game is fifty points.

Throughout the game each player should have his cards standing up on their edges on the table in front of him, so that while he can see them clearly their faces are not visible to other players.

All Fives is exactly the same game in principle as *All Threes*, except that fives are reckoned instead of threes.

The object of each player is therefore to obtain end totals that will divide by five.

Supposing, for instance, that the first player puts down, or poses, a double-five, that would score two points for him. The second player might have nothing better than five-two, and the fives being placed together his end totals would give twelve, which not being a multiple of five would score nothing. The next player might put two-blank, gaining a score of two, from the transverse double-five.

Scoring is not so rapid as in the *All Threes* game, for fives do not turn up so readily. Game should be thirty-one points.

One of the most popular games is **Fives and Threes,** a combination of the Three and Five varieties. Two to four players take part, and, as is evident, there are a wide range of scoring possibilities. The highest possibility is eight points—from a total of fifteen pips—for there are five threes and three fives in fifteen. The fifteen can be achieved from a double-six at one end and a three at the other, or a double-five and a five. Six points are gained from eighteen pips—a double-six and a six, for three goes into eighteen six times.

Game consists of sixty-one points. When no player can "go," each counts up the pips on his remaining cards, and the one with the lowest total is awarded one point.

THE MOST POPULAR TYPE OF DOMINOES

The Block Game is for two players. After the shuffle and draw for first pose, each player draws seven cards.

Each poses a card in turn, and as a general rule it is wise to get rid of those with the largest numbers of pips first. Any card can be put down at the start, and the next player must match one end of it. There is no question of counting up end pips; the main idea is to get rid of all one's cards before the opponent. If either should be unable to follow on, the other takes his turn. When neither can go, the game is over. It is likewise finished when either player has posed his last card. When a block occurs—neither being able to follow on—each player totals his remaining pips, and the difference between their totals is counted as score points by the one with the lower total. If one, for instance, has eleven pips and the other only four, then this latter scores seven points.

If the game finishes by one player running out, after putting down his last card, he scores the number of pips on his opponent's remaining cards. Should, for example, the opponent have only the five-four remaining, the winner scores nine points.

Game is any agreed number of points, generally one hundred.

TACTICS IN THE BLOCK GAME

It is a good plan to get rid of doubles as soon as possible, particularly the high numbers, for a double is just twice as difficult to pose as another card, since it can only match one number. Also, if you have a lot of one number it is good to play that frequently, as your opponent is bound in consequence to have only few of the same number and so will not be able to follow on so readily, while each time he is forced to call "go," you have an extra opportunity of getting rid of a card.

The **Draw Game** is like the *Block Game*, except that when a player is unable to "go" he can, if he chooses, draw one from the reserve stock of cards, and play that if it will match. But two must always remain in the stock.

The player can only learn by experience when it is advisable to draw an extra card. Remember that what turns up when you draw is entirely a matter of chance, and you may find yourself still unable to follow on and so be landed with another lot of pips which may count against you at the end of play. On the other hand if you draw a good card, in all probability it will enable you to play out all your cards, as you would not otherwise have been able to do.

Another very popular form of the domino game is **Matador.** A " matador " is either a double-blank or any card whose pips added together total seven: four-three; six-one; five-two.

Each player, at the outset, draws seven or some lesser number of cards. There is no matching of ends; the object is to make sevens all the time, so that any card can be put down providing that when it is down the two ends of the line add up to seven.

For instance, if a five-two is played first, then the end half of the domino posed next must be either a two or a five, so that the total of seven for the end pips is maintained.

But a matador can be put down at any time, irrespective of other numbers. Thus, if you cannot follow in the instance just quoted, with any two or five, then you might pose any of the four matadors should you chance to have one. The other alternative, when you cannot " go " at all, is to draw from the pool or stock. Such drawing is compulsory.

SCORING FOR MATADOR

The game is won by the first player to get rid of all his cards. Should a block occur, and the stock be down to two, so that no more can be drawn from it, the game is won by the player with the smallest number of pips.

The winner scores points according to the number of pips over and above his own on the cards of his opponents. If he is played out he scores all the pips the others hold; if he still has cards he first subtracts his pips from their total.

Game is usually one hundred points.

Bergen is an interesting variant of dominoes in which the aim is to make the two ends of the domino line match. When this is achieved twenty points are scored.

It is thus usual to begin with a double, which scores twenty.

In putting down further cards the joining ends must also match. It is therefore impossible for the second player to score. For instance, if the first player poses double-three the second must join a three to one end—there is no need for the *à cheval* or transverse placing—and as there is no other double-three there will be a different number at one end. Supposing he puts down a four-three. The two end numbers will now be three and four, and as the four-three is already down and cannot be repeated, this third posing still cannot score. Instead, perhaps, a five-three is played. This gives four and five as the end numbers, and if the five-four is next posed it will score twenty. If the fours have been joined, there will then be a five at each end. Should the double-five be

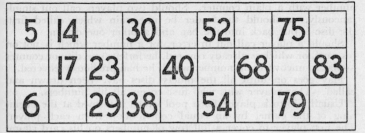

Fig. 15.   *One card of a Lotto set.*

played next it will score thirty points—a double following on ends
which already match always takes this score.

If at any point a player cannot go, he is allowed to draw one
domino from stock. The game concludes when no player can
follow on or when one has played out. The one who first uses up
his cards takes ten points; if both have cards left the ten points go
to the one with the lowest total of pips.

Two or three players take part in *Bergen.* If there are four, the
pool or stock is apt to run short—since, as we have already said, it
must never be reduced below two.

A TEST OF ALERTNESS

The equipment for the old and popular game of **Lotto** consists
of a set of special cards, and a bag of ninety numbered discs—the
numbers running from one to ninety. On each card are twenty-seven
squares, in three rows of nine. Five squares in each row have
numbers in them : they may be any numbers from one to ninety.
In the first vertical row of three squares are units; in the second,
tens; in the third, twenties, and so on. Plain counters are also
sometimes supplied with lotto sets, but they are not essential. A
typical lotto card is shown in Fig. 15. Each card is different from
the rest of the set.

A leader is chosen. It is his duty to shuffle the cards and deal
them out to the players, one or more to each according to the
number taking part. The players put their cards face upwards
on the table in front of them. If plain counters are being used
these are left in a heap at the middle of the table, so that all can
draw from them at will.

The leader then begins to draw the discs from his bag, one at
a time, but rapidly. As he does so he calls out each number. The
player who first sees this number on his own card and calls out,
" wins " that number, and either takes the disc from the leader
to put on the appropriate square of his card, or covers his printed

number with a plain counter. Should two players call out simultaneously, or should the leader be uncertain which called first, the disc is put back into the bag and another one drawn.

Should a player call out in error, for a number which is not on his card, or which is already covered, he forfeits one disc or counter —that is, uncovers one number which he had previously covered.

Play goes on until all the ninety discs have been drawn and called. That player wins who first covers all his numbers.

Usually, lotto is played for a pool which is formed at the beginning of the game, by an equal contribution from each player. The first player to cover a full row of numbers on his card claims one quarter of the pool. Play then continues, and the first player to complete two rows on a card similarly claims another quarter. Finally, the player who first completes a whole card, covering all the numbers in his three rows, takes the rest of the pool.

The pool is then made up again, and a new round begins, with the discs mixed again in the leader's bag.

Lotto is widely played in many countries, and is generally considered to be an excellent test of quick observation.

A NOISY CARD GAME

There are many varieties of cards for the game of **Snap,** but all have one thing in common, that their pictures run in sets of four.

Two to six players take part, seated round a table. The cards are served round to them in equal numbers, and face downwards. All players pick up their cards, but do not look at them. Then each in turn puts one down on the table, face upwards in front of him. This placing down continues without pause, every player making a pile of his own cards.

When, at any point, two similar cards appear, any player who notices the fact can call out " snap." The first to call takes both the piles on which the two similar cards are lying. Of course the caller may be, and usually is, the owner of one pile, so that he will merely take the cards from in front of the other player. But all cards in both piles are picked up from the table and placed at the bottom of the cards in the player's hand.

Should a player call " snap " wrongly, when there are not two cards alike showing, he forfeits all the cards which he has on the table, and they are put into a " pool " in the middle of the table, face upwards like all the rest. When a similar card to the top one in the pool is turned up by any player, the player who first notices this and calls " snap pool " takes all the pool and also the table cards of the player who turned the similar card up.

After a player has placed down all his cards, those who still have cards in hand continue to put them down, and the one who has

finished is still at liberty to call " snap."
When a player has emptied his hand
he picks up his cards and begins over
again.

So the game continues, player after
player losing all his cards, until one
person holds the lot—and so wins the
game. Even after he has had all his
own cards snapped, a player can still
watch for and snap others, thus bringing
himself back into active play.

Ordinary snap cards are generally of
humorous design, with all sorts of
caricatures in colour. But simple playing cards may also be used for the game,
" snap " being called whenever two
similar numbers appear, irrespective of
their suits. Any two kings, queens or
jacks in the same way would be liable
to snapping.

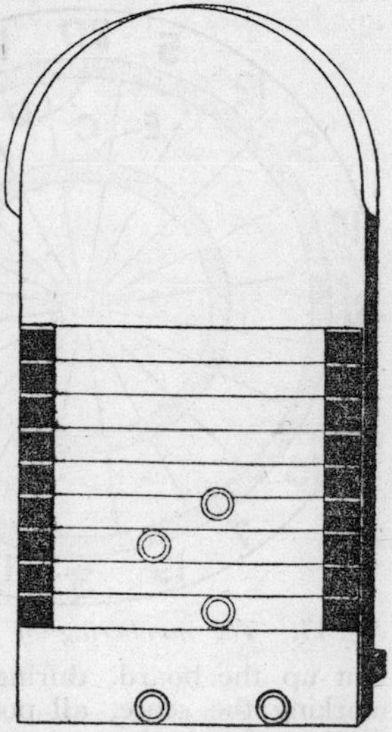

Fig. 16. *A Shove-ha'penny board with three discs played.*

Shove-ha'penny is played on a board
of wood or slate which lies flat on a
table. The board is divided by transverse lines into nine sections or " beds."
Worn halfpennies or metal discs of
similar size are " shoved " up the board by the ball of the thumb,
the aim being to make them rest in the beds (a shove-ha'penny
board is shown in Fig. 16) without touching the lines. Each player
plays the five discs in turn; there are two players or teams.

To start the game the two opponents, or team leaders, shove
the discs up the board, and the one who gets into the ninth bed,
or nearest to it, has the choice of beginning first.

Each player sends the five discs up the board at one " turn."
Play goes on in this alternate fashion until one of the players has
had three discs in every bed. This wins the game.

The method of playing is to place the disc at the bottom end
of the board, so that part of it projects over the edge, then to
" shove " it. Each disc remains where it stops until all five have
been sent up. Scoring then takes place in this way. Every disc
which is resting on a bed and is not touching either dividing line
counts for scoring. Near each side of the board is a row of marking squares, one corresponding to each bed. A chalk mark is
put in each of these—upright like a figure 1—for the first and
second discs which come to rest in the same bed. When a third
is scored by the same player into the same bed a line is crossed
through the other two marks, and that bed is " closed." Should

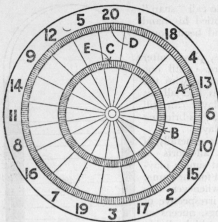

Fig. 17. *The numbering of a Darts board.*

the same player later get another disc into a bed he has already closed, his opponent may mark it down on his own scoring square.

If any discs " cannon " or strike together it does not matter—only their final " lie " at the end of the five shoves counts, for all scoring is done then.   But, if at any point in the game a disc happens to touch the cushion at the side of the board, it can score nothing.

Should a player touch any disc that has been sent up the board, during his turn, or remove any disc before marking the score, all points made during the turn of the five discs are forfeited.

A disc driven off the board cannot be used.

When only one point is needed to finish a game, it must be scored in regular fashion, by a new shove.   The last point cannot be gained by a forfeit from an opponent through his driving into a bed that is already closed.

Although a bed is closed to one player, after his three entries into it, that does not, of course, mean that it is similarly closed to his opponent.   Each player endeavours to get three discs in every bed.

The game is sometimes varied by agreeing that the beds must be gained in a particular order, for instance from the ninth down to the first.

The standard board for **Darts** is divided into sections, as shown in Fig. 17.   Each line inside the marked numbers represents a strip of wire, the thick outer line being the edge of the board.   It will be seen that there is a " bull " at the centre.   When a dart lands in this it scores fifty points.   But the bull, or " dosser " as it is generally called, is only half-inch across, i.e., it has a quarter-inch radius.   Marked round the dosser, with a five-eighths inch radius, is another ring, called the " outer."   This counts for twenty-five points. At a distance of $3\frac{1}{2}$ inches from the centre is the " treble circle," which is three-eighths inch wide.   Darts falling within this score treble the number belonging to the segment or section of the board in which it lies. Another $2\frac{1}{8}$ inches out is the "double circle," within which darts score double the number of the segment. This "double" is also three-eighths inch wide. In the diagram, A shows the double ring and B, or rather the arrow running from it, the treble.

Fig. 18. *How to hold a dart for throwing.*

It will be noticed that the numbers round the board do not run in consecutive order. Each number applies to the segment of circle running inwards from the number to the middle, as far as the "outer." For example, if a dart fell on C it would be reckoned as a score of twenty; if on D, forty; if on E, sixty; if in the "outer," twenty-five; if in the dosser, fifty.

Two or four players generally take part, or sometimes two teams. The score required for the game depends on how many are playing. When there are two players it is generally 101 or 201; for four players 301 or 501; for teams 1,001. The commonest game is for 301.

Darts may be either of wood, and light; or of brass, and heavy. The wooden are usually regarded as being the more accurate. The player has three darts, and throws all three at each turn, standing nine feet from the board, which is hung so that the centre is 5 feet 8 inches from the ground, and the 20 division is at the top.

HOW TO THROW A DART

Hold the dart lightly, between thumb and forefinger, the other fingers being bent down as shown in Fig. 18. Most players poise the dart at the front just above the shoulder level before throwing. Throw easily and let the arm move with a smooth follow-through action. Don't jerk the hand to a standstill when the dart has been released.

In any ordinary game no scoring is allowed until a double has been scored, so that the player's first object is to land his dart somewhere in the outside "double" ring. This score of a double, of course, counts towards the game. Incidentally the easiest place to begin play is in the double ring of 14, 11, 8, or 13, 6, 10. It will be seen that each of these is an upright section, so that if, for example, the dart happens to drop too low for the 13 it may land in the 6.

Not only must a game begin with a double, but it must also end with one, and it must be exactly the right number to reach the

A	B
301	301
256	245
203	158
173	130
110	82
47	35
20	17
10	6

Fig. 19.   *A completed Dart score.*

necessary score. Thus, if ten points are needed to complete the 301, then a double five might be thrown. If eleven were needed, a one could be thrown first and then the double five. Other possible ways of finishing for a required score of eleven would be three and double four; five and double three; seven and double two; nine and double one.

The thrown scores are not themselves written down for scoring purposes. Instead, the game total, perhaps 301, is put down at the top of the board or paper, for each player; then as each score is made it is subtracted from the top figure, which is crossed out, and the new required score is written below. So the numbers gradually decrease until the final double allows the winner to cross off his last entry. A complete dart score board is shown in Fig. 19. In this game A has won.

As each player throws three darts every time his turn comes round, the total score of the three is naturally reckoned when making the deduction from the previous number of needed points.

If, when a certain number is required to finish, a player scores more than that number, or only one less than that number, his throw is ignored and his score stands as before.

OTHER DART GAMES

Another popular form of the dart game is **Round the Clock**. In this each player has to score every number from one to twenty, and finally the double twenty. A player is allowed to continue with his turn so long as he is advancing, but if he fails in three successive throws to get the number he is aiming for, then his opponent carries on.

Shanghai is another dart game, in which the segments one to twelve of the board are used.

Three darts have to be thrown at each number in turn, by each player, and singles, doubles, or trebles of the number are scored from each successful throw. Darts which fall in other numbers than the one aimed at score nothing.

Thus it is possible that a player might score three trebles with his three darts on any number.

The game begins by the first player throwing his three darts at one—he may try for a double, or treble, or be content to play for safety in the larger section of the number. Then the next player follows on, also with three darts at one. When all have taken their turn the first begins afresh, this time at two.

So the game goes on, and the player wins who gets the highest total score, when all twelve numbers have been played. The game has plenty of excitement, for its chances are uncertain right up to the end, because of the steadily increasing scores which the bigger numbers make possible.

Cricket is still another popular form of darts. Teams of not more than six take part. The " batting side " goes in to begin, each throwing three darts. All scores of more than forty, made with the three darts, count as runs. For instance, if a player scores sixty-four he reckons twenty-four runs for his team : if thirty-six he counts none. The " bowlers " try always for the "dosser." An " inner bull " takes two wickets, an " outer " one. A wicket also falls if the bowler throws a double in the number equal to the remaining wickets. If, for example, there are six wickets left, from the total of ten, and the bowler scores a double in the six, he thereby takes a wicket towards the eleven needed.

GAMES WITH TIDDLEY-WINKS

For the game of **Tiddley-winks,** each player has a set of discs, rather smaller than a sixpence, and of a distinctive colour. Each also has one large shooting disc, the size of a penny, of the same colour as the small discs. If the shooting disc is pressed hard on the edge of a small disc the latter will jump forward—especially if the game is played on a thick table-cloth. In the middle of the table is placed a wooden cup, about two inches high and 1½ inches across the top. The game consists in making the small tiddley-winks jump into this cup.

At the beginning the players stand round the table, each with his tiddley-winks in a row in front of him, and with these rows at equal distances from the cup. Then each in turn takes one shot. No discs may enter the cup from any set until all of that set have been shot off from the starting line. When, afterwards, a disc does go into the cup another shot is allowed.

So the play continues, until one player has got all his tiddley-winks in the cup. He may be declared the winner, or, alternatively, each may count the number of discs he has put into the cup and the game may recommence, the numbers being scored to the credit of each so that the one with the biggest final total wins.

Should one tiddley-wink fall on another, even if only a small part is resting on top, the disc underneath cannot move until the upper one is played away—and this can be at the owner's discretion. When a disc leaves the table, it is replaced at the point of leaving. If you should have eight players, and only four sets of discs, then arrange for pairs to play together, each with one colour, and taking alternate shots. If there is one odd player when pairs have been settled let him take double turns, just as if he had a partner.

Klondyke is an exciting variation of the game, based on a "gold rush." All players start together from their equidistant lines, but after that each is for himself. There is no waiting for turns; each plays as fast as he can, and continuously.

Bunkers is another variation, in which all take their proper turns as in the ordinary game. But around the cup, at varying distances, six or eight " bunkers " are marked with chalk—they can be about the size of a match-box, or they may be actual match-box interiors. Whenever a tiddley-wink falls in a bunker the player loses a turn and must take his disc back to the starting line.

A die, a throwing cup, and a cribbage board (Fig. 20) with scoring pegs, are needed for the game of **Sixty-one.** It is played by two people.

Each player has one throw in turn, and starts from his own end of the cribbage board, pegging all the numbers thrown on the die. The peg has to travel up the board in one row of holes, and down in the companion row, landing finally into the sixty-first hole in the middle of the board at the starting end.

Every time a peg lands in the fifth or last hole of a section—the holes are arranged in groups of five—the player loses a throw.

The exact number must be thrown to " get out."

GAMES WITH LETTER SETS

With a set of **Word Making and Word Taking** letters, several different games can be played. These sets consist of small squares of wood or cardboard; on each square is clearly printed or stamped a capital letter. The number of cards with the same letter varies according to the frequency of their use in ordinary words.

The commonest form is to give each player a certain word, such as " pomegranate," and then to see who can make up the largest number of other words from this. In this game each player will begin with the word spelt out in front of him in letter blocks. From that point two procedures are possible. The problem may be to form other words which completely use up the " pomegranate " letters—in which case the end of play will find the same set of letters simply rearranged in front of each player; or each player in turn builds a word from letters selected out of the original eleven and each such word is written down by the leader and scores one point. No word should have fewer than three letters, and proper nouns and singular and plural forms of the same word should not be permitted. Naturally the starting word should be long, so that a good number of letters are available for play. No player may give a word which has already been given; if he cannot think of a word, he misses his turn. Play continues until no one can think of any more words, or alternatively a time limit may be set.

A second game is called **Find it.** In this the letters are put face upwards in a pile in the middle of the table. The first player draws whatever letters he needs from the pile and forms a word, perhaps in his hand, so that no one sees what it is. He then throws the letters on to the table, turning them face upwards, in any jumbled order. No other person is allowed to touch them, so the rest sit round looking at the letters—until someone guesses what the word

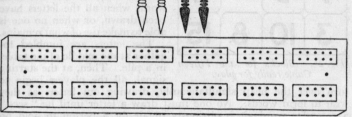

Fig. 20. A Cribbage board and pegs, as used for Sixty-One.

is. When a correct guess is made the successful player puts the letters back into the pile and draws others which spell a word of his own choice.

Spot is another variation. All the letters are placed face upwards in the middle of the table, thoroughly jumbled, and of course, facing in all directions. The players sit round, and each in turn calls out any word which he sees can be spelt by the letters in front of him. He at once draws out these letters and spells the word on his bit of table. There must be no pause in play; a player who cannot follow on immediately loses his turn.

When play has proceeded long enough, or when no other words can be drawn from the remaining " pool " of letters, players count up their scores. One point is allowed for every letter of every word, and the highest score wins. All drawn letters remain spelt out into their words in front of each player throughout the game. Any player detecting a spelling fault in another player's word scores two points, and the incorrect word is put back into the pool.

Spot and Take is a variant of the preceding game. Everything proceeds as in Spot, but should any player see that, by adding letters from the pool to any word lying on the table in front of someone else, a longer word can be formed, he is free to take the letters from the pool and the word from the other player and put them down in front of himself.

For instance, supposing the first player has drawn " main " from the middle, the second player might spot " re " in the pool, and

Fig. 21.   *Blocks for the Fifteen Game ready for play.*

take this together with his neighbour's word to make " remain " for himself. A later player might draw " ing " from the middle, and with it take " remain " to form " remaining."

Jumble Sale can be quite exciting, because all play together as fast as possible, the winner being he who has most words when all the letters have been drawn, or when no one is able to make use of what remains.

The letters are jumbled together at the middle of the table, in a pile. Then, at the starting signal, all the players begin to turn over the heap simultaneously, drawing out letters as they wish to form words. No one must draw a letter until he " sees " a complete word—it is obviously unfair for a person to hold on to two or three letters in the hope that they may be useful.

In **Time Limit** each player is allowed to draw thirty letters from the pile, then three minutes are allowed for word making. That player wins who is able to form most of his letters into complete words. Words of two letters are permissible. It is not the number of words formed that determines the winner, but the fact that he has used all of his letters, or more than any one else.

The Fifteen Game is a very old game for one player. It goes under a variety of names, **Boss** being one of the commonest.

The game consists of a square flat box large enough to hold sixteen cubes or squares of wood each measuring about three-quarters of an inch across. These blocks are numbered from 1 to 15 on their upper surfaces.

But there are only fifteen blocks, numbered 1 to 15, so that there is one blank space in the box, allowing one block at a time to be moved.

At the beginning of the game these blocks are put into the box, numbers upward, in any order. Only one player takes part, his object being to move the blocks, one at a time, by sliding into the empty space, until all are in proper order. Fig. 21 shows how blocks might possibly be placed at the outset.

The game, you will find, generally becomes increasingly difficult as you complete your top rows and it is not always possible to work out a complete solution. For instance, if all are right but the bottom row, and these run 13, 15, 14, or 15, 14, 13, then you will not be able to finish without a completely new start.

CHAPTER 6

FUN FOR THE CHILDREN

IN one way, children are the easiest people in the world to entertain; once they are interested in a game, they will entertain themselves. The secret of getting them to do this is to interest them right from the start, and not to organize them too much. Anything over-complicated will bore them. So make your games simple, and don't keep too firm a hand on them once they are started.

Let us begin with some of the more active children's games suitable for playing indoors in a fairly confined space.

ACTIVE INDOOR GAMES

Any number of children can take part in the game of **Workers,** and quite small youngsters will enjoy it.

Each player in turn goes to the middle of the room and performs some action characteristic of some particular work or occupation. The others then try to guess what it is. Whoever guesses right first goes to the middle and gives a new performance.

If no one guesses correctly the same player may stay in the middle and imitate some second kind of work belonging to the same trade, and so on.

Feeding Time is most fun if the whole house can be used for the game. Any number can join in.

Before the game starts the play leader hides paper-wrapped sweets about the house. Then she divides up the players into pairs—each pair playing the part of an " animal " with its " keeper."

Only such animals must be chosen as make a distinctive noise, such as—cow, donkey, pig, sheep, dog, cat. Each " keeper " is provided with a paper bag. Then the game begins.

The animals dash off together to find as many sweets as they can, and the keepers, at first, all stay together in the starting room. Whenever an animal finds a sweet he makes the noise appropriate to him, and as soon as the keeper hears it, he hurries to the spot. The " animal " then gives him the sweet he has found and the keeper puts it in his bag. As soon as this is done the partner goes off to search for another sweet, the keeper remaining at the spot where he has just arrived, until called once more.

When the game is over, the pair who have most sweets have won, but the losers will probably eat what they have found, all the same !

Hand Football is very strenuous. A clear room is necessary for it, and there should be a goal at each end, perhaps two chairs, with about two yards between the " posts." Any large heavy ball will do; perhaps the best is a football cover stuffed with rags. Two single players or two teams can take part.

The game is played as much as possible like ordinary football, except that there is no kicking. Instead the ball is propelled about the floor by hand. It must be pushed and knocked, not lifted or thrown; and only one hand at a time may touch it—that is, no player may use both hands.

After each goal the ball is started off afresh from the centre. Should a " throw-in " be required the ball can be knocked in from the side of the room. A free hit should be the penalty for lifting or knocking the ball up from the floor.

AN OLD GAME BUT A GOOD ONE

Though **General Post** is an old game, it is always a popular one. The more who take part the better.

One player is blindfolded and stands in the middle of the room. The rest sit in rows down opposite walls, facing each other, or even round all four walls. Each is given the name of a town, and every one retains his name right through the game, unless he happens to go to the middle. There should be a leader who keeps control of the game.

The leader calls out any two names, in this fashion : " There is a letter from Kingston to York."

Immediately the two players with these names stand up and clap their hands once, so as to let each other, and the one at the middle, know where they are. Their aim is to run and change places, without being caught by the blindfolded player. If they succeed they take the new seats, though retaining their original names. Then the leader calls two other names—perhaps " Carlisle to Paris "—and these two players stand, clap, and change places in the same way. So the game goes on until the one at the middle succeeds in capturing someone.

When one is captured he becomes the blindfold player in the middle, while the person who is released takes over the other's name and goes to his seat.

Now and again, especially if the one at the middle is having bad luck and cannot make a capture, the leader may call " general post." At this order every player must jump up and get a new seat, anywhere. Naturally, with so many dashing round him the blindfold one has an excellent chance of capturing somebody.

The game of **Giddy Walk** (Fig. 1) is always popular, as most children like to be made giddy sometimes.

One at a time takes part. First you must have a walking stick. The player who is to try the " giddy walk " holds the stick upright with its point on the floor, and bends forward so that his forehead is pressed on the handle, or on his finger-tips holding the handle,

Fig. 1. A player getting ready to try the Giddy Walk.

and standing near the top end of the room. Then, keeping the stick upright, he walks round it three times, the handle being a sort of pivot for his head. As soon as he has completed the third round he lets the stick fall, stands up, and walks to the far end of the room to blow out a candle which is burning there.

He may, of course, get to the candle all right—or he may arrive anywhere. It is best to have a few people standing near to take care that he doesn't sprawl to the floor immediately he tries to stand up after the turns.

Black and White Tag is a novel and very amusing game, needing not fewer than eight players, and one leader. The leader is supplied with a slate or square of cardboard which is white on one side and dark on the other. A piece of white cardboard with brown paper stuck over one side serves very well. The players are divided into two teams—the " blacks " and the " whites."

At the beginning of the game all the players are standing up, where they can see the leader. He suddenly holds the card up with one of its sides towards the players. If it is the dark side, all the blacks promptly sit down on the floor—before the whites can tag or touch them; if it is the white side, the whites sit down and the blacks try to catch them first.

Any player who is touched before he gets down, drops out.

Then all stand up again, and watch for the next signal. The leader, of course, will continue to flash up the card, but changing the colour irregularly so that no one ever knows what is coming. Players can move about the floor as they like, to get nearer to or farther from opponents. So gradually the teams will be diminished until one is wiped out completely.

The success of the game depends largely on the speed and unexpectedness of the signals.

Handkerchief Tag is a game that is always popular with boys and girls of any age. One of them is It, and he tries to tag or touch any other player, who then will become It in his place. But a handkerchief is being tossed about the room, and only a player who is actually holding it can be tagged.

When the handkerchief falls to the floor, it must always be picked up by the one who threw it, unless it has touched someone else, when that person must recover it.

Elbow Tug-of-war is another strenuous game. The players begin by forming up in a line down the middle of the room. If possible there should be a straight chalk line marked along the floor, on which they can stand. They number down in turn from one end to the other, then all the odds form one team with the evens as their opponents. The evens turn about so that they are facing the opposite way to the odds. Finally all crook their arms and link them together at the elbows with their neighbours.

Now the struggle begins. The odds strain forward, and so do the evens, each pulling in opposite directions. The tussle goes on until the whole of one team is dragged across the line.

If one team always wins, then let the players mix up afresh and form a new line, so that different teams can be made.

FOR SMALLER CHILDREN

Smaller children like playing **Old Man Wind,** and quite a lot can join in. Slips of paper are needed, one for each player. On one is written " old man wind," and on each of the others the name of some bird. The slips are then mixed up together, and every player draws one. The player who draws " old man wind " goes to the middle of the room; the rest stand round in a large ring, facing to the centre.

Those in the ring call out, " ' old man wind,' what bird will you catch today? " " Old man wind " calls back the name of any bird he likes. That player must at once drop back from his place and try to run twice round the ring without being caught by " old man wind." If the run is successfully made, the player goes back to his place; but if he is touched, his place in the ring is taken by the one from the centre and he has to go to the middle as " old man wind," leaving his name to the one who has taken his place. The same name must not be called twice in succession.

When " old man wind " is in pursuit, he can, of course, get

between players in the ring quite freely and run round on the inside or the outside—but he must not wait at the vacant place and touch the runner just as he arrives.

Circus is a game which appeals to the younger children. A leader is made ringmaster. If he can have a silk hat and whip, he will be all the more real. He should certainly have some sort of whip. It is his job to call out the " performing animals " and put them through their performances. No one knows beforehand what he or she is supposed to be, the ringmaster settling all that.

Every one sits or stands round the walls of the room, and the ringmaster begins with a little speech telling of the wonderful circus of trained animals which he is going to introduce. Then he cracks his whip and, pointing to any player, announces, " Here is my wonderful bucking broncho, straight from the prairies. Never been ridden and never on the ground for more than three seconds at a time. Whoa, my beauty ! "

The player indicated must at once come out and begin to perform in accordance with the character given him, until the ringmaster sends him back to his place, and calls out someone else. With imagination the ringmaster can keep the game going for a long time, with all sorts of varied performances. The same players can be called out again, and pairs or groups can be made to perform.

A GAME FOR A LARGE ROOM

Any number from six up can take part in **Astride Ball,** providing the room is large enough. A football or similar large ball is needed, and the players all stand in a ring, facing inwards, with one at the centre. All forming the ring bend forward and put their hands on their knees and their feet astride.

The one in the middle holds the ball, and, turning about as he pleases, rolls or throws it in any direction. His purpose is to make it pass between the widespread legs of some other player. A player who sees the ball coming to him can drop his hands and stop it, but otherwise his hands must remain on his knees. When the ball is caught it is rolled back to the centre and the player there throws it afresh. When he succeeds in getting it through someone's legs, he changes places with that player.

Be very careful all through that hands are kept on knees and that legs are properly astride. It is best for players in the ring to stand sufficiently close together for their feet to touch their neighbours'; this will save much running after the ball.

Children always like " playing shop." **Starting Shop** is a very fresh form of it, for the aim of every " shopkeeper " is to get in his stock before the other players.

Each player is given a name—grocer, confectioner, chemist, draper, and so on, and for each a dozen slips of paper must be

Fig. 2. Spoon Hockey should be played on a table you don't mind scratching.

prepared beforehand. On each slip is written the name of something stocked in that particular shop. Then, before the players come in, the slips are hidden about the room or, better still, about the house.

All start off together to " collect their stock," and the first to get his dozen slips wins. Every slip should be taken back to the " shop," which is a chair, and displayed " on the counter." If there is any doubt which shop an article belongs to, it can be made clear on the slip; for instance, " Toothpaste—Chemist."

The game of **Spoon Hockey** (Fig. 2) is played on a smooth table. From two to eight players can take part. Each has a teaspoon for a hockey stick, and this must be held with rounded side downwards all the time. Instead of a ball, a wooden draughtsman or checker is used; this stays flat on the table like an ice-hockey puck and slides about without rolling.

If there are two players only, one should be on each side of the table; with four, have two goalkeepers (the goalposts should be cotton reels and about six inches apart); with more players, see that there are members of each team on each side of the table.

The rules of ordinary hockey, with starts and restarts at the centre, and so on, are followed as much as possible.

The **Water Drinking Contest** is just a kind of competition or race game in which any number can take part.

All you have to do is to put a tumbler of water on the floor for each competitor, and supply each boy and girl with a teaspoon.

Start them off together, and see who can empty a tumbler first. It takes a surprisingly long time to drink water in this fashion.

To play **Hunt the Orange** four or more players sit in square formation holding a sheet or table-cloth stretched out tightly between them, at their shoulder level. On the cloth is an orange, which rolls about as they tilt their hands up or down. And round behind them, trying to seize the orange, dodges another player. He runs round quite freely, darting his hand over whenever he sees a chance.

The aim of those who are seated is to keep the orange out of his reach, by tilting the cloth so that it always runs away from him. But when he catches it, the player over whose shoulder he caught it changes places with him. Similarly, should any player allow the orange to run off the cloth, he must change with the " hunter."

On the Bridge of Avignon. This is a charming old French singing game, and here the music is given as simply as possible. An experienced pianist of course, will fill in more harmony.

ON THE BRIDGE OF AVIGNON

Six to a dozen players take part. During the verse they clasp hands and dance round in a ring, singing these words :—

> On the bridge of Avignon
> They are dancing, they are dancing
> On the bridge of Avignon,
> They are dancing in a ring.

After this they halt, and take the chorus standing still, fitting to it the proper action. The first time, for instance, when it is " the

H.E.—D*

young men " every one turns to the right and bows with the words " do this way," and with the later words " again do this way " they turn to the left and bow again.

Thus the chorus is different each time, and following it the players join hands afresh and dance round to the original verse.

Here are ten chorus lines, with the actions belonging to them :—
The young men they do this way (bow to the right).
Then again do this way (bow to the left).
The ladies they do this way (curtsy).
The old men (raise their hats).
The children (skip one way, hop the other).
The nursemaids (rock baby in arms).
The fiddlers (play violin).
The pipers (play pipe).
The organ men (turn organ handle).
The beggars (hold out hands).
The sailors (do hornpipe steps).

If the order of items cannot be remembered, or the song is not very well known, the leader may herself sing the first part of each changed chorus and do the first action, all the others coming in with, " Then again do this way."

Or a different child may go to the middle for each part and invent some new character and action which the others will imitate in the repetition to the left.

Rooting is a game particularly suited to the very young ones. Quite small children know how animals " root " about for food and how fowls scratch and peck and search, so this game will appeal to all of them.

All you have to do is to hide wrapped sweets about the house, preferably on the floor—under chairs, against skirting boards, and so on—and then let the children search for them.

Allow perhaps five minutes, and then see who has found most in that time.

Ankle Pull is strenuous, and can be used for single contests, team events, or knock-out bouts. Two at a time compete. Each hops on his right foot, holding his left ankle with his left hand and gripping with his right hand the right hand of the opponent. Then they pull and push and struggle until one—the loser—is compelled to put his left foot to the floor (Fig. 3).

See that the contestants keep in the middle of the room, well clear of chairs and furniture. The winner of one bout can take on the next comer.

Blindman's Circle is a game like General Post, but is better for a small number of players.

Those taking part sit in a ring, and the blindfolded one squats on a stool or hassock at the middle. The ring must be of such size that

Fig. 3. *Ankle Pull depends on your ability to keep your balance.*

he has a fair chance of touching any one who passes in any direction. Those in the ring are numbered round, whispering their numbers so that the blind man does not know which is which.

Then he calls out any two numbers, and these two change places, as silently as possible, the blind man hoping to touch one of them as they do so. If he succeeds, he changes places with that one; if not, he calls two other numbers.

When a new blind man goes to the middle, he will naturally know where all the numbers are, so as soon as he is in his place, all the players stand up and move round, sitting in new seats so that their whereabouts is no longer known. Then the game goes on as before. The players will retain the same numbers all through.

Push is vigorous and often exciting. Two at a time take part, and the only preparation needed is a line on the floor a yard long.

The two stand facing each other, on opposite sides of the line. Each has his hands on the other's shoulders, or they may stand very close to each other with forearms doubled up in front of them so that each can press his palms flat against those of his opponent.

Only straightforward pushing is allowed; hitting, or trying to twist your opponent sideways, is forbidden.

Then the tussle begins. It is the aim of each to step forward over the line so as to stand on the opponent's side of it, and that player wins who first does this. But, of course, the other person has to be pushed back before you can step over, and it is necessary for both

feet to be fairly on the floor before the contest is reckoned to be over
—it is not enough merely to get one foot momentarily across.

Players must remain upright and squarely facing each other
throughout.

For the game of **Big Brother,** two players are chosen to stand in the
middle—" big brother " and " little brother." It is the task of the
former to protect the latter.

All the other players stand round in a ring and try to torment or
tease " little brother," by pushing, pinching, slapping. " Big
brother " dodges round, trying to shield his companion. If he
succeeds in touching any of the attacking players, that one comes
to the middle as " big brother," choosing some " little brother "
to accompany him.

As a variant, " little brother " too may be able to touch any one
of those who surround him, and his touch, like that of " big
brother," may release him from the middle and bring another pair
of players to the centre to start another round.

TWO GAMES FOR TWO TEAMS

A large room is needed for **Rats and Rabbits.** Any number of
players can take part.

They are divided into two equal teams, and line themselves in
two rows across the middle of the room. Each team should be
facing its own end of the room, and opponents are thus back to back.
The members of one team are " rats "; the others are " rabbits."

At the side of the room stands the leader. He begins to call out
one of the names, rolling the first *r*, so that the teams are at first
uncertain which word is to be called. When he does finish the
name, either " rats " or " rabbits," that team makes a dash for its
end of the room. The opponents, at the same time, spin round and
follow in pursuit. Any one who is overtaken must join the team of
his captor—he is captured if he is touched before he can reach his
end wall.

Then the two teams, altered as they may chance to be, take up
their places again at the middle and the game begins afresh.

It is important for the leader to give equal opportunities to each
team, though, of course, he must preserve sufficient unexpectedness
in his calls.

If the room is not wide enough to allow for augmented teams after
each run, then all those who are touched by pursuers should drop out
of the game until one team is completely eliminated.

Two teams take part in **Table-cloth Squeaks.** One lot goes out of
the room, taking a large table-cloth with them. Then one of the
number, draped under the cloth so as to be invisible, crawls back
into the room on all fours, and proceeds to emit a series of squeaks.
The team which has remained in the room is only allowed to have

two guesses at the identity of the concealed opponent. If either of the guesses is right the teams change places, and the new " outs " send in a member similarly hidden. If both guesses are wrong, the player crawls out and a fresh team member is sent in.

The " in " team should not touch the concealed squeaker.

Every player in the game of **Dumb Orchestra** is allotted some imaginary musical instrument. The conductor takes his place in the middle and begins to lead the concert. Each time his hand, which is beating time, points to any person, the latter must immediately begin to perform on his instrument without making any sound.

When both hands join in the beating every member of the orchestra begins to play, and continues until the left hand ceases to beat with the right.

Any solo player can be stopped by the conductor snapping his fingers near to the player's face, and the whole band can be silenced by both arms being raised towards the ceiling.

The game should go at a brisk pace, and strongly contrasted pieces of " music " performed, if the best effects are to be had.

Musical Numbers is a game for a large number of players. All march round the room in single file, while music of some sort is being played.

Then the leader calls out a number, the music stops, and all rush to form into groups of that number. If, for instance, the leader has called " five," then all try to get into groups of five, and any who are finally left out have to leave the game.

The music restarts, the leader calls some other number—perhaps " six "—and the same break-up into groups, this time of six each, occurs.

The leader must watch carefully and call out such a number each time as will allow a few players to be put out. Thus the marching line is gradually lessened until the game is over.

A TEST OF ALERTNESS

In **Eena, Meena, Mina, Mo** the leader has to be very alert, for it is so easy for him to get mixed up himself. He speaks one of his four words and waits for the players to obey it, then speaks another, and so on. The words are used in any order, and play is very brisk.

For " eena," all stand up; for " meena," all sit down; for " mina," all stand on the right leg; for " mo," all stand on the left leg.

Any player who does the wrong thing, or fails to do the right, drops out of the game, until only one, the winner, remains. The leader may, if he likes, make the game still more difficult and confusing by taking part himself, doing any actions, wrong or right, to mislead the others. The faster the game is played the better.

There are many children's games which, while they can be quite as exciting as the ones given above, call for less movement and are often useful, if you want to keep the children you are entertaining amused without any strenuous activity. Here are some games which fulfil these requirements.

Shops is a game which calls for quick thinking and a good leader. The leader sits in the ring and tells everybody to choose some trade —grocer, draper, chemist, house-furnisher, ironmonger, and so on. Then he begins to tell a story, about a shopping expedition, and at frequent and unexpected intervals mentions the name of some shop, stating that here he bought something beginning with a certain letter of the alphabet. When he says this he halts, and the player " owning that shop " must at once mention some article which he or she sells, beginning with that letter. The leader counts ten while waiting, and if the article is not mentioned within that time the shop is considered to be " out of stock," and a " black mark " scored against it. Any player getting five black marks is considered " bankrupt," and has to pay a forfeit.

It is sometimes better for the leader to mention each shop in turn, round the ring of seated players, for in this way there is no danger of any one being left out.

The story might begin thus :—

" It was Saturday, so of course I had to go to the butcher for something beginning with S."

Butcher—Steak.

" And the greengrocer had said that he would have in, nice and fresh, something beginning with C."

Greengrocer—Cabbage.

" So I took the bus down to the town and got off by the iron-monger's, where I left an order for something beginning with S."

Ironmonger—Saucepan.

For **Cook in the Kitchen,** one player is chosen as the " cook." He stands in the middle of the room, with the others in a large ring round him. Each of the others is given a name, that of something used in the kitchen—saucepan, oven, rolling-pin, flour, currants, dish, pantry, and so on.

Then the cook throws a " dish-cloth "—which may be a handkerchief—at one of the others, and calls his or her real name three times. The one who has received the cloth tries to call out the name which has been given to her, before her own name is spoken the third time. This may sound easy, but in the excitement of the game it is not.

When a player fails to reply in time, she changes places with the " cook," who goes into the ring and takes over the name of the one who has gone to the middle.

In **Animal Buff,** one player is blindfolded. He stands in the middle of the room, holding a walking stick. All the others sit

Fig. 4. Card Toss only requires a hat and some pieces of card.

round in a ring. The blindfolded one turns about three times, then points his stick in any direction he pleases. The player at whom the stick is pointing must grip the end of it. The one at the middle then asks him to make the noise of some animal or bird—cow, cat, pig, owl, cock, dog—and the one holding the stick end must promptly obey. The sound must be made twice.

If the blindfold player guesses the name of the one who replies in this fashion the two change places; if the guess is wrong, the stick is pointed elsewhere and another attempt made.

There is no need for the blindfold player to turn round three times after each attempt; it is only when he first goes to the middle that this is necessary in order that he shall lose his bearings.

Target Flip is a good table game—but it must be a table on which you may mark four circles, one inside the other, with chalk. The innermost circle should be about two inches across, and each outer one about two inches bigger.

Wood draughtsmen, or pennies, are used, each player having his own. If there are four players they stay always in the same order.

The game consists in shooting or flipping the disc of wood or metal up the table, and trying to land it in the middle of the target. No score is counted until all the discs have been sent up, for often one played later may knock out or alter the position of one already lying. The scoring is as follows : five for the centre circle, four for the next ring, three for the next, and so on. A disc must be lying clearly in a section to take the score belonging to it; if it is touching a line then it takes the score of the circle on the outer side of that line.   Game is fifty points.

Basin Ping-pong is a quiet, pleasant little game, requiring just a pudding basin and a ping-pong ball. The basin is placed in the middle of a table, and round it is drawn a circle, with chalk, measuring about a foot across.   Any number of players take part.

The game consists in tossing the ball so that it hits the table outside the marked ring, and falls into the basin—to stay there. Each time this happens the successful player counts one point, and is allowed another throw. Game is eleven points. Each player takes his throw in turn.

Card Toss is very like the previous game, but is played with pieces of card. Put down a hat or basin in the middle of the floor, and let the players kneel in a ring two yards away from it (Fig. 4). Each player has six cigarette cards, or postcards cut in halves and every one in turn tries to toss these cards into the hat. Any player whose card goes in the hat, picks up all the cards that are lying on the floor. Then, when any player has thrown all his cards, he is out of the game, and play continues until only the winner remains.

The best way to throw a card is to hold it flat between the knuckles of the first and second fingers and then to send it spinning forward by a flick of the wrist.

STUNT GAMES FOR CHILDREN

Children can always be relied upon to appreciate a stunt game— that is, a game with a " leg-pull " at the end. Here are one or two. One warning : think carefully before you use any of them. For instance, except for " The Mummy " and " Aeroplanes " they are obviously unsuitable for children in their best party frocks. But used at the right moment in the right party, they can be a great success.

For **I See a Ghost,** the leader forms all the players into a straight line, standing side by side and shoulder to shoulder. He himself is at the head of the line. He starts off by looking dramatically in front of him and exclaiming :—

" I see a ghost ! "

" Where? " the player next to him must ask.

" There ! " says the leader, and raising his right arm, points to the front.

The second player now repeats the same dialogue with the third, and finishes up in the same way with his right hand raised and finger pointing.   So the thing goes down the line.

Next the leader begins afresh : " I see a ghost ! "   " Where? " " There ! "—and this time the left arm is raised. At the end of this round, therefore, the whole line of players will have both arms

Fig. 5. A victim being initiated into the Ancient Order of Jackdaws.

raised to the front and, of course, will be staring straight in front.

The third round begins. The leader goes through the same dialogue yet again, and this time goes down on his right knee. All the others follow in turn, still keeping their arms pointing. At this stage it is important that they shall be all in line—there should be an assistant who takes care that they are shoulder to shoulder and close together.

The leader begins for the fourth and last time : " I see a ghost ! "

" Where ? " asks his neighbours.

For answer the leader gives a hearty shove with his shoulder, which sends the second player, and the whole row following him, toppling over sideways.

The **Ancient Order of Jackdaws** is a stunt game requiring a fairly slippery floor, a rug, and one chair (Fig. 5). When the victim comes into the room, he is told that he is to be initiated as a member of the Ancient Order of Jackdaws. The Grand Master is sitting on the chair with the rug in front of him. The Members of the Order kneel in a semicircle behind the rug. Nobody smiles. The victim is led to the rug and told to kneel down.

" You wish to become a member of the Ancient Order of Jackdaws ? " asks the Grand Master.

" I do."

" You will observe its rules faithfully, treat your superiors with respect, keep its secrets until your dying day, and remember always the oath you are about to take? "

" I will."

" You will bow to its decisions? "

" I will."

" Good," says the Grand Master—and at that moment the two who led the victim in silently jerk the rug backwards by its corners. The victim can be relied upon to bow with this initiation !

A SCRAMBLE AND A SURPRISE

Feeding the Zoo is another game with a surprise ending. All the players who do not know the game stand in a large ring, facing inwards. At the centre, on the floor, a piece of chocolate or biscuit is placed. The leader announces that he is going to give the name of some zoo animal to each player, but each must keep his name secret.

He then goes round the ring, and whispers the same word, " bear," to every player. No one, of course, will suspect that any but himself is a bear, and the leader can ensure that there is no suspicion by seeming to hesitate now and again, as if he finds it difficult to think of enough names.

When all have been named he explains that he is now going to call out various animals, and each player in his turn must, when his name is called, dash to the middle and break off a scrap of the biscuit or chocolate, returning to his place with it before the next name is called.

The leader begins : " Lion," " puma," " antelope." No one moves. " Bear," says the leader, and immediately the whole crowd of players find themselves on top of each other in the middle, to their immense surprise.

There can be a great deal of fun in playing **The Mummy,** if it is well prepared.

Every one is sent out of the room except the leader and one other. This one lies flat on the floor and the leader covers him with a sheet. His hands are stretched beyond his head, and on them he holds his shoes, upright, as if they were on his feet. These shoes must just protrude from the end of the sheet. With a little adjustment, and maybe the help of a cushion, the leader will be able to make the " mummy " look as though he is lying the other way round, and as though the shoes really contain his feet and his head is where his feet actually are. A " mummy " arranged in a suitably convincing manner is shown in Fig. 6.

The leader then calls in the first victim, explaining in an awed voice that here is a mummy who is said to be able to answer any question addressed to it with proper respect.

So the new-comer kneels down by the mummy, by what he

Fig. 6. " The Mummy " arranged ready for a visitor.

supposes to be the head, and proceeds to ask his questions, say:—
" Oh mummy, can you hear me ? "

" Surely ! " replies the mummy—the voice, to the astonishment
of the kneeling person, coming from near what he had assumed
to be the feet. If the mummy, at the same time, sits up, from the
" wrong end," the surprise is the more complete.

For **Lucky Sign,** a sheet is suspended between two chairs, or
across a corner of the room, its top edge being about a yard from
the floor. Behind this sheet crouches a player equipped with an
electric torch and a wet sponge. The room must be in darkness.

One by one the victims are led in and instructed how to " try
their luck," by " following their nose."

The new-comer is made to kneel down in front of the sheet, close
up against it. At the same time the person behind switches on
his torch, shining it close against the other side of the sheet. The
one in front is instructed to press his nose against this ring of light,
and see if he can ensure good luck by making the lucky sign which
the torch itself is about to describe.

So the torch begins to move about the sheet, and the intent
victim moves his face about with it. Slowly the light moves upward,
by a zigzag course, until at last it reaches the top edge of the sheet,
and still goes up. The nose of the victim in front follows, and as
his face rises clear he finds the wet sponge pressed against it.

Aeroplanes is a favourite stunt game. A short wooden plank is held some six inches from the ground by two fairly strong adults, and the victim is blindfolded and told that he is going for an aeroplane ride. He stands on the plank, with his hands on the shoulders of two others who stand on the floor.

The two holding the plank, with appropriate noises and remarks wobble the plank very slightly and pretend they are lifting it higher and higher. The two on the floor gradually bend their knees until they are crouching; the blindfold victim feels their shoulders sinking lower and lower, and naturally believes that he is going up.

After a while he is told that the aeroplane's engine has failed, and that he must jump. " Don't worry—we'll catch you " the two whose shoulders he holds assure him.

He gathers up his courage to jump what he imagines will be four or five feet—and only when he reaches the floor after a jump of six inches, may the audience be allowed to break its silence !

GAMES FOR THE GARDEN

All the games described in this section can be played in the garden, and some of them in a large room.

Tournaments (Fig. 7) is a good game if the children are not dressed in their best. Two pairs of children should be picked, the smaller of each pair riding on his companion's back. Then they should attack each other with the object of dislodging the " horse's " rider. Only pulling or pushing is allowed—no butting or strangling.

For **Balloon Battle** you need half as many balloons as there are players. Pairs of boys or girls, or both, take part in this, and any number can join in at once; you may prefer to play it tournament fashion, two couples at a time—though this will cost you more in balloons !

Each couple consists of a mount and a rider, the latter sitting on the back or shoulders of the former. The mount will have all his attention occupied in gripping the legs of his rider and holding him on firmly. The rider holds a balloon in his left hand, and his right hand is free. His aim is to burst the balloon of his opponent, before the opponent can burst his.

This game is very exciting, and very tiring too!

Bell Battle is exactly the same as the preceding game, except that this time each rider carries a small bell, instead of a balloon. The object of each rider is to make the bell of the opponent sound.

This game is not strenuous, but immensely amusing, for each couple creeps about with great care so as not to shake and sound their own bell. Any vigorous movement is as likely to put them out as to defeat the other pair.

Small sleigh bells, or bells from toy reins, are suitable.

Pick-a-back Polo is a magnificent game for playing on a lawn— as long as it is not bordered by fragile plants! The heavier members

Fig. 7. Tournaments is a strenuous and tiring game, but great fun.

of the party carry the lighter ones pick-a-back. These pairs divide into two teams. Each jockey has a walking stick, which is used to knock a tennis-ball through the enemy's goal. The teams should change ends at half-time. Barging an opposing pair is allowed, but holding them with the hands or tripping them up are fouls. The victims of a foul are given a free shot from the place where it was committed.

Those who like a rough game will enjoy **Body-guard**, for it can be very strenuous and hard, and energetic.

One player is the "chief." He is surrounded by a "body-guard" of three, who clasp hands and remain round him, facing outwards. It is their duty to protect him from being touched. All the other players dodge round, darting in when they see a chance, and trying to reach the chief. Any one who succeeds in touching him becomes the new chief, and the former one takes the place of one of the body-guard.

Each of the body-guard in turn thus drops out, and every one gets his chance.

Fox and Geese is a game that requires plenty of room; a fairly big lawn is just right.

One player is chosen to be "fox." His aim is to catch the "geese." These geese—there may be six of them—stand in single file, one behind the other, and behind the leader. Each has his hands on the shoulders or hips of the one in front. The leader.

at the front of the file, cannot be caught. His task is to spread his arms widely and try to prevent the fox dodging past and capturing any of the geese behind.

So the fox begins trying to get past, and the leader to dodge, trying to keep in front of the fox. The string of geese behind can swing and twist about as they like, but they must not loose their holds. When the fox succeeds in getting by and touching one of the geese, that one drops out of the game—or alternatively becomes fox. The one who previously was fox takes his place at the head of the line of geese, becoming leader.

Every boy and girl knows how to play ordinary **Tag**, in which one is It and chases the rest until he touches one of them, who must then become It.

Cross Tag is the same, except in one important respect. When It is chasing someone, another player may dodge between the two. It must at once leave the first player alone and start chasing this new player. When a player is tagged he or she, of course, becomes It.

A FRONT GARDEN GAME

Spotting is a restful outdoor game. It can give plenty of amusement played in front of the house, overlooking a street or road. Individuals can play, each scoring his or her own marks, or play can be arranged for teams.

First you must draw up your scoring table, which will be based on the frequency with which people or vehicles, or other things, pass in the road.

In a town the conditions are quite different from in the country, and so the list would be different. Here is a sample table : Bearded man, 10 points; bare-legged girl, 9; furniture van, 8; walking stick, 7; tradesman's van, 6; lorry, 5; horse, 4; baby, 3; dog, 2; pedestrian, 1.

Each player " takes " whatever comes along the road, in turn, and marks down the score corresponding to the marks table. If teams are competing the same method is used, though on a busy road it may be more fun to let one team score down all that passes from left to right, and the other team the things that are travelling in the opposite direction.

In the individual game first described, for example, there might be three players. After the start a tradesman's van might first go by, and the first player would accordingly mark down 6 points. Then a man carrying a walking stick might pass—and the second player would score 7. A baby in a pram might be next—giving the third player 4 points—3 for the baby, and 1 for the pedestrian pushing it. If a man with a beard were pushing the pram the fortunate third player would score 13. The first player would take whatever next went by, and so on.

This game can of course only be played if you can keep the

players sufficiently in order—otherwise it can be very embarrassing to the passers-by !

Game can be 100 points.

A fair space is needed for the game of **Ten-step Blindman**; the lawn is ideal if it is wide enough.

One player is blindfolded, and stands at the centre. By him, to begin with, stand the other players—any number of them. After a while they silently walk away from him, in any direction they choose, each taking exactly ten steps. At the end of the ten steps they stand still, and are not again allowed to move their feet— though they may bend or twist their bodies later if they wish.

Then the blind man takes his turn. He is permitted to take ten steps in any direction, and during these he can reach out with his hands, hoping to touch some other player. If he succeeds the two change places; if not, all come to the middle and a new start is made.

For **Jousting**, a ring two or three inches across is suspended from the branch of a tree, or some other convenient place, so that it is about four feet from the ground. Half the players are "jousters" and the rest "mounts." Each mount takes a jouster on his back, and each couple in turn then "charges" the ring, the jouster carrying a "lance"—which is a stick about four feet long.

The run should be several yards, and should be made without stopping. If the point of the lance goes through the ring, 5 points are scored; if the ring is touched, but not pierced, 3 points are counted. Game should be 50 points.

A TRIANGULAR CONTEST

Three players at a time take part in the **Three-cornered Tug-of-war**. A rope is needed, at least six yards long, and the ends of it are knotted together. Then the three players stand about two yards apart, forming a triangle, and hold the rope stretched out between them, each grasping it behind his back with one hand. The players face outwards, away from the rope, and in front of each of them something is placed on the ground, perhaps a handkerchief.

The winner is the first to pick up his handkerchief with his free hand.

For a **Ring Race,** a ring is marked on the ground, with chalk, stones, pegs, or something similar. The players form up round it, with gaps of about two yards between them. When the signal is given they all start running round together, in the same direction. Any one who is overtaken and touched by the boy or girl behind drops out. Any player who steps inside the circle must also drop out. There is no pause in the race; all keep on running, and one by one they drop out, until at last only the winner is left.

Touch the Tail is a little like Fox and Geese, except that every player joins into the single file line, each holding the shoulders or waist of the one in front. And it is the leader of the file, instead of a separate player, who tries to make the capture.

The aim of the leader is to catch the tail player of the line, and to effect this he twists and dodges about, while the line swings behind him. Most of the players between the two ends follow helplessly, according to whether they are nearer to the head of the line or to the tail. It is important that players should not release their holds, for the game is interrupted each time the line breaks.

When the leader succeeds in touching the tail player he goes on to the tail himself, and in turn is chased by the new leader of the line. So, providing captures occur with fair regularity, every player has his chance of being leader and chasing the tail.

A HUMAN SKITTLE GAME

Boys' caps are needed for the game of **Egg Cap,** one for each of the four to six players who take part. The caps are placed in a row on the ground. Five yards from the row of caps a line is marked, parallel with the caps, and along this line the players stand.

One boy has a ball, which he rolls at the caps. If it goes into one of them, he dashes forward and snatches up the ball, while the other players scatter in all directions as soon as they see the ball go into the cap. They can run anywhere they like for safety. Meanwhile, the ball is thrown at any player the thrower chooses. If the thrower succeeds in hitting any one, he puts a stone or "egg" in that one's cap. If he fails to hit any, he puts an egg in his own.

Should the ball have failed to go into a cap the other players will not have scattered, and the same player recovers the ball and rolls it up again. When he hits someone, the person who is hit is the next to roll the ball up.

A player who gets three eggs in his cap drops out of the game.

For **French Cricket,** one player—the batsman—stands in the middle of a lawn or open space and protects his legs with a small bat, stick or cricket stump. The other players stand round in a ring, a reasonable distance out, and roll a ball at the batsman's legs. He strikes at the ball to protect himself, and the ball is recovered and thrown afresh by any one in the ring. The batsman can turn in any direction he likes so as to face whoever is throwing, but once a player has the ball, the batsman must keep his feet still until the ball has been thrown. There is no pause in the play. The ball must be thrown from wherever it was picked up.

When someone hits the batsman's legs, the two change places, and play restarts by the ball being hit by the batsman.

Rhubarb Race is an outdoor game for two or more teams. The size of teams can suit one's convenience, but six is a good number.

The players forming one team stand close together, in a cluster, and are then fastened into a bunch by a cord which is passed round their waists, tying them together like a bundle of rhubarb sticks. At the word " start " the competing bundles set off down the lawn or field. If they are lucky, they will arrive at the end of the " course " without falling over—but generally they don't !

Instead of using a cord, you may have just three or four in a team, all of them squeezed inside a hoop or old motor tyre. The smaller the children the more you can get in!

GARDEN PASTIMES THAT NEED EQUIPMENT

In this section are described games which children can play in the garden, but for which equipment of some sort is required. For some you will have to buy the things needed, for others you can make your own.

The popularity of the old game of **Bat, Trap and Ball** never lessens, and the equipment is never expensive. It consists of a wooden trap —which is a shoe-shaped block containing a seesaw-like trigger. A ball is balanced on one end of this trigger at the heel end of the trap, and when the other end is struck by the bat, the ball is thrown into the air, and so can be driven by the bat. The ball is small and hard, the bat stubby and solid.

The best method of play is for teams of four or six to take part. It is then played in the same fashion as cricket, with one team " in " at a time, and all the others fielding until all the batting team are out.

The player who goes in to bat strikes the trigger and hits the ball in any direction he chooses, trying to get it through the line of fielders. If the ball is caught before it bounces, the batsman's whole side is put out. But more often the ball is stopped on the ground. When this happens the fielder who gets it stays at the spot where it was seized and throws the ball at the trap. If the trap is hit the batsman is put out; if it is missed the batsman counts one point. Should no fielder manage to stop the ball before it crosses the boundary the batsman counts two points.

So one after another of the batting team gets his innings until all are out; then they take a turn at fielding while the other side bats.

In a game in which two players only take part, the method must be different, as fielding in the former sense is not possible.

Two stones or sticks should therefore be placed down the " pitch," about three yards apart, and the batsman must always drive the ball between these if he is to score a point. This gives the fielder his chance. If he catches the ball before it bounces the batsman is put out, but if he merely stops it on the ground nothing happens, except that he is allowed to throw at the trap, and his opponent is out if he hits it. But every throw must be taken, not from where the ball is caught, but from a fixed " throwing line " about twenty paces from the trap. It should be agreed beforehand whether the trap is to be " end-on " or " broadside " to the throwing line; the former is more convenient for the batsman using the trap.

There is plenty of fun in **Bottle Fishing,** though like most fishing it is not strenuous. The " fish " are bottles, and they are " caught " with ordinary lines to which ordinary curtain rings instead of hooks are attached.

Lemonade bottles, or similar bottles with long necks, are needed —as many bottles as players. For the fishing rod, use a walking stick or long cane, and to the end of it tie about five feet of string. To the end of the string is fastened a metal curtain ring of about two inches diameter.

The game consists in getting the ring over the neck of the bottle, so that the bottle can be pulled over. Getting the ring over is not nearly so simple as one might imagine.

Take care that no player winds his line on his rod, for the shortened string would give him an unfair advantage.

Competing players should start off simultaneously. When a bottle is dragged over all halt. A point is then scored to the successful angler, and all begin afresh. You may arrange that the first player to catch five bottles wins one game.

HOW TO MAKE A CHUTE

A **Chute** is a fine addition to any garden. It can be simple, short and low, and quite inexpensive, for the smallest children; or it can be big and elaborate to give thrills to much older boys and girls. Whatever sort you decide to have, it must be well made. There must be nothing shaky or fragile about it or it will be a source of danger rather than fun.

The simplest form of chute is a straight, plain plank, perhaps ten feet long, very smooth, and with raised edges formed by strips of wood screwed on each side. The top end of the slide should then be five feet from the ground, and the lower end right on the ground. Some firm staging will be needed at the mounting end; a ladder or steps to get up to it; also, for extra safety, a rail on one or both sides to safeguard the child, while getting into position at the top of the slide.

As a chute cannot be painted, but only stained and polished, it is best to use a hard wood which will withstand the weather, for even if you bring it under shelter sometimes it is bound to endure considerable exposure. Elm is best for the chute itself, though the ladder and staging can be of deal, which is cheaper. Be sure that every part that can be touched by the child, especially during the actual slide, is rounded and smoothed, so that there is no possible danger from splinters.

A bigger and more elaborate chute should be lined with some non-rusting metal, like brass or copper, and where the fall is steep and swift, the chute end is generally flattened out to make the landing easy.

If you do not wish to construct your own chute, any sports dealer will quote you a price for one.

Bell and Hoop is popular with children of all ages, and it is very easily contrived.

Suspend from the branch of a tree, or the crossbar of a swing, a small hoop. In the middle of the hoop hang a bell. That is all. Players now take it in turn to toss a ball through the hoop, trying to hit the bell. They should stand not nearer to the hoop than about five yards.

Every time the bell is rung, 5 points are scored; if the ball goes through the hoop without ringing the bell, 3 points; if the ball hits the hoop but does not go through it, 1 point. Game can be 25 points.

Opposing players can stand on opposite sides of the hoop, at proper throwing distances. The ball can then be caught by the one on the far side, and much running about saved. A bean bag is even better than a ball, for it does not roll out of reach so annoyingly. To make a bean bag you simply sew two five-inch square pieces of strong material together and fill the interior with dried beans or maize. The bean bag is ideal both for throwing and catching, and it can be used for a great many games beside this one.

A GARDEN CUBBYHOLE

For quite small children, a **Cubbyhole** in the garden is a constant source of enjoyment. It keeps youngsters out of doors, and affords scope for endless make-believe games—for it can be ship, house, aeroplane, engine, tree-top, or anything the juvenile imagination happens to desire. You can make your own cubbyhole with little trouble, or a skilled carpenter will very soon fix one for you.

The essential thing is that there shall be a platform, preferably roofed in, at some height from the ground. The easiest way to arrange this is to take a large wooden box and put it on props, lying on its side, about a yard from the ground. If the top is raised to give a sloping roof and covered with roofing felt, so much the better. The cubbyhole should be reached by a ladder, and it is a good idea to remove one end of the box so that a sloping plank can be attached as a second mode of entry.

Your cubbyhole can be usefully fixed against a fence or on the back of a house, garage or shed. Let the wood be smoothed and free of nails, and creosote rather than paint it, for it will not then become shabby so quickly with constant use and exposure to the weather.

The plank leading from the end or side of the cubbyhole may be smoothed into a proper chute, so that you have the two things

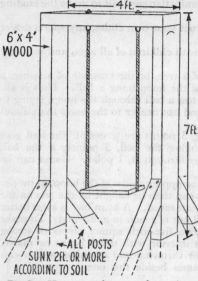

6' x 4' WOOD

4 ft.

7 ft.

ALL POSTS SUNK 2ft. OR MORE ACCORDING TO SOIL

Fig. 8.   How to make a garden swing (for explanation see text).

combined, and you may even have a "jungle climb" built on to the other end of it.

Most children like climbing, and a well-built **Jungle Climb** is safer than the average tree, and offers more interesting possibilities.

Roughly, it is a tangle of bars or spars among and over which the youngster can climb. In its simplest form it is a square frame, measuring perhaps six feet each way, with ladder-like cross pieces which afford steps to the top of it. On top, or near the top, may be a flat platform, which serves as a sort of goal for every climb, or here may be just more bars on which the climber may sit. A platform is of course more comfortable.

The most satisfactory jungle climb is made of galvanized iron tubing, so that joints are strong and the whole frame quite rigid. With a little trouble in finding second-hand piping, it is surprising how cheap such a frame can be, even if you call in a plumber to put it together for you. Alternatively, you may have a frame of strong timber, three by two or four by two, with bars of lighter wood—perhaps broom handles.

Allow for really complicated routes about the framework, so that skill and athletic ability are given plenty of scope.

A wooden frame should be kept under cover during the winter; a metal one, well painted, will be secure all the year round, and can therefore be a more permanent structure built into the ground

HOW TO MAKE STILTS

Girls like **Stilts** as well as boys, and there should certainly be a pair available for use about the garden and round the house.

Don't have them too high. Just a foot or so above the ground will be quite enough for the foot-rests, unless the children are getting towards their teens. Stilts can, of course, be bought, but they are easy enough to make from broom handles or slim strong poles of ash or some hardwood, with foot-rests protruding about three inches,

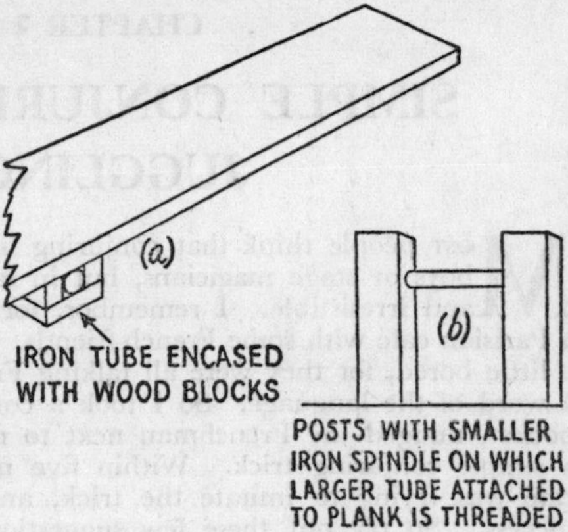

crewed on very firmly.
The parts of the poles
above the rests should
be quite smooth and
easy to grip.

In walking on stilts
the poles should be kept
stiffly by the legs, and
the feet prevented from
straying outwards. Steps
taken should not be too
long, and the poles
should be held tightly
all the time and kept
close in to the shoulders
or sides of the body.

No garden in which
children can play is com-
plete without a **Swing**.
The whole swing can be

IRON TUBE ENCASED
WITH WOOD BLOCKS

POSTS WITH SMALLER
IRON SPINDLE ON WHICH
LARGER TUBE ATTACHED
TO PLANK IS THREADED

Fig. 9. *A seesaw is even easier to make
than a swing but it must be well constructed.*

bought ready-made, with a frame of wood or iron, or it can be
quickly erected by a carpenter. If you prefer to make your own,
be sure to make it strong and rigid; for there is always considerable
strain on a swing when a youngster is swinging vigorously, and a
fall from a swing can be very painful.

Fig. 8 shows a sturdy swing which is easily made at home. The
wood should be of six-inch by four-inch section. There must be struts
for each post, and the posts and struts should be sunk at least two feet
into the ground and well packed with soil rammed firmly in. Ropes,
safety hooks, seats, and suitable bolts and screws can be bought
quite cheaply.

A **Seesaw** is another worth-while addition to any garden. One
of the simplest forms—if you want to make your own—is with a
plank and a carpenter's splay-legged stool.

The most satisfactory seesaw is one with a fixed plank, turning on
an iron spindle held rigidly between two upright posts, as is clearly
shown in Fig. 9.

It is not difficult to make; two posts are fixed firmly in the ground
with a two-foot length of strong galvanized iron piping between
them as the spindle. Then fasten a short length of piping one size
larger to the underside of the plank and thread it on the spindle,
and the seesaw will work with perfect freedom, and yet be incapable
of slipping or twisting. The short length of larger tube can be
fastened to the underside of the plank by enclosing it with three
strips or blocks of wood, one at each side holding it in, and another
joining these two and covering the pipe.

CHAPTER 7

SIMPLE CONJURING AND JUGGLING

Most people think that conjuring is of interest only to small boys or stage magicians, but in fact its appeal is universal and irresistible. I remember, for example, once sitting in a Parisian café with some French friends. After some time I became a little bored, for they were all talking French and I speak hardly a word of the language. So I took a couple of matches from my pocket, nudged the Frenchman next to me, and proceeded to do a simple conjuring trick. Within five minutes every one in the café was trying to imitate the trick, and I was a raging social success. So try out these few suggestions, memorize them, and make a habit of bringing them out at odd moments.

THE SIMPLEST TRICK IN THE WORLD

We will start with the world's simplest trick—so simple that a child of six can do it perfectly, yet I've seen a brilliant scientist beaten by it for over an hour. You need a pack of cards and a hat. Introduce the trick as a matter of psychic ability ! Hand about a dozen cards to someone in your audience, and ask him to drop as many cards as he likes into the hat, remembering carefully whether he drops an even or an odd number in. He can do this whilst you leave the room. When you enter, announce that you know by telepathy whether he dropped in an odd or even number, and knowing this you are now able to drop in a few more cards with the effect of reversing his number. Then drop in the cards, saying : " Now if what you put in was an odd number, you'll find it changed to even, and, if even, then changed to odd ! " And sure enough you are always right. The explanation is that you simply drop in an odd number yourself every time, changing about from three to seven, five to nine and so on. Obviously, when you examine it, odd plus odd makes even, and odd plus even makes odd.

Telepathy. Whilst we are on the subject of thought-reading, you may as well try a few other effects. Here is one. You enter the room, sit down before a low table on which are arranged four or five articles, and ask your audience to blindfold you. Now ask someone to step forward quietly and touch any article on the table. As soon as this has been done, you pass your hands lightly over the articles and at once call out the name of the article touched. Now for the solution. Black cotton ! Tie a loop round your wrist, and tie the other end round the wrist of your confederate. Leave the cotton long enough for your friend to go into the room and sit down well away from your table. The door will close easily, despite the fact that your confederate is in the room and you outside, and when you do enter, no one will suspect you are connected in any way—least of all by black cotton. Once inside the room, your friend winds up the slack in the cotton—this is easy whilst every one is

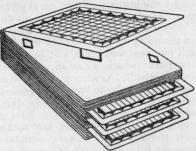

Fig. 1. *A pack of cards prepared for the Spotting the Winners trick.*

watching you being blindfolded—and then, when your left hand is poised above the right article, the pull of the cotton on your right wrist tells you to stop. You can do this in a well-lit room under their very noses—and they still look at the articles carefully!

Then work out some variations. You stay outside the room and call out the moment any one touches a particular article—say the clock. Your confederate will pull the cotton. In fact, this piece of cotton is a perfect substitute for real thought-reading.

Spotting the Winners. Here is a simple card trick. Take a pack of cards and offer it in turn to three people, asking them each to take any card. Give them time to memorize their card, and then taking their cards from them, insert them face downwards in the pack so that they can be satisfied that you haven't left any edges sticking out. Square up the cards after you have replaced all three in different positions in the pack, and then, turning your back on them for a moment—say while you walk back to your table, quickly separate the three cards and throw them on the table. Are those the right ones? Thank you very much. Now my next trick, ladies and gentlemen !

How is it done? Well, when they have taken the three cards and whilst they are looking at them, quickly turn over the bottom card of the pack so that it is face downwards while the rest of the pack are face upwards. Now hold the pack in your hand with this one card on top *face downwards* and the rest of the cards face upwards but hidden by the top card (as shown in Fig. 1). Now when you slip in the three cards face downwards and turn your back on the audience, all you need to do is to turn the top card into its correct position and the three chosen cards will be face downwards in the pack with all the others face upwards.

Before you get far with your conjuring, you must find some way in which you can make a person take a given card from the pack, under the impression that he is pleasing himself instead of pleasing you. Here is the simplest way to do this.

Place the card which you wish him to choose at the bottom of the pack, but slide it back a little way as shown in Fig. 2. Now tell him that you are about to withdraw cards from the bottom of the pack (which, naturally, you hold face downwards) until he calls " Stop." As soon as he does this, he takes the next card, which will of course be unknown to you—or so you say. Actually when you hear his shout you simply slide out the card which is really at the bottom, the cards you have previously been taking having come from above it. By this means you can make him choose, say, the ace of diamonds, without his realizing that you made him do it ! This isn't of course a trick in itself, but with some suitable finish you can make an effective demonstration.

Counting Cards. Here is a trick which sounds very complicated but is actually quite simple once you have got the hang of it. But you'll need to take a pack and go through these instructions a few times before you have got it off pat.

Turn over the first few cards in the pack, one at a time, and ask your audience to choose one card in the first ten, remembering its position in the pack—say the fifth card—but without telling you which he chose or where it was. Take care to keep the cards in

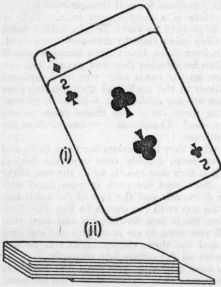

the same order by placing the first card face upwards on the table, the second card face upwards on top of the first, and so on. When you have counted out ten cards, pick them up and reverse their order on top of the pack, and transfer six cards from the bottom.

Now ask your audience to add one to the number of the chosen card, and beginning with that number, to count to themselves as you deal out the cards. The

Fig. 2. How to make someone " choose " any one particular card.

card they choose, you say dramatically, will be the seventeenth. And the seventeenth it is!

How is this worked? Think this out.

They had to choose from the first *ten* cards which you dealt and reversed, then you transferred *six* from the bottom of the pack to the top, and then you added *one* when they did. That made *seventeen*.

You can vary this trick each time. Let them choose from the first *eight*, transfer *five* cards from the bottom of the pack to the top, and add your *one* as usual and this time they should count to *fourteen* when they will find their card. But if you vary your numbers every time, they'll never find the secret.

HOW TO "DOUBLE YOUR CAPITAL"

Money Making is one of the most popular tricks ever devised. When you start, you apparently have a sheet of blue paper about two feet square, on top of this a slightly smaller sheet of red paper, on top of that a smaller sheet of yellow paper, on top of that a smaller sheet of white paper, the white paper being only about six inches square and the remaining sheets being graded in between these figures. At the start of the trick the sheets are lying loosely one on top of the other.

Suppose we start this business with a capital of one threepenny piece. Afford that much? Right! Allow your audience to see clearly that you place the threepenny piece on top of the sheet of white paper. Whilst discussing the various matters and problems which concern business men today, such as the risk of being found out and thrown into prison, etc., fold the small coin carefully in the white paper. Don't crumple it, just fold over each end of the paper to the centre and press it flat with your hand. Now continue to talk and fold the white packet up in the sheet of yellow paper. At this point, pretending to hear a suggestion from your audience that the trick is simple and the threepenny piece has already vanished, say that this is not the case. Indeed the threepenny piece is still there, and you may go to the trouble of unwrapping the papers and demonstrating the fact. Now wrap them up again, this time continuing until the whole package is wrapped in the outer sheet of blue paper. Then pick up the parcel and ask some member of the audience to lend his brains. Remarking that two heads are better than one though the particular head you have chosen is better than none, place the package upon the head in question. Allow it to remain there for a moment, adding as many remarks as you can make up on the spur of the moment to the effect that you can hear the till rattling and so on, and then remove the packet. On unwrapping the blue paper, the red one is visible. Inside that we find the yellow, and inside that the white. But inside the white one, to your audience's great astonishment, is a nice bright sixpence!

H.E.—E

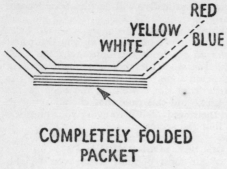

COMPLETELY FOLDED PACKET

Fig. 3. One set of paper is already folded.

No, there's nothing up your sleeve ! That's just how money is made. It isn't just a flash in the pan, either. Wrap up the sixpence in exactly the same way, place it once more on someone's head (try another assistant this time for a change) and on unwrapping it once more the sixpence has become a shilling ! But you'll have to resist attempts to continue " doubling " your capital like this on the ground of avoiding the National Defence Contribution. The solution? Simple. The blue sheet is double and the centre of the two sheets is gummed together. You also have two red sheets, two yellow sheets and two white ones. First prepare your trick by wrapping up the sixpence as we have seen, and then when you place this on the table, with the outspread blue sheet on top of it, no one can see it. On this place your second set of coloured sheets ready for the trick. But whilst you certainly had the threepenny bit there to start with, you took care to change it for a shilling when you went back to show your audience that it was still a threepenny bit. This is quite easy. Try it out in front of a mirror. Now, when you place the blue packet on the head of your " assistant," you simply turn it over so that the side in which the sixpence is wrapped is now uppermost. Unwrap the sixpence, wrap it up again, turn it over once more on the head of your second business friend, and you can unwrap the shilling which you substituted for the threepenny piece ! Take a look at Fig. 3, and it will seem as easy as falling off your magician's table.

MAKING YOUR FRIENDS LAY EGGS

Egg Production is one of the oldest tricks in the world, but it never fails because it is so funny. The audience sees the assistant sitting in the conjurer's chair whilst the conjurer takes a constant stream of eggs out of the other's mouth. Each egg is heralded by a tremendous cackling and choking. In a few seconds the egg protrudes from the mouth of the unfortunate assistant, the conjurer takes it from him and thanks heaven that that is safely over. But even as he places the egg on the table another burst of cackling followed by the sight of another egg falling out of the assistant's mouth sends the audience into fresh fits of laughter. How is it done?

Of course there is only one egg. Choose a small china egg—I need hardly say the smaller the better—and place that in the mouth of your assistant. It feels uncomfortable at first, and indeed within a few seconds your assistant will be forced to start pushing out the egg. In your right hand you hold concealed another egg (real, if possible) and at once you place your right hand over the assistant's mouth. While it is still hidden by your hand, this pushes back the china egg into his mouth (and, I may add from experience, affords the assistant a moment's relief) and when a moment later you remove your hand and display the egg which had previously been concealed within it, the audience are satisfied that it is the one which you have just removed from the mouth of the human hen (Fig. 4). Place this egg on the table, and whilst doing so your side will be away from the audience and you will have an opportunity of removing another egg from your pocket. With this egg concealed in your hand, repeat the process. If the trick goes well, it is possible to continue until your assistant has laid a dozen eggs and is almost purple in the face. Remember, the important thing about this is not really to deceive your audience—lots of them could guess the process if they thought seriously—but to keep them amused.

Thought Reading is an amusing trick with a wireless set and a microphone. If you have no microphone, a pair of old headphones with their tops screwed on slackly will do just as well. Run a double wire (under the carpet) from your loudspeaker to your wireless set and connect your microphone or headphones to the gramophone pick-up terminals on your set. If you haven't got a lead for a gramophone pick-up, then take one wire to one of the filament terminals of the detector valve and the second wire to the grid of the same valve. Now if you switch on the set, you'll find that anything spoken into the phones or the mike will be reproduced through your loudspeaker. And the simple plan is this. Hide the improvised microphone in the room in which the party is, and install your wireless set in the next room. Inform them that you can thought-read anything which they may discuss, and ask them to try and think of something really difficult—say something for you to do—and make it complicated. Slip out of the room and listen to their discussion. When

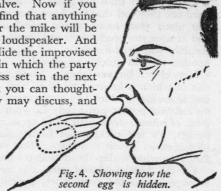

Fig. 4. *Showing how the second egg is hidden.*

they call for you, simply go in and act in accordance with their instructions ! To make sure that the mike picks it all up, have a confederate stationed near it so that he can make sure someone near the mike really says what you have got to do. They'll be amazed. And if you want to give this trick away (a thing which in the ordinary way of business you should never do) you might let them all try broadcasting to the rest of the company.

A SIMPLE TRICK THAT NEVER FAILS

Picking Your Own Pocket is another simple trick which is always popular. Obtain three coloured handkerchiefs, say red, white and blue. Show them to your audience and invite someone to tie the three handkerchiefs together in one string. Allow the knots to be tested carefully so that every one is quite sure that there is no deception. (That's an important point in conjuring—if ever you really are doing what you say, take care to let people satisfy themselves about it as much as they like—and since in this case it doesn't matter how securely the knots are tied well, let them all have a go !) Now invite them to feel inside the *inside* pocket of your jacket. Quite empty. No holes. And now, ask them to place the knotted bundle of handkerchiefs inside that pocket. All satisfied? Then ask the audience which colour did they really prefer? " The red," says someone. " Ah," you say, " the blue? " Immediately your hand goes to your pocket, but the cries from your audience stop its progress. You are informed that they prefer the red, not the blue. But surely, you protest, someone said blue, and really if they said blue, then blue they must have. Finally, you will be forced to give in, since every one is now convinced that you *want* the blue one to be mentioned. (It doesn't matter which colour they choose, but try to make them think that one colour is much harder than the other. When you do finally produce the hard one they feel that you have done something clever.) At once you insert your hand, sleeve rolled up, into that inside pocket, and at once you produce the red handkerchief, unknotted and alone. Rapidly you produce the others, also unknotted, and move on to another trick as quickly as possible.

Very clever, but very simple. You have two sets of handkerchiefs, one of which is knotted together, and the other set, neatly folded and in an order which you can remember, tucked away inside your *top waistcoat* pocket just handy for your fingers, as shown in Fig. 5. And, of course, when your hand appears to be in your inside jacket pocket, it's just picking out from your waistcoat pocket the one handkerchief which you want. But you must be careful not to forget in what order the duplicates are arranged.

For the **Mental Marvel** trick, you need a confederate, a supply of papers (one for every one), pencils, and someone else in the know. Ask every one to write down a short message on his paper, fold it up, and then hand it to the assistant. These are placed in a small heap where everybody can easily see them.

Now take your seat facing your audience and ask your assistant to pick out a folded paper and hold this on the top of your head whilst the "picture soaks through." Sure enough, in a few seconds you are able to read out the message written and the writer in the audience admits that it was correct. Your assistant unfolds the paper and confirms that this was so. Again he takes

DUPLICATE
HANDKERCHIEFS

KNOTTED HANDKERCHIEFS

Fig. 5. *How the duplicate handkerchiefs are concealed in the waistcoat pocket.*

up a second hidden message, and again you are able to read it through the folds of paper and the top of your head. And so you can go on, reading every message in turn until your supply runs out or your audience begins to suspect the reason for your remarkable ability.

And what is the reason? Your first answer is a fake. You simply call out a fictitious message, which you have previously mentioned to uncle. He admits that he wrote that. Your assistant unfolds the message to verify it, and shows it to you. Actually, of course, you are now reading a genuine message—which you pretend to " read " telepathically from the second piece of paper. The other messages are dealt with in the same way. The last piece of paper must, of course, be an extra piece secretly added by your assistant.

The Four Pack Trick. Here is a demonstration which, whilst it will amaze your onlookers, is at the same time extremely simple to do effectively. Take a pack of cards, invite some gentleman present to shuffle them and then to spread them before you on your table in four packs face downwards.

You now rest your finger tips lightly on the top of the first pack and after a judicial frown say slowly : " H'm. The ten of diamonds."

You then pick up the top card of the pack upon which your finger has rested and place it, still face downwards before you. You now transfer your attention to the second pack and once more, without seeing the top card, you call out its name : " The seven of spades " and once again pick up the card in question from the top of the second pack and place it on top of the first card which is before you. Then to the third pack, where once more the process is repeated and you name the card without seeing it and remove it from the pack. Finally you repeat the process with the fourth pack, and now having before you four cards turned face downwards, you pick them up and offer them to the gentleman, once more repeating their identities. He will find that you were right. This trick can be at once repeated and indeed performed with any number of packs. Your audience will be convinced that you can tell the value of the cards by some marking on the backs, but in fact there is a much simpler explanation.

TELEPATHY THROUGH PLAYING CARDS

When the pack has been shuffled, hold out your hand for its return and take the opportunity of glancing at the top card of the pack. As soon as this is known, and as if changing your mind about the performance of the trick, hand the pack back. Now as soon as the cards have been cut into four packs, remember which pack has on top the card which you know—that is, the card which was top of the original pack before cutting. Leave that pack to the last. Let us suppose that the ace of diamonds was the top card of the pack. Rest your finger on the first pack and slowly say : " Yes. . . . The ace of diamonds." Pick up the card and place it before you. Now as a matter of fact, this card is not the ace of diamonds, but since your audience are not allowed a glimpse of it, they are none the wiser. But as you pick it up, glance quickly at the corner of the card, bending it slightly to bring it in to view. Let us suppose it turns out to be the three of hearts. Turn your attention to the next pack, and inform them that its top card is the three of hearts. As you pick it up, glance at it. It may be the seven of clubs, in which case, name the top card of the third pack as the seven of clubs and once more get a glimpse of it as you transfer it to the little pile before you. Call out its name as you pick up the top card from the fourth pack (which top card, is of course, the ace of diamonds). In this way you have named all the four cards which are before you. Put briefly, you always call out the name of the card which you last picked up, and the last card of all is the one known to you, which you called out first of all.

Juggling is the art of performing tricks by sleight-of-hand, that is, by lightness or nimbleness of hand. The conjurer deliberately deceives his audience; but in juggling there is no trickery. Very real skill is demanded, and this is what makes juggling so fascinating. Once you have learned the principles of juggling, you can juggle with anything—plates, knives, or balls, it makes no difference. For practice, however, it is better to use balls for they are cheap, easily handled and incapable of hurting any one.

Rubber balls are the best for practice work although the glistening metal kind can be used. Preferably they should be of fair weight and not too large. Tennis balls will serve, but they are rather big—little rubber balls the size of a golf ball are best.

A PRACTICE COURSE IN JUGGLING

Get half a dozen balls. Some prefer to have them in different colours so that they can be conveniently distinguished when they are being used together, but this is a point of small importance. As likely as not, the most frequent way in which you will exhibit your skill will be with a few oranges, and they will look all the same.

Here is a progressive course of practice which will carry you through to fair proficiency. Systematic work is essential, but though it may be long it need not be dull or particularly arduous, for the steps from stage to stage are small and easy. It is not necessary for you to keep exclusively to the balls; you may usefully intersperse your practice, for instance, with the plate juggling dealt with later.

Exercise 1.—Take a ball in one hand and practise tossing it up and catching it again. See that it goes quite vertically, and begin with a moderate height of about two feet. At first you will need to keep your eye on the ball and to adjust your hand and arm in order to catch it as it descends, but you must persevere until it falls exactly to the same spot from which it rose, so that your hand can remain motionless, certain that the ball will fall into it (Fig. 6, a).

As you gain skill, vary the height of the throw until you are equally safe with the ball rising anything from one foot to six feet. The ability to toss to any desired height is also of great importance. One good plan is to begin with the lowest throw and to toss a few inches higher each time until the maximum height is reached, then gradually to reduce the force until the original height is recovered.

HOW TO CATCH THE BALLS

Remember that in catching a ball the hand must always be slightly yielding, otherwise the ball bounces from it before the fingers can grasp the rubber. So let the palm " give " the tiniest bit each time, with softened muscles; then fling the ball upwards again with a sort of steel-spring recovery.

These simple yet fundamental exercises should be continued until they can be performed just as surely with the eyes shut; that will be the proof that you are ready, with that hand, for the next stage.

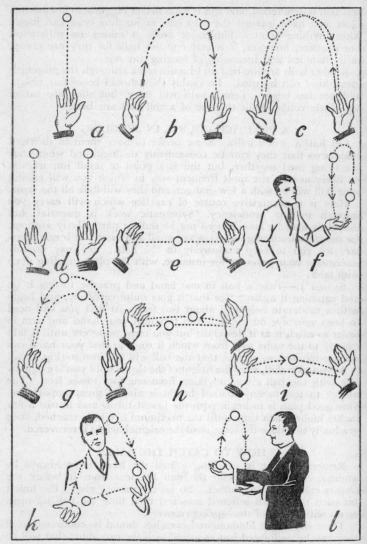

Fig. 6.   The principles of Ball Juggling.

But first you must gain the same skill with the left hand as with the right, for juggling demands equal dexterity in each.

You can now try a further stage, getting the same vertical fall of the ball first in front of the right hip, then in front of the left, still using only one hand. Begin with the right hand, in its normal position in front of the right hip. Make an ordinary toss. As soon as the ball is caught, move the hand swiftly across the front of the body until it is in front of the left hip and make a similar throw and catch there. At once come back again to the original position, and so continue, smoothly, without pause. Afterwards do the same work with the left hand. Soon you will get a clean, mechanical movement of the hand across the body and complete accuracy of throw in the two positions.

Exercise 2.—Now the ball can be made to describe an arch instead of the vertical rise and fall.

Stretch both hands comfortably to the front, in their normal positions, and toss from one hand. Send the ball to the customary height, but in a curve across the front of the body. It must descend, nearly vertically, into the other hand (Fig. 6, b). The force of the throw, and the size of the arch described, must be such as will bring the ball exactly to the waiting hand. Try this toss from right to left until you get the same accuracy that you have with a plain one-hand vertical throw. Then go on with the reverse action— left to right. As soon as you can do this perfectly, try to develop the easy backwards and forwards—or, rather, side to side—movement between the two hands, throwing with the right, catching with the left; throwing with the left, catching with the right; and on and on without a pause (Fig. 6, c).

As a further practice, learn to do this throw with one hand only —throwing with the right hand and catching it on the left side of the body with the same hand. Then try this with the left hand.

Practise also the reverse of the movement, tossing from the right hand in front of the left hip, and bring the hand back to its normal position on the right side for the catch.

NEED FOR A STANDARD THROW

By this time you will have settled to a sort of standard height for your throws, probably between two and three feet. Keep to this, so that you come to judge it with absolute precision, for that will help a great deal when you have to toss more than one ball at different heights. In practising continue your throws for a fairly long period; this makes them become automatic and accurate. For instance, in the work just described, the right hand will cross from the right hip, catch on the left side; toss on the left, catch on the right; and so on without any pause. The mechanical timing of an action, without any variation, is another very important part of juggling, for when several balls are in the air the hand must not only be always at the right spot, but be there at the right moment.

Exercise 3.—You can now begin with two balls simultaneously, making vertical throws with both hands (Fig. 6, d). At first you may time them together, so that it is easier to get the same force with each. Then go on to work them alternately, so that while the right ball is descending the left is going up.

Just one more preliminary stage, with a single ball. In *Exercise* 2 you did plain arched passing from one hand to the other and back again. Now you have to get a flattened, almost horizontal pass (Fig. 6, e). Naturally, the ball will have to move quicker, especially when the hands are well apart. But at first have the hands fairly close, and just toss the ball backwards and forwards between them, making it rise as little as possible. Gradually separate the hands until they are in their normal positions, about a couple of feet apart, in front of the hips. You may even, for practice, spread the hands as widely as three feet apart in this exercise.

JUGGLING WITH TWO BALLS

Of course, this passing, like all other juggling work, is easy enough to do just once, but when you continue, the ball is apt to stray a little from its course—and that must not happen. If, when you are using several balls, one of them goes just a little astray and the hand has to adjust itself for the catch, then the following balls will drop to the floor.

Exercise 4.—Now begin real juggling, by the tossing of two balls with a single hand.

Take the two in your right. Toss one straight up, four or five feet, and the instant that it begins to drop again throw up the second. The first will thus be caught by the empty hand and tossed up afresh just at the time the second begins to descend. A good deal of repetition will be needed to do this neatly, for obviously if the balls are thrown precisely vertically, they will collide with each other in the air. To prevent this, you will toss each ball so that it covers a narrow arch and falls a few inches from the spot where it rose. This will allow just sufficient clearance, but it will make it necessary for the hand to move backwards and forwards for each throw and catch (Fig. 6, f).

With increasing proficiency, you will not need to throw so high, for the long pauses will be unnecessary. Shorten your throws, therefore, until the balls rise no more than two feet.

When the right hand can do its work, train the left hand in the same way—for at every stage the two hands must keep pace.

If you like, you may go right on to four-ball juggling. That may sound rather frightening, but it need not be. It will certainly look very impressive, and will also add a great deal to your confidence.

Simply perform the two-ball juggling which you have just mastered, in both hands simultaneously. At first you will have some difficulty, but it will be due to nervousness rather than lack of ability if you have really mastered the separate hand work.

By this time your throwing and catching will not depend on watching the ball closely, so that it will be no drawback that you cannot possibly concentrate attention on all four balls together. You may find it a help, however, to toss your balls in unison, and perhaps to count one, two, one, two, so that rhythm is helped. But if the four-ball exercise seems particularly troublesome, leave it alone till later.

Exercise 5.—This is the simplest and most attractive feat of plain juggling, and you should certainly give plenty of time to it. Two balls are needed, one in each hand, and they are simultaneously tossed in opposite directions. The one thrown by the right hand goes across the body and is caught by the left, and the left-hand ball is caught by the right. Each travels over a high arch (Fig. 6, g).

This feat is simply a two-ball version of tossing from one hand to the other, with which you are already familiar. But now both balls travel at the same time and both hands work together. To prevent the balls striking each other at the highest point of the throw, it is necessary that one shall go over the other. The best plan is to throw a trifle harder with the right hand than with the left, so that the right-hand ball always goes a few inches above the other; the right hand, being the stronger, is the most natural one to give the additional force necessary for this.

ALWAYS THROW IN A STRAIGHT LINE

Now, for a little while, revert to the plain horizontal passing of a single ball, the hands being turned inwards instead of having their usual palm-upward position. Be quite sure that you can send the ball rapidly backwards and forwards in as nearly a straight line as possible and with the hands about two feet apart.

Then you will be ready to try the same passing with two balls. Let the hands be near together at first, and keep to the rule of making the right-hand ball pass above the other in a flat curve, while the left-hand ball goes almost straight (Fig. 6, h and i). Gradually widen the space between the hands until they are at hip width. Having mastered this horizontal pass you will be well prepared for the next feat.

Exercise 6.—This consists of juggling with three balls in such a way that they travel round all in the same direction.

The left hand must be held slightly higher than the right. You begin with one ball in the left hand and two in the right. Think the whole movement out before you attempt to perform it, picture every part of it clearly, and if necessary make a few pencil diagrams.

There is little time for thinking when the three balls are in motion, but you will be much helped by having foreseen all the things you will be required to do during the feat.

Start by tossing the first right-hand ball fairly high, and in the familiar big arch to the left. When it is up, follow with the second right-hand ball—we will call these two balls *one* and *two*. The right hand is now empty, and so the left hand tosses *three* down into it. *Three* is not held, but tossed up promptly by the right, by which time the left hand has caught *one* and tossed it down also to the right, the left hand being consequently free to receive *two* which has just completed its arch. So it goes on, the balls following each other round, evenly spaced apart (Fig. 6, k).

The only new movement in this feat will have resulted from the high position of the left hand which necessitates a downward slant for the throw across to the right hand. The raised position of the left is necessary to get a more even division of times in the movements of the balls, and you will have to discover for yourself by experiment the exact height that best suits you. Incidentally, remember that the left hand must be turned neither upwards nor across to the right, but midway between these positions, so that it is equally able to catch the vertically falling ball and to make the horizontal pass in a straight line across the body.

HOW TO GET THE SPECTACULAR CASCADE EFFECT

You may like to practise the slightly downward body pass with a single ball, tossing in the high arch from the right hand to the left, then passing down from left to right.

And now for a cascade effect with three balls—the balls working in opposite directions, backwards and forwards, instead of following round as just described.

Begin, as before, with two balls in the right hand and one in the left. The hands will be spread in front of the body in their usual positions, and at the same height. Toss one ball from the right hand, making it travel over towards the left in the familiar manner. As it passes the highest point and begins to fall, the left-hand ball is thrown.

Thus, at the very moment the left hand receives the first ball, the second ball will have reached its highest point and be starting to drop towards the right hand—which is the signal for the right hand to throw up the third ball (Fig. 6, l).

You will see that the complete action works in with perfect rhythm and symmetry. And remember that right-hand throws must be slightly higher than those of the left.

Quite probably you will find that this " cascading " is easier than the other form of three-ball work.

A very good way of deciding when you have mastered any juggling feat, is to count the number of times that you can repeat it without failing. As soon as you can get up to fifteen counts without breakdown, then it is fair to assume the thing is done. But reasonably constant practice is naturally required to keep yourself in good condition so that you will always give sure performances.

JUGGLING WITH CUPS AND PLATES

Juggling with plates always looks impressive and spectacular, yet plates spin easily, keep their equilibrium, and are very easy to catch.

Don't use crockery—at any rate, in the early stages. Enamel or heavy tin plates, of medium size, are the best. They should have smooth edges and a well-raised rim.

Begin by plain tossing and catching in each hand, in much the same way as the earliest ball exercises. The plate should be held vertically, by the edge nearest to you, then flung upwards so that it rises straight into the air, rather higher than your head. The hand will remain still, and the plate should fall so that its edge drops again between your thumb and fingers. All the time it is spinning in the air the plate should remain upright and spin over towards you.

Practise this with each hand in turn. Then go on to both hands together, each dealing with a single plate.

Incidentally, don't practise on a hard floor or your plates will get chipped and damaged. Stand on a lawn, over a bed or settee, or spread a rug on the floor. The same thing applies with balls, for even their frequent impact on a hard floor can become irritating —and the softer and rougher the surface beneath them the less they will roll when they fall on it.

When you feel at ease juggling with single plates, go on to two-plate work with one hand. This will not be difficult if you have already mastered with balls the habit of making the slight adjustment of forward and backward movement of the hand, though now the movement will need to be rather greater (Fig. 7, a). Remember to keep the plates spinning strongly, otherwise they will not keep properly upright. It is the original upward fling of the hand, which sends the outer edge of the plate up a fraction of a second before the fingers and thumb release the inner edge, that causes this revolving of the plate.

Go on to juggle with two plates in each hand, just as you did with two balls, and when the four-plate work goes smoothly you can try something entirely new, by way of relaxation from your other exercises—say a little **Balancing** for example.

Use just one plate, and see if you can keep it upright on your chin (Fig. 7, b).

Put it into position on its edge, as you stand with head leaning well back. Release it cautiously from your hand and be prepared to move lightly on your feet. Keep your gaze fixed on the top edge of the plate and try to anticipate when it is losing its balance, so that you may correct it by moving. In this anticipation of when and in which direction overbalancing is likely to occur lies the secret of good work.

You may also balance your plate on the palm, the back of the hand, the nose. And you may use both hands and two plates.

PLATE SPINNING IS ALWAYS EFFECTIVE

Now another complete change—**Plate Spinning.** This is a very fascinating trick, and being even more unusual than ball juggling, makes a strong appeal to onlookers.

You will need a light stick about two feet long, with one end sharpened to a rounded point. A piece of rounded curtain stick, or " dowel," serves well. Having shaped the end with knife or chisel, smooth it with glasspaper.

The point of your stick must be put against the inside, or concave, edge of the plate. First hold the plate flat, and upside down, at about the level of your head, with the left hand. The blunt end of the stick will be in your right hand, and the stick remains as nearly vertical as possible; the pointed end will thus come up under the plate. Now begin to work the stick round rapidly, with a circular movement of the fingers and wrist, at the same time releasing it from your left hand. This will set the plate spinning. After a little practice you will be able to keep the plate flatly balanced on the top of your upright stick (Fig. 7, c).

A very swift, smooth, continuous movement is what you need. It is not necessary to make a wide sweep of the stick; its lower end, which you hold, should scarcely move at all, and the pointed tip need only describe a small circle, not more than a few inches in diameter. The edge of the plate will prevent the stick slipping clear.

As you gain proficiency you will be able to reduce the sweep of the stick and so bring the point nearer to the middle of the plate. This will give increased speed and steadiness. Keep your fingers supple and firm or the plate will wobble.

THE NEED FOR PATIENCE

Don't be impatient to proceed to something else. Persevere with this simple exercise until the plate never falls or gets out of control.

When you can get a plate spinning really strongly you may toss it from the point of your stick and catch it again. Make the toss with a quick lifting movement of the whole arm. Similarly, after some practice, you will be able to start off by throwing the plate into the air from your hand, imparting a good spinning motion as you do so, and catching it on the point of your stick and working

Fig. 7. Juggling and balancing with difficult objects: a to f, various tricks with plates; g, an effective hat trick; h, the ball and parasol illusion.

up to a greater speed. For this hand throw, of course, the plate must be kept flat, not vertical as in ordinary juggling.

Your next stage will be to develop plate spinning equally with each hand. After that it will be possible to spin two plates simultaneously—quite an imposing spectacle. To start such a feat toss a plate up from the right hand and take it spinning on your left stick. Then follow by throwing up the second and receiving it on your right point. Both plates and stick will have been held in the right hand at the outset—that is not very troublesome. And when the second plate is tossed the stick is, naturally, still in the right hand ready to catch it and keep it spinning.

STEADINESS DEPENDS ON SPEED

A strongly spinning plate, you will find, will keep revolving for a long time and will have a surprising steadiness, like a gyroscope or top; and it is this quality of steadiness, dependent mainly on speed, which you must primarily aim at developing. Thus when you have got a plate going well, it is no very difficult matter to raise the stick and balance the whole on your chin. Your chin will naturally impart no added motion, but the stick will be kept steady by the whirling plate—exactly as a top might similarly spin, but the stick end will not itself be revolving as the point of a top would be.

Having reached this stage of ability with balls and plates, you will be able to develop juggling along lines of personal preference, for all sorts of combinations of feats already described will suggest themselves.

Here are one or two feats which will make a juggling display more interesting and impressive to the spectators.

OTHER INTERESTING TRICKS

Catching the Plate is an odd moment trick, which looks well when done as if by accident. Fold the right arm across the body and let a plate lie in the crook of the elbow, immediately above the wrist.

The trick consists in letting the plate fall, and then catching it just at the instant before it reaches the floor (Fig. 7, d). If you move your right arm downward the plate will slide off. But the back of your hand, also dropping downward, will thus remain close behind the plate. At the final instant it will only be necessary for the hand to lift slightly, to allow the thumbs and fingers to grip the top edge of the plate. Practice will soon give the knack.

Plate Spinning and Juggling, a very showy feat, consists of spinning a plate on a stick held in the right hand, and at the same time tossing one or two plates with the left (Fig. 7, e). To start off the spin, rest the plate on the flat knuckles of the right hand, as shown in Fig. 7, f, and then fling it upwards with a twist of the right wrist. This hand will have been holding its stick in readiness, and now has simply to catch the plate on the point.

If you find that plate spinning is very troublesome because of this, or at any other early stage of your practice, you may make a flat indentation at the centre of a tin plate, rather larger than a half-crown, and the point of your stick will lodge more safely in this little niche.

The **Top Hat Trick** is a neat way of starting a juggling display. All you have to do is to kick a silk hat into the air and catch it on your head. This is easier than it sounds. Put your toe inside the hat to begin, then kick it gently upwards and in the direction of your head.

With practice, you will be able to make it turn over once in the air, towards you, as it rises, and so come exactly into the right position for dropping on your head (Fig. 7, g). Almost no adjusting of the head position will be necessary, though of course you will be ready to move a few inches, in a natural, easy manner. And don't look pleased and surprised when the trick comes off—leave the showing of appreciation to the onlookers.

JUGGLING WITH A SUNSHADE

Sunshade Juggling is a real trick, in which the audience is deliber-ately deceived, though it can very effectively be introduced among some genuine juggling feats. Fasten a ball, by a piece of thread, to the point of sunshade—Fig. 7, h, shows how to do this. Then hold the sunshade and spin it round at a good speed, by the handle. The ball will retain its position, rolling round the flat top, and the onlooker will be led to believe that it is somehow held in position by the rapid movement of the sunshade.

You must be careful how you begin the feat. The best plan is to hold the ball in the left hand and the sunshade handle in the right. Then you can release the ball and begin twisting the sun-shade at the same instant, making some show of balancing the ball with great difficulty, until smooth speed is attained.

We have now given you the basic principles of juggling; once you have mastered these, you will be able to devise many tricks of your own, and to try juggling with many different objects. " Practice makes perfect " has become a platitude, but in few things is it more true than in the art of juggling. When you can perform the simple movements almost without thinking, you will still have to practise constantly to remain expert.

CHAPTER 8

AMATEUR THEATRICALS

HOME theatricals are one of the few forms of home entertainment that have a definite social value. Those who are inclined to be shy and backward at parties and similar functions will soon discover that, by devoting some of their spare time to amateur theatricals, they will not only pass an hour or two in a most enjoyable manner, but will also begin to lose their self-consciousness and nervousness.

A side of home theatricals that is very popular on the Continent but is only just coming into vogue in England is the open-air theatre. On grounds of expense alone, this form of the amateur stage is to be welcomed. It requires even less scenery than its indoor counterpart : the trees, bushes and natural surroundings give sufficient background. All that is needed is a fair-sized lawn with a background of bushes. If you have a few bushes or other natural cover, it is perfectly simple to rig up a small canvas screen at both sides of the stage. The screen can be painted some pleasing shade, or if any member of the party feels sufficiently artistic he can paint a suitable scene upon it. If the natural background is not considered to be sufficient, an additional screen can be placed at the rear of the stage (Fig. 1). The actors play their parts on one end of the lawn and the audience are seated at the other. To get the right perspective, it is advisable for the audience to be seated upon the grass, but that is a minor point.

While many plays exist that have been written especially for outdoor presentation, there are also a great number of plays which, though intended for a covered theatre, can with very little alteration be adapted for outdoor performance.

GENERAL HINTS ON PRODUCTION

For home indoor shows too, the amount of scenery should be cut down to a minimum. Scenery seems a little out of place in all but the largest drawing-room or small hall. But this is a matter for every producer to decide for himself. In any case, quite satisfactory effects may be obtained by the judicious use of screens. These can be prepared from three or four clothes-horses covered with canvas, or better still, with some neutral-coloured material. The most appropriate of all places for an indoor stage is a double room with dividing doors or curtains. A " drop " curtain, however, is not a very difficult contrivance to arrange. All that is required is a stretched wire or stout bamboo pole, of sufficient length to reach from wall to wall, and some means of supporting its ends very firmly. A large hook sunk in either wall is ideal, if it is at all practicable.

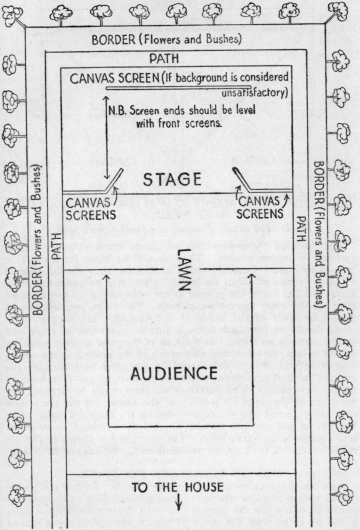

Fig. 1. *An effective plan for an open-air theatre in a suburban garden, showing how the stage should be laid out.*

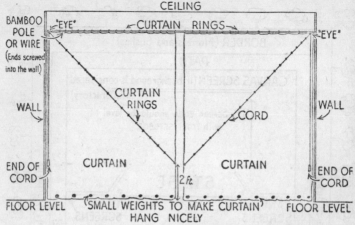

Fig. 2. Full details of curtain construction (back view).

The curtains themselves can be made quite cheaply. Dark cretonne is recommended. They should be hung from the pole or wire by means of curtain rings; in addition rings should be sewn on each curtain at about six inches apart, in a diagonal line from about two feet above the ground at the edge where the two curtains meet, to the outer top corner of each. The rings, needless to say, should be sewn on the inside of the curtain. On each curtain, cords should be threaded through this diagonal line of rings and passed through an " eye " at the end of the pole or wire, allowing a loop to hang down within easy reach of the ground in the wings. The other end of the cord should be threaded back through the eye and through the rings at the top of the curtain, and then fastened to the top corner. The curtains can then easily be drawn from each side of the stage by pulling on the loops : at the same time they are gathered well out of the way by the diagonal cords. The bottoms of the curtains should be slightly weighted in order to make them hang attractively. These points are shown in Fig. 2; cords for closing the curtains are omitted for the sake of simplicity.

HOW TO CONSTRUCT THE STAGE

Now for the construction of the stage itself. In this connexion it is as well to consider whether it is possible to do without a special stage and to use just the normal floor. In the vast majority of cases it will be found that if a piece of 6-inch wide planking is placed across the part of the room intended to be used as the theatre, and the footlights placed into position behind it, the effect will be quite satisfactory (Fig. 3). If the amateur producer is keen on having a real stage, and is prepared to spend both the time and money necessary, the following specification will be of great help. It should be remembered, however, that it applies only to a stage ten feet by twelve, and eighteen inches high. If the stage proposed differs from these dimensions, a little simple arithmetic will soon reveal the correct proportions.

First of all, the materials required are : one 15-foot length of 5-inch square wood; six 10-foot lengths of 6 inch by 1 inch section; and lastly, eight 12-foot lengths of 15-inch by ⅝-inch section. Saw the 5-inch square wood into ten pieces each 16 inches long. Place them in upright positions along the floor at intervals of 3 feet in two parallel lines 10 feet apart. On top of these nail the five 10-foot lengths firmly into position, and nail the eight lengths of 12-foot timber on top of this (Fig. 4). Then fix the remaining piece of 6-inch timber across the front edge of the stage on its edge. Behind this the footlights can be placed. Paint the last piece of timber the same shade as the curtains; run a small curtain across the front of the stage as shown in Fig. 5, and you have your small home stage. It must be remembered, however, that the preparation of this stage will cost both time and money, but if you can spare this it is well worth the attempt.

The next important consideration is the lighting of the stage.

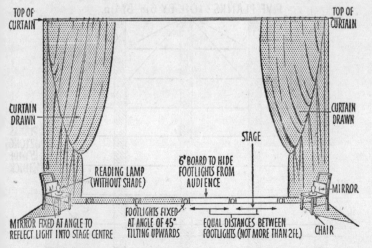

Fig. 3. *The curtains* (*drawn*) *from the stage, showing how the footlights and sidelights are placed.* (*See also the stage plan in Fig.* 6.)

Footlights of some kind are absolutely essential. For a very small stage, electric bicycle lamps will do quite adequately, provided that they are placed not more than two feet apart across the front of the stage. They should be fixed firmly into position and should tilt upwards at an angle of approximately forty-five degrees. In addition to the footlights, the stage should be lit from the sides. The best way to light it here is to fix a small reading lamp (without its shade) at either side of the stage, with a mirror propped into position behind it, for as much light should be reflected towards the centre of the stage as possible (Fig. 6). Finally, it must be remembered that no light should be left burning in the auditorium. The effect of the last two precautions will be that though the stage may not be very well lit, the difference between the darkness of the auditorium and the light of the stage will help to make your audience forget everything but the stage and the people on it.

CHOOSING A PLAY

The next thing to consider is the furniture of the stage. It is important to remember that in a limited space as little furniture as possible should be used; actors cannot move about naturally if they are obliged to keep one eye on the furniture the whole time they are on the stage, to avoid banging into it. The producer will therefore, be well advised to go through the script of his intended

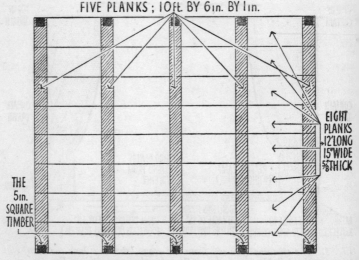

FIVE PLANKS; 10 ft. BY 6 in. BY 1 in.

EIGHT PLANKS 12' LONG 15" WIDE ⅝ THICK

THE 5 in. SQUARE TIMBER

Fig. 4. *Full constructional details for building a simple wooden stage.*

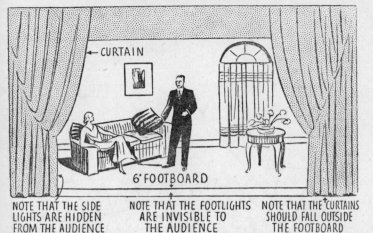

NOTE THAT THE SIDE   NOTE THAT THE FOOTLIGHTS   NOTE THAT THE CURTAINS
LIGHTS ARE HIDDEN   ARE INVISIBLE TO   SHOULD FALL OUTSIDE
FROM THE AUDIENCE   THE AUDIENCE   THE FOOTBOARD

Fig. 5. How the curtains and stage should look from the auditorium.

play, and to cut out all furniture that is not essential to the action.
Another warning : Do not make use of very low chairs if it can
be avoided.   No one has yet discovered a method of rising gracefully
from a low chair !

The choice of a play requires a great deal of thought.   So many
factors must be considered.   Of these, the most important are :
the cast, what facilities are available for production, the length,
the type of audience you will be playing to, and, last but by no
means least, the cost.   The size of the stage, too, must govern the
choice.   If you can only have a small stage avoid a play that requires
a large number of lesser characters, for they will clutter up the
stage horribly.   If scenery and funds are limited, choose a play that
requires only one set or scene throughout.   There are a host of
these.   Some are one act only, but there are numbers of two, three and
four act plays that can be produced without a change of scene.

As soon as rehearsals begin, the producer will come up against
a stumbling block.   Quite a number of amateur actors and actresses
detest rehearsing and will do anything to shirk it.   If the play is to
be a success, the producer must prevent this.   One of the best methods
of doing this and ensuring regular attendance, is to employ a system
of fines for non-appearance.   Another nightmare to every con-
scientious amateur producer is the actor who puts in a regular
appearance but makes no attempt to learn his lines.   The only
thing to do with this sort of person is to give his part to another
player, or you are likely to find that, when the play is performed,

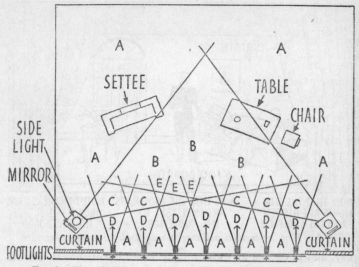

Fig. 6. *Stage lighting arrangements (for explanation see text).*

he misses his " cues," forgets his lines, and turns an otherwise excellent production into a complete " flop."

IMPORTANCE OF THOROUGH REHEARSALS

Only one, or possibly two, rehearsals should be allowed with the text. After this, the players should have memorized their lines sufficiently to dispense with the script. Any slip should henceforth be corrected by the prompter, who should be one of the most punctual and reliable members. An old but effective way of memorizing one's part is to copy it out. Many odd moments in bus, train or tube can be spent in this way.

As soon as the actor is more or less word-perfect, he should begin rehearsing alone. In this connexion the pitch and expression of the voice is every bit as important as the words themselves. Remember that it is fatal to let the voice drop at the end of a sentence, as is often done in ordinary conversation; be sure to keep the voice " up." Remember, too, that in lines that express great emotion or stress, the pitch of the voice should be lowered. In the same way, lines expressing excitement or hysteria should be spoken in a higher tone. Another fault in delivery is that of gasping out the lines in a spasmodic fashion. To remedy this, the actor should practise taking deep breaths until he can speak steadily and evenly.

Facial expression is another factor which must be taken into consideration. Rehearsing in front of a mirror is an excellent way of improving your performance in this respect. Above all, try to be natural; act as though the play were really an occurrence in the lives of the actors, and the audience will believe it as well.

WATCH THE ENTRANCES AND EXITS!

Walking naturally on the stage is another art to be acquired only by constant practice. In the somewhat restricted space of a stage, the normal tendency on the part of men to take long strides is one which must be checked. The best thing to do is to find the approximate dimensions of the stage and, when practising in private, rehearse one's part in an area of similar size. Again, it is necessary to learn to tread lightly, for the floor of a stage acts as a sounding-board and distorts the sound of normal footsteps. Entrances and exits must be carefully watched. Finally, when producing costume pieces it is best to have more than one full-dress rehearsal to accustom the cast to their unusual clothing.

A word to the prompter. Remember that the audience are listening intently. If your services are required—as it is to be hoped that they won't—speak in the lowest tones that the actors can hear or your voice will carry beyond the stage into the auditorium.

Don't forget that full make-up must be used for the dress rehearsal, and not left until " the night " before it is tried out.

Greasepaint is obtained at most chemists in numbered tints. The most important thing to remember is that, for amateurs, too little is better than too much greasepaint. For most female parts—except, of course, for " characters " or old age—a slight accentuation of ordinary day make-up is enough. A vivid lipstick, a faint touch of rouge, powder to tone and rather heavy mascara will do, with a dab of carmine on the end of an orange stick at the inside corners of the eyes to add brilliancy. Only use eye-shadow if your eyes are large and not deep set, otherwise the effect is that of a bad-tempered mole! A pale green shadow will help to give brilliancy.

HOW TO MAKE UP THE CAST

For straight male characters a blend of Nos. 5 and 9 greasepaint is the standard base. First faintly grease the face, jaw and neck with a very little cold cream. Wipe it off with a soft rag or tissue and then smear on the yellow and brown pigments not too heavily, work to an even tone with the fingers, taking care to fade off at the ears and scalp, as well as avoiding bare patches in the hollows of the jaw. Next a touch of carmine on the cheeks. If you are playing a young man work this round and up to the side of the eye and temple—but not too high. If older, keep it on and slightly below the cheekbones. A smear of No. 5 down the centre of the nose carefully smoothed away on each side will emphasize its shape. Lines are best made with a pointed match or an orange stick that has been thrust into the end of an amber or deep carmine greasepaint. *Don't overdo the lines*, and don't try to produce lines where there are no indications on your own face already. For old age, darken the eyelids with carmine and create shadows at the temples and below the cheekbones with amber or deep carmine very lightly applied. Remember to touch up the hands as well. Finish with a light application of rachel or peach powder. Don't forget to powder the throat. Then do the lips. For a middle-aged part, use No. 9 with the slightest admixture of carmine. Use a light carmine for youth, but with discretion, and keep to the natural contours of your lips. Lastly, the eyes. A light blue shadow on the lids gives brilliance and youth. Lashes should be darkened with mascara or black greasepaint, applied with a small brush or orange stick. Carry the line slightly beyond the outer corners of the eyes and place a dab of bright carmine at the inside corners.

Finally, don't forget to tone your hands with the rest of your make-up. Use wet white in an ochre or rachel tint.

Costume plays, needless to say, are slightly more difficult to produce than those in modern dress. But a little extra care is all that is required and it will be very well repaid.

PRODUCING CHILDREN'S PLAYS

Children's plays are very popular. They can be produced in much the same way as adult plays, but need rather more care and attention. If the following hints are carefully followed, however, there is no reason why children's plays should not be equally successful. First of all, bear in mind the age of the children. The younger they are, the more excited they will be about acting. The wise parent, therefore, will try to damp their ardour a little. But be very careful not to damp it too much. If the children are under the age of ten, avoid a play that has long speeches in it, or else the actors are liable to " dry up " in the middle. If they are very young, a play that is written in rhyme is the more suitable, because it is easier to remember. Above all, keep the play simple. If the plot is too involved, the children will lost interest.

Again, once the roles have been cast, stick to them. Never change parts unless it is unavoidable. All children, whether they show it or not, are very sensitive and are likely to consider the loss of a part as a slur upon them, and tears, quarrels and jealousy will be the inevitable result. In assigning the parts, it is a good idea to give them to the children as though one's mind has been made up on the spur of the moment; for some unknown reason, it tends to avoid arguments.

The next step is to explain the play to the children, i.e., to make sure they know what it is all about. If there will be someone in the audience of whom they are very fond, point out how happy that person will be to see them act. This line of reasoning will tend to turn excitement into enthusiasm, which is all to the good.

As soon as they are word-perfect, not before, start rehearsing the movements of the play. The final step is to get them into costume. In this connexion, it is wise to have as many dress rehearsals as possible in order to accustom the children to their different dresses.

HOW TO PLAY CHARADES

Another form of home entertainment, which in more ways than one is a modified kind of play-acting, is the charade. The idea, in brief, is this. The party splits into two groups. One group leaves the room and chooses a word, returns to the room, and proceeds to act that word portion by portion, then reacts the whole word, while the second group do their best to discover the word that has been secretly chosen.

Let us take an example. The group that has left the room has chosen the word "catastrophe." The word is split up from its sound into three parts—"cat," "ass," "trophy." The group returns to the room and proceeds to act a short scene on any subject they like, probably with improvised props and costumes. During the conversation, which should be as confusing but as funny as possible, the word "cat" is mentioned. Next follows a second scene—perhaps a mock quarrel, in which one person calls another an "ass." The procedure is repeated with the word "trophy." Then finally follows a short impromptu playlet in which the whole word "catastrophe" is mentioned. The second group is then asked to try to guess what word was chosen. The second group then leave the room and choose a word, and the whole process is repeated.

With a little thought, charades can be very entertaining indeed. There are thousands of words that can be used in this way, but to aid the beginner, here are a few words split up ready for use :—

Con-script-ion	Sit-u-a-tion	Cott-age
Con-nex-ion	De-light-ful	Di-rector-ship
Tel-eg-ram	Min-or-it-ies	In-vest-ment
Cat-ar-act	Holi-day	Gal-van-ize
Butt-on	Cap-it-al	Supp-le-ment
Honey-comb	Labor-a-tory	Thou-sand
Ed-i-tor	Ann-ounce-men	

CHAPTER 9

COMMUNITY SONGS

MOST organizers of sing-songs make the mistake of assuming that everybody knows the words, and far too many songs begin bravely and peter out miserably half-way through, just because nobody knows any more.

With this collection, you will be safe. It has been designed specifically to overcome this difficulty. We give a number of the most popular songs in English—more than enough for any sing-song —with a complete set of words for each. The book can be shared by a group or the words read out before each song.

Where music is given it is purposely a mere skeleton of melody and bass. Thus it can be played by an absolute novice; the more expert performer will amplify the harmony as he or she pleases.

SOME FOLKS DO

Some folks like to sigh,
  Some folks do, some folks do;
Some folks long to die,
  But that's not me nor you.

Chorus:
Long live the merry, merry heart
That laughs by night and day,

Like the Queen of Mirth,
No matter what some folks say.

Some folks fear to smile,
  Some folks do, some folks do;
Others laugh through guile,
  But that's not me nor you.
                    Chorus.

Some folks fret and scold,
  Some folks do, some folks do;
They'll soon be dead and cold,
  But that's not me nor you.
                    Chorus.

Some folks get grey hairs,
  Some folks do, some folks do;
Brooding o'er their cares,
  But that's not me nor you.
                    Chorus.

Some folks toil and save,
  Some folks do, some folks do,
To buy themselves a grave,
  But that's not me nor you.
                    Chorus.

AULD LANG SYNE

Should auld acquaintance be forgot
  And ne'er brought to mind?
Should auld acquaintance be forgot
  And days of auld lang syne?
For auld lang syne, my dear,
  For auld lang syne,
We'll tak' a cup o' kindness yet
  For auld lang syne.

And here's a hand, my trusty frien',
  And gie's a hand o' thine,
We'll tak' a cup o' kindness yet
  For auld lang syne.
For auld lang syne, my dear,
  For auld lang syne,
We'll tak' a cup o' kindness yet
  For auld lang syne.

THE ASH GROVE

How dear are these haunts, when at even I hear
The breeze fall in sighs on my fanciful ear,
And Philomel warbling the branches among,
In sympathy pours her melodious song.
How dear are these haunts, how delightful the grove
Where first I held converse with her that I love;
How dear are these haunts, how delightful the grove,
Where first I held converse with her that I love.

Ah! 'tis but an image; my fair Ellen's gone!
And still shall I wander unconscious alone,
Can regret furnish mem'ry with pleasing employ,
And the mind brood with fondness on scenes of past joy?
Still dear are those haunts, still delightful the grove,
Tho' 'twas here that I parted from her that I love;
Still dear are those haunts, still delightful the grove,
Tho' 'twas here that I parted from her that I love.

COME LASSES AND LADS

Come, lassies and lads, take leave of your dads,
  And away to the maypole hie,
For every he has got a she,
  And the fiddler's standing by;
For Willy has got his Jill,
  And Johnnie has got his Joan,
To trip it, trip it, trip it, trip it,
  Trip it up and down,
To trip it, trip it, trip it, trip it,
  Trip it up and down.

" You're out," says Nick. " Not I," says Dick,
  " 'Twas the fiddler played it wrong."
" 'Tis true," says Sue, and so says Hugh,
  And so says every one.
The fiddler then began
  To play the tune again,
And every girl did trip it, trip it,
  Trip it to the men,
And every girl did trip it, trip it,
  Trip it to the men.

Now there they did stay the whole of the day
  And tired the fiddler quite,
With dance and play without any pay
  From morning until night;
They told the fiddler then
  They'd pay him for his play,
And each a twopence, twopence, twopence,
  Gave him and went away,
And each a twopence, twopence, twopence,
  Gave him and went away.

" Goodnight," says Harry. " Goodnight," says Mary.
  " Goodnight," says Poll to John.
" Goodnight," says Sue to her sweetheart Hugh.
  " Goodnight," says every one.
Some walked and some did run,
  Some loitered on the way
And bound themselves by kisses twelve
  To meet the next holiday,
And bound themselves by kisses twelve
  To meet the next holiday.

THERE'S A HOLE IN THA' BUCKET

There's a hole in tha' bucket, dear Liza, dear Liza,
There's a hole in tha' bucket, dear Liza, a hole.

Then mend it, dear Georgie, dear Georgie, dear Georgie,
Then mend it, dear Georgie, dear Georgie, mend it.

With what shall I mend it, dear Liza, dear Liza,
With what shall I mend it, dear Liza, mend it?

With some straw, dear Georgie, dear Georgie, dear Georgie,
With some straw, dear Georgie, dear Georgie, some straw.

If the straw be too long, dear Liza, dear Liza,
If the straw be too long, dear Liza, too long?

Then cut it, dear Georgie, dear Georgie, dear Georgie,
Then cut it, dear Georgie, dear Georgie, cut it.

With what shall I cut it, dear Liza, dear Liza,
With what shall I cut it, dear Liza, with what?

With a knife, dear Georgie, dear Georgie, dear Georgie,
With a knife, dear Georgie, dear Georgie, with a knife.

If the knife be not sharp, dear Liza, dear Liza,
If the knife be not sharp, dear Liza, not sharp?

Then sharpen it, dear Georgie, dear Georgie, dear Georgie,
Then sharpen it dear Georgie, dear Georgie, sharpen it.

On what shall I sharpen it, dear Liza, dear Liza,
On what shall I sharpen it, dear Liza, on what?

On a stone, dear Georgie, dear Georgie, dear Georgie,
On a stone, dear Georgie, dear Georgie, on a stone.

If the stone be too dry, dear Liza, dear Liza,
If the stone be too dry, dear Liza, too dry?

Then wet it, dear Georgie, dear Georgie, dear Georgie,
Then wet it, dear Georgie, dear Georgie, wet it.

With what shall I wet it, dear Liza, dear Liza,
With what shall I wet it, dear Liza, wet it?

With water, dear Georgie, dear Georgie, dear Georgie,
With water, dear Georgie, dear Georgie, with water.

In what shall I fetch the water, dear Liza, dear Liza,
In what shall I fetch the water, dear Liza, in what?

In a bucket, dear Georgie, dear Georgie, dear Georgie,
In a bucket, dear Georgie, dear Georgie, in a bucket.

There's a hole in the bucket, dear Liza, dear Liza.
There's a hole in the bucket, dear Liza, a hole.

OH DEAR ! WHAT CAN THE MATTER BE?

Oh dear ! What can the matter be?
Oh dear ! What can the matter be?
Oh dear ! What can the matter be?
   Johnnie's so long at the fair.

He promised to buy me a bunch of blue ribbons,
He promised to buy me a bunch of blue ribbons,
He promised to buy me a bunch of blue ribbons,
   To tie up my bonny brown hair.

  Chorus:
Oh dear ! *etc.*

He promised to buy me a basket of posies,
A garland of lilies, a wreath of red roses,
A little straw hat to set off the blue ribbons
   That tie up my bonnie brown hair.

  Chorus:
Oh dear ! *etc.*

THE VICAR OF BRAY

In good King Charles's golden days,
When loyalty no harm meant,
A zealous high churchman then was I,
And so I got preferment;
To teach my flock I never missed,
Kings were by God appointed,
And lost are they that do resist
Or touch the Lord's anointed.

Chorus:

And this is law that I'll maintain
    Until my dying day, sir,
That whatsoever king may reign
    I'll be the Vicar of Bray, sir.

When royal James possessed the crown
And Popery came in fashion

The penal laws I hooted down,
And read the Declaration;
The Church of Rome I found would fit
Full well my constitution,
And had become a Jesuit
But for the Revolution.
                    Chorus.

When William was our King declared,
To ease the Nation's grievance,
With this new wind about I steered
And swore to him allegiance;
Old principles I did revoke,
Set conscience at a distance,
Passive obedience was a joke,
A jest was non-resistance.
                    Chorus.

When good Queen Anne became our Queen,
The Church of England's glory,
Another face of things was seen,
And I became a Tory;
Occasional Conformists base,
I blamed their moderation,
And thought the Church in danger was
By such prevarication.
                    Chorus.

When George in pudding-time came o'er
And moderate men looked big, sir,
I turned a cat-in-pan once more,
And so became a Whig, sir;
And this preferment I procured
From our new Faith's Defender,
And almost every day abjured
The Pope and the Pretender.
                    Chorus.

The illustrious House of Hanover,
And Protestant succession,
To these I do allegiance swear,
While they can keep possession;
For in my faith and loyalty
I never more will falter,
And George my lawful King shall be—
Until the times do alter.
                    Chorus.

CLEMENTINE

In a cavern in a canyon,
    Excavating for a mine,
Dwelt a miner, forty-niner,
    And his daughter Clementine.

Chorus:
Oh my darling, oh my darling,
Oh my darling Clementine,
Thou art lost and gone for ever,
Dreadful sorry, Clementine.

Light she was and like a fairy
    And her shoes were number nine,
Herring boxes without topses
    Sandals made for Clementine.
                              Chorus.

Drove she ducklings to the water
    Every morning just at nine.
Kicked her foot against a splinter;
    Fell into the foaming brine.
                              Chorus.

Saw her lips above the water
    Blowing bubbles mighty fine.
But alas, I was no swimmer—
    So I lost my Clementine.
                              Chorus.

Then the miner, forty-niner,
    Soon began to peak and pine;
Thought he oughter join his daughter—
    Now he's with his Clementine.
                              Chorus.

In my dreams she still doth haunt me,
    Robed in garments soaked in brine,
Though in life I used to hug her,
    Now she's dead I draw the line.
                              Chorus.

How I missed her, how I missed her,
    How I missed my Clementine,
But I kissed her little sister,
    And forgot my Clementine.
                              Chorus.

THE WHALE

Did you ever, ever, ever, ever, ever,
   Did you ever, ever, ever, see a whale?
No I never, never, never, never, never,
   No I never, never, never saw a whale.

Well if you ever, ever, ever, ever, ever,
   If you ever, ever, ever, see a whale,
You must never, never, never, never, never,
   You must never, never, tread upon its tail.

For if you ever, ever, ever, ever, ever,
   If you ever, ever tread upon its tail,
You will never, never, never, never, never,
   You will never, never see another whale.

YE BANKS AND BRAES OF BONNY DOON

Ye banks and braes o' bonnie Doon,
How can ye bloom sae fresh and fair,
How can ye chant, ye little birds,
And I sae weary, fu' o' care?
Ye'll break my heart, ye warbling birds,
That warble on the flowery thorn,
Ye mind me o' departed joys,
Departed never to return.

Aft hae I roved by bonnie Doon,
To see the rose and woodbine twine,
And every bird sang o' its love
As fondly sae did I o' mine.
Wi' lichtsome heart I pu'd a rose,
Fu' sweet upon its thorny tree,
And my fause lover stole the rose,
But ah, he left the thorn wi' me.

ONE FISH BALL

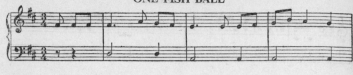

There was a man walked up and down
To see where he could dine in town;

There was a man walked up and down
To see where he could dine in town.

And when at last he found a place,
He sat him down with modest grace.
(*Repeat.*)

He took his purse from pocket hence—
And found he'd only five halfpence.

He searched the menu through and through
To see what five halfpence would do.

And at the very end of all
Saw "five halfpence for one fish ball."

He called the waiter down the hall,
And softly murmured : "One fish ball."

The waiter bellowed down the hall :
"This gen'leman here wants one fish ball."

The people all turned round to see
Whoever such a man could be.

The wretched man all ill at ease,
"A little piece of bread too if you please."

The waiter bellowed down the hall :
"We don't serve bread with one fish ball."

The moral is for one and all
Don't ask for bread with one fish ball.

LOCH LOMOND

By yon bonnie banks and by yon bonnie brae,
Where the sun shines bright on Loch Lomond,
Where me and my true love were ever wont to gae,
On the bonnie, bonnie banks of Loch Lomond.

Chorus:
Oh, you'll take the high road and I'll take the low road,
    And I'll be in Scotland afore ye,
But me and my true love will never meet again
    On the bonnie, bonnie banks of Loch Lomond.

I mind where we parted in yon shady glen,
On the steep, steep side of Loch Lomond,
Where in deep purple hue the Highland hills we view,
And the moon coming out in the gloamin'.
Chorus.

The wee birdies sing and the wild flowers spring
And in sunshine the waters are sleeping,
But the broken heart can ken nae second spring again,
Though the waeful may cease from their weeping.
Chorus.

ONE MORE RIVER

Old Noah once he built the ark,
    There's one more river to cross;
He patched it up with hickory bark,
    There's one more river to cross.
One more river, and that's the river of Jordan,
One more river, there's one more river to cross.

He set to work to load his stock,
    There's one more river to cross;
He anchored the ark with a great big rock,
    There's one more river to cross.
One more river, and that's the river of Jordan,
One more river, there's one more river to cross.

The animals went in one by one,
The elephant chewing a caraway bun.

The animals went in two by two,
The rhinoceros and the kangaroo.

The animals went in three by three,
The bear, the flea, and the bumble bee.

The animals went in four by four,
Old Noah got mad and hollered for more.

The animals went in five by five,
With travelling trunks they all arrive.

The animals went in six by six,
The hyena laughed at the monkey's tricks.

The animals went in seven by seven,
Said the ant to the elephant: "Who are you shovin'?"

The animals went in eight by eight,
They came with a rush, 'cos it was late.

The animals went in nine by nine,
Old Noah shouted : " Cut that line ! "

The animals went in ten by ten,
The ark she blew her whistle then.

And then the voyage did begin,
Old Noah pulled the gangplank in.

They never knew where they were at,
Till the ark it bumped on Ararat.

The ark it landed high and dry,
The cow it kissed the ape goodbye.

Now all, remember well the text,
To be continued in our next.

JOLLY OLD PALS

Dear old pals, jolly old pals,
    Always together in all sorts of weather;
Always game, ever the same,
    Give me for friendship the jolly old pals.

ANNIE LAURIE

Maxwellton braes are bonnie,
Where early falls the dew,
And 'twas there that Annie Laurie
Gie'd me her promise true.
   Gie'd me her promise true,
   Which ne'er forgot will be,
   And for bonnie Annie Laurie
   I'd lay me doon and dee.

Her brow is like the snawdrift,
Her throat is like the swan,
Her face it is the fairest
That e'er the sun shone on.
   That e'er the sun shone on,
   And dark blue is her e'e,
   And for bonnie Annie Laurie
   I'd lay me doon and dee.

Like dew on the gowan lying
Is the fa' o' her fairy feet,
And like winds in summer sighing,
Her voice is low and sweet.
   Her voice is low and sweet
   And she's a' the world to me,
   And for bonnie Annie Laurie
   I'd lay me doon and dee.

HOME SWEET HOME

'Mid pleasures and palaces though we may roam,
Be it ever so humble, there's no place like home !
A charm from the skies seems to hallow us there,
Which, seek through the world, is not met with elsewhere.

Home ! Home ! Sweet, sweet home !
There's no place like home, there's no place like home !

An exile from home, splendour dazzles in vain,
Oh give me my lowly thatched cottage again !
The birds singing gaily, that came at my call,
Give me them, with the peace of mind dearer than all.

Home ! Home ! Sweet, sweet home !
There's no place like home, there's no place like home !

SWANEE RIVER

Way down upon de Swanee ribber,
  Far, far away,
Dere's where my heart is turning ebber,
  Dere's where de old folks stay.
All up and down de whole creation
  Sadly I roam,
Still longing for de old plantation
  And for de old folks at home.

Chorus:
All de world am sad and dreary
  Eb'rywhere I roam,
Oh darkies, how my heart grows weary,
  Far from de old folks at home.

All round de little farm I wandered
  When I was young,
Den many happy days I squandered,
  Many de songs I sung;
When I was playing wid my brudder
  Happy was I,
Oh take me to my kind old mudder,
  Dere let me lib and die.
                              Chorus.

One little hut among de bushes,
  One dat I love,
Still sadly to my mem'ry rushes,
  No matter where I rove.
When shall I see de bees a-humming
  All round de comb?
When shall I hear de banjo strumming
  Down in de good old home?
                              Chorus.

KILLARNEY

By Killarney's lakes and fells, em'rald isles and winding bays,
Mountain paths and woodland dells, mem'ry ever fondly strays.
Bounteous nature loves all lands, beauty wanders everywhere,
Footprints leaves on many strands, but her home is surely there.
Angels fold their wings and rest in that Eden of the West;
Beauty's home, Killarney; Heaven's reflex, Killarney.

No place else can charm the eye with such bright and varied tints,
Every rock that you pass by, verdure broiders or besprints.
Virgin there the green grass grows, every morn Spring's natal day;
Bright-hued berries daff the snows, smiling Winter's frown away.
Angels often pausing there doubt if Eden were more fair;
Beauty's home, Killarney; Heaven's reflex, Killarney.

EARLY ONE MORNING

Early one morning, just as the sun was rising,
I heard a maid sing in the valley below:

Chorus:
Oh don't deceive me, oh never leave me.
How could you use a poor maiden so?

Oh gay is the garland and fresh are the roses
I've culled from the garden to bind on thy brow.
Chorus.

Remember the vows that you made to your Mary,
Remember the bower where you vowed to be true.
Chorus.

Thus sang the poor maiden, her sorrow bewailing,
Thus sang the poor maid in the valley below.
Chorus.

POLLY WOLLY DOODLE

Oh I went down South for to see my Sal,
  Sing Polly-Wolly-Doodle all the day,
Oh my Sally am a lively gal,
  Sing Polly-Wolly-Doodle all the day.

Chorus:

Fare thee well, fare thee well,
Fare thee well, my fairy fay,
For I'm off to Louisiana for to see my Susy Anna,
  Singing Polly-Wolly-Doodle all the day.

Oh my Sal she am a maiden fair,
  Sing Polly-Wolly-Doodle all the day,
With laughing eyes and curly hair,
  Sing Polly-Wolly-Doodle all the day.

                         Chorus.

Oh I came to a river and I couldn't get across,
   Sing Polly-Wolly-Doodle all the day,
And I jumped on a nigger for I thought he was a hoss,
   Sing Polly-Wolly-Doodle all the day.
                   Chorus.

Oh a grasshopper sitting on a railroad track,
   Sing Polly-Wolly-Doodle all the day,
A-picking his teeth wid a carpet tack,
   Sing Polly-Wolly-Doodle all the day.
                   Chorus.

Behind the barn, down on my knees,
   Sing Polly-Wolly-Doodle all the day,
I thought I heard a chicken sneeze,
   Sing Polly-Wolly-Doodle all the day.
                   Chorus.

He sneezed so hard, wid de hoopin' cough,
   Sing Polly-Wolly-Doodle all the day,
He sneezed his head and his tail right off,
   Sing Polly-Wolly-Doodle all the day.
                   Chorus.

SWEET LASS OF RICHMOND HILL

On Richmond Hill there lives a lass,
   More bright than May-day morn,
Whose charms all other maids' surpass.
   A rose without a thorn.
This lass so neat, with smile so sweet,
   Has won my right good will,
I'd crowns resign to call her mine,
   Sweet lass of Richmond Hill.

Sweet lass of Richmond Hill,
Sweet lass of Richmond Hill,
I'd crowns resign to call her mine,
Sweet lass of Richmond Hill.

Ye zephyrs gay that fan the air
   And wanton through the grove,
Oh whisper to my charming fair—
   "I die for her I love."

This lass so neat, with smile so sweet,
    Has won my right good will,
I'd crowns resign to call her mine,
    Sweet lass of Richmond Hill.

Sweet lass, *etc.*

How happy must the shepherd be
    Who calls his maid his own.
Oh may her choice be fixed on me;
    Mine's fixed on her alone.
This lass so neat, with smile so sweet,
    Has won my right good will,
I'd crowns resign to call her mine,
    Sweet lass of Richmond Hill.

Sweet lass, *etc.*

DRINK TO ME ONLY

Drink to me only with thine eyes
    And I will pledge with mine,
Or leave a kiss within the cup
    And I'll not ask for wine;
The thirst that from the soul doth rise
    Doth ask a drink divine.
But might I of Jove's nectar sip
    I would not change for thine.

I sent thee late a rosy wreath,
    Not so much hon'ring thee
As giving it a hope that there
    It could not wither'd be.
But thou thereon didst only breathe
    And sent'st it back to me—
Since when it grows and smells, I swear,
    Not of itself but thee.

ONE MAN WENT TO MOW

One man went to mow, went to mow a meadow;
One man and his dog, went to mow a meadow.

Two men went to mow, went to mow a meadow.
Two men, one man and his dog, went to mow a meadow.

Three men went to mow, went to mow a meadow,
Three men, two men, one man and his dog, went to mow a meadow.

Four men went to mow, *etc.*

Five men went to mow, *etc.*

Six men went to mow, *etc.*

Seven men went to mow, *etc.*

Eight men went to mow, *etc.*

Nine men went to mow, *etc.*

Ten men went to mow, *etc.*

COMIN' THROUGH THE RYE

Gin a body meet a body,
  Comin' thro' the rye;
Gin a body greet a body,
  Need a body cry?

Chorus:
Ilka lassie has her laddie,
Nane, they say, ha'e I,
Yet a' the lads they smile at me
When comin' thro' the rye.

Gin a body meet a body,
  Comin' frae the well;
Gin a body meet a body,
  Need a body tell?
                    Chorus.

Amang the train there is a swain
  I dearly lo'e mysel',
But whaur's his hame and what's his name
  I dinna care to tell.
                    Chorus.

WHAT SHALL WE DO WITH THE DRUNKEN SAILOR?

What shall we do with the drunken sailor?
  What shall we do with the drunken sailor?
What shall we do with the drunken sailor
  Early in the morning?

Hooray and up she rises,
Hooray and up she rises,
Hooray and up she rises,
Early in the morning.

Put him in the scuppers with a hosepipe on him, *etc.*
                                              Chorus.

Throw him in the long-boat until he's sober, *etc.*
                                              Chorus.

Heave him by the leg in a running bowline, *etc.*
                                              Chorus.

Tie him to the taffrail when she's yard-arm under, *etc.*
                                              Chorus.

SWING LOW, SWEET CHARIOT

Swing low, sweet chariot,
  Coming for to carry me home;
Swing low, sweet chariot,
  Coming for to carry me home.

I looked over Jordan and what did I see,
  Coming for to carry me home?
A band of angels coming after me,
  Coming for to carry me home.

Swing low, *etc.*

If you get there before I do,
  Coming for to carry me home,
Tell all my friends I'm coming too,
  Coming for to carry me home.

Swing low, *etc,*

The brightest day that ever I saw,
  Coming for to carry me home,
When Jesus washed my sins away,
  Coming for to carry me home.

Swing low, *etc.*

I'm sometimes up, I'm sometimes down,
   Coming for to carry me home,
But still my soul feels heavenly bound,
   Coming for to carry me home.

Swing low, *etc.*

THE GRAND OLD DUKE OF YORK

Oh the grand old Duke of York,
He had ten thousand men,
He marched them up to the top of a hill,
And marched them down again.

Chorus:
And when they were up, they were up,
   And when they were down, they were down,
And when they were only halfway up,
   They were neither up nor down.

Oh the grand old Duke of York
He had ten thousand men,
They beat their drums as they marched up the hill,
And they beat them down again.
                                        Chorus.

Oh the grand old Duke of York
He had ten thousand men,
They blew their horns as they marched up the hill,
And they blew them down again.
                                        Chorus.

Oh the grand old Duke of York
He had ten thousand men,
They waved their flags as they marched up the hill,
And they waved them down again.
                                        Chorus.

ROUND

London's burning, London's burning,
Look yonder, look yonder,
Fire, fire, fire, fire,
Oh bring me some water.

CHAPTER 10

SIMPLE CARD GAMES

In this chapter are given descriptions of, and rules for what may be called the classic card games, as well as of many popular round games. Between them they provide something for every taste and every occasion.

Until the advent of its offshoot Bridge, **Whist** was *the* card game, played by all classes of the community.

The whole pack of fifty-two cards is used, and in the standard game, four players—two in partnership against the other two—take part.

The first move is to cut for partnership and the deal. The two cutting the highest cards play against the two with the lowest, and the player who picks the lowest card takes the first deal. In cutting, the ace counts as the lowest card, though in play it counts as the highest. Partners sit opposite each other.

DEALING AND SHUFFLING

The player with the lowest card in the cut is the first dealer. If the two lowest cards cut were of equal value, the player who drew the first of the two cards is dealer. In the second game the player on the left of the first dealer is the new dealer, and so on.

The usual procedure is for the player on the left of the dealer to shuffle, and then for the player on the dealer's right to cut. The cards are then dealt to the four players, one at a time, in rotation, thirteen to each, starting with the player on the left of the dealer. The last card which of course comes to the dealer, is turned up and put before him to indicate the trump suit. This card remains exposed until the first trick is taken.

The player to the left of the dealer starts the game, the object of which is to take as many tricks as possible. Players must follow suit if possible, but, if they cannot, they can either trump, or discard a card which seems of little value. The winner of each trick leads off for the following trick. The made tricks are kept by two of the players, one for each partnership. Six tricks makes a " book," and each trick taken after that counts as one point in the game which is, of course, of seven points, there being thirteen tricks in the pack. The result of the hand is calculated by deducting the loser's score from seven. The game is for ten points. The honours, i.e., the ace, king, queen and knave of trumps if held in partnership add to the score. If two partners between them hold three honours they score an extra two points, and if all four, four points. In scoring, honours count before tricks, so that if a set of partners has already scored six in a game and one of them holds all four honours in his hand, he may call (show) them and win the game without further play. Similarly if they have scored eight and one partner holds three honours, he can show them and win the game. Furthermore, when a partnership has scored eight, if one of the partners holds two honours in his hand, he may ask the other " Can you one? " and if the reply is " Yes," they show them and win the game. But if one pair has already scored nine, they can no longer count honours towards the game.

PENALTIES FOR REVOKING

If a player in error, throws down two cards on a trick, he must indicate which one he wishes to play, and the other card may be " called." A called card must be left, face upwards, on the table by the side of the owner. If either of the other players wish, he can call for it to be led or played—unless, in the latter case, it would mean revoking. The owner of a called, exposed card can lead or play that card himself at any time if he desires.

For a " revoke," i.e., omitting to follow suit when the player has a card of that suit in his hand, two tricks are transferred to the other partnership. This can be enforced for as many revokes as are made during the hand, and the side making a revoke cannot win that game. If both sides revoke neither win that hand. A revoke may be corrected, if the trick has not been completed and turned over, but such a correction leaves the card incorrectly played as a called, exposed card. The player of a revoke, and his partner, can demand that the game should be played out, but they can only score points up to six. A revoke may be claimed any time before the cards have been shuffled and cut for a fresh deal.

PLAYING WHIST WITH TWO PEOPLE

The rules for Whist for Two, a variation of whist proper, are much the same as for the parent game. The cut for deal comes first, and this goes to the holder of the lowest card. As in ordinary whist, the ace counts as the lowest card in a cut, but as the highest card in play.

The dealer having been decided on, he shuffles, his opponent cuts, and the dealer proceeds to deal thirteen cards each to his opponent and himself, starting with his opponent, and dealing the cards one by one.

The twenty-six remaining cards are put face downwards in a heap on the table in a position convenient to both players, and these cards are now drawn into the game, one by one. The top card, however, is exposed, and the suit of this card determines trumps.

The opponent leads the game, his adversary replies. The winner of this and of each ensuing trick takes the top card from the pack and adds it to his hand. The loser takes the next card, shows it to his adversary, and then adds it to his hand. The card below is then exposed, to be played for in the next trick. The winner of each trick sets it by his side, as in whist proper, but he has to take thirteen tricks to make a book. Each trick taken after the book is made counts towards the player's score, and the final score and win is to the player who takes the most tricks.

There is some skill and a nice element of chance in playing this game. For instance, if the turned-up card is a trump, the player will risk a good deal (according to its value, and to the number which he already holds in his hand) to win it. On the other hand, if the turned-up card is a low one of no obvious value, it may be worth while to lose the trick, in the hope of picking up something better.

Trumps and dealer are changed with each hand. Any total agreed upon may constitute a game, but fifty is generally accepted.

AN OLD VICTORIAN FAVOURITE

Bezique, a game for two people, is played with sixty-four cards, namely the aces, kings, queens, knaves and tens to sevens of two packs. The ace ranks as the highest card, the ten next, and the rest in normal order, with the seven as the lowest. If two cards of the same suit and the same value fall on the same trick, the first one played wins.

The players cut for deal, and the highest card wins; in the case of a tie a re-cut is made. Either or both players may shuffle, the dealer last. Eight cards are dealt to each player, three, two, and three at a time. The top card left in the remaining pack is turned up and determines trumps. If it is a seven, the dealer makes his first score at once of ten points. The cards left in the pack are put face downwards on the table, with the trump card by the side.

The game consists of trying to make up certain sets of cards, and to take tricks containing aces and tens—these two are called brisques. The combinations to be made are :—

	Points
Marriage—the king and queen of any suit but trumps	20
Royal Marriage—the king and queen of trumps	40
Sequence—ace, king, queen, knave, ten of trumps	250
Bezique—queen of spades and knave of diamonds (Fig. 1)	40
Double Bezique—two queens of spades and two knaves of diamonds (Fig. 2)	500
Four aces	100
Four kings	80
Four queens	60
Four knaves	40

Each brisque scores ten points for the player winning it and should be scored at once, and the winner of the last trick also scores an extra ten points. A scoring card for bezique is shown in Fig. 3.

The opponent starts the play by putting any card he likes on the table and the dealer plays another card.

Fig. 1. *Bezique.*

This may be any card he likes, i.e., he need not follow suit and he need not trump. The higher card played wins the trick unless a trump is played, in which case the trump wins. Before leading for the next trick the winner of the former one takes the top card from the pack on the table, and the opponent takes the next card.

Before drawing these cards either player can declare and lay upon the table any combination he may hold, and he scores whatever the value is at once. Only one combination can be shown by either player after each trick, but combinations may be held if desired and declared after later tricks; they need not be declared in the order in which they were made. Cards from the exposed combinations may be played or led at any time, but they must not be taken into the hand again until the table pack is spent. The king or queen of trumps can be used in a sequence after they have been used to declare a royal marriage, but if they are used in a sequence first, they cannot be scored afterwards as a marriage.

WHEN YOU DRAW THE SEVEN OF TRUMPS

The player who holds or draws the seven of trumps may exchange it for the exposed trump card on the table, if he wishes, and scores ten points for so doing, but this can only be done *after* taking a trick, and once it has been done with one seven of trumps, it cannot be done with the other. However, the second seven of trumps scores ten for its holder, if it is " shown " after taking a trick, but the player may not then make a declaration until he takes another trick.

If a player makes an incorrect declaration, his opponent can call

Fig. 2. *Double Bezique—two queens of spades and two knaves of diamonds.*

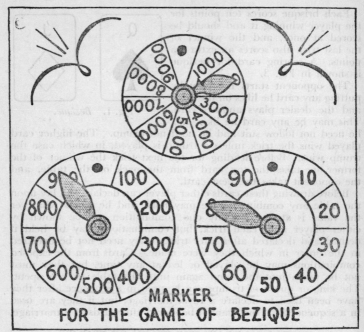

Fig. 3. *The usual type of marker used for Bezique.*

for any of such cards to be led. He may correct the declaration if it is possible, but not after he has drawn a fresh card from the pack on the table.

The winner of the last trick takes the remaining covered card and the opponent the exposed trump. No more declarations may be made, and each player takes into his hand whatever cards he has remaining on the table.

The game now continues by the winner of the last trick leading. He must be replied to in suit and the opponent *must* take the trick if he can, trumping if necessary. The winner of the last trick scores ten points, apart from any brisques he may hold.

All scores made during the game are made at once, and the game is usually one of 1,000 points.

There are several variations of this game. One is known as **Without a Trump.** In this case the first marriage declared settles the trump suit. The combinations are the same as in the parent game, save that there is no score of ten points for the seven of trumps.

Three-handed Bezique requires three packs of cards, from which the aces to the sevens of each suit are used. The game is played for 2,000 points, and with the exception of triple bezique, which is three spade queens and three diamond knaves, and counts 1,500 points, the scores for the combinations are the same as in the two-handed game.

For **Four-handed Bezique** four packs of cards are needed, and the same cards are used in play, the aces to the sevens of each suit. Triple bezique again counts 1,500, and the other combinations are of the same value as in the two-pack game. Play may be for the four as individuals, or for two and two as partners. When a partnership is arranged, any player after having taken a trick may either announce combination in his hand, or may pass the right on to his partner. Only one combination may be scored after having taken a trick. Partners can make use of cards shown by one another in forming extra combinations.

HOW TO PLAY CRIBBAGE

Cribbage is a game for two or three, or for four as partners, but is best played by two people only, and we will take this two-handed game as a basis for purposes of description.

A full pack of fifty-two cards is required; the king ranks as the highest card and the ace as the lowest. A cribbage board and four pegs (Fig. 4) two of one colour and two of another (each player needing two), are also wanted.

The object of the game is to form different scoring combinations, and the game consists of 61 or 121 points. If either player reaches 61 before his opponent gains 31, or 121 before his opponent gains 91, it is called a " lurch," and counts as two games won.

The players cut to determine the deal, the lower cut winning. Both players may shuffle if they so wish, but the dealer takes the last shuffle, and the opponent then cuts. Six cards are dealt to each player, one at a time, alternately, beginning with the opponent. The loser of the first game deals the next hand, and so on, the loser always taking the ensuing deal. The penalty for a mis-deal is

Fig. 4. Cribbage board and markers.

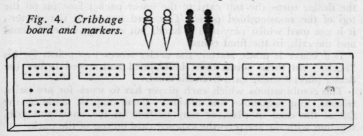

two points. A mis-deal may be called if the cards are not cut by the opponent immediately before the deal, for exposing a card or cards whilst dealing, or for dealing too many, or too few, cards to either hand. If a mis-deal is called, the opponent has the right of calling for an entirely fresh deal if he wishes, but he must decide before looking at his hand. The exception to this is when either hand has been dealt too many or too few cards. If the dealer has too many cards, and the opponent decides either before or after he has seen his own hand to claim a re-deal, he may do so; but if he decides to leave the deal, he may take the extra card or cards from the dealer's hand and look at it or them, if the dealer has seen his hand, and then place it, or them, on the top of the remaining pack. If too few cards have been dealt, the dealer supplies them from the top of the pack. If the opponent has too many or too few cards, he must decide before looking at them whether to claim a fresh deal or not. If the deal stands, the extra cards must be placed on the top of the pack, and in the case of too few having been dealt, the dealer must hand out as many as are required, always from the top of the pack.

PENALTIES FOR MIS-PLAY

If a card is exposed during the deal, the same dealer must re-deal.

If the pack is found to be wanting, the same dealer must re-deal, but scores already made with the incorrect pack stand.

Dealing out of turn must be " called " before the opponent touches his cards.

If either person plays in error, a penalty of two points is scored, at once, by the adversary.

At the start of play, each person discards two cards from his hand and places them on the table, face down. These cards are the *crib* and now belong to the dealer. They remain hidden until the end of the game, when the dealer claims them and scores any points they may contain. The non-dealer scores three points for having lost the crib.

After the crib has been made, the opponent cuts the pack, and the dealer turns the top card of the lower packet face up on the top of the re-assembled pack. This card is termed the starter : it is not used whilst playing the hand, but counts with each hand and the crib, in the final count.

If a knave is made starter, the dealer scores two points for his "heels," but these points must be claimed and scored before the dealer plays a single card from his hand.

The combinations which each player has to work for are pairs, triplets, four sequences and fifteens. These may be made by the fall of the card in play, or may be held in the hand and crib, together with the starter—the exposed card on top of the pack.

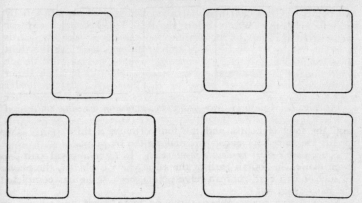

Figs. 5 and 6. How triplets (Fig. 5, left) and fours (Fig. 6, right) in the game of cribbage should be laid out on the card table.

Play starts by the opponent playing any card from his hand, face up on the table, in front of himself, and he, at the same time, calls its value (in pips), kings, queens, and knaves counting as ten points. The dealer then places a card face up in front of himself, and calls the combined value of his card and that of the card already exposed. The game continues, each player calling the amassed value of the exposed cards, but this value must not exceed 31. If, as the game progresses, either player has no card which will keep the value under 31, he calls " Go," and the opponent then continues, if possible, until he, in his turn, can play no further without passing 31.

The player who gets nearest to 31, scores one point; if he gets exactly 31 he scores two points. If the score only reaches 15, the last player scores three points.

When the play has gone as far as it can, and the scores are pegged, each player turns the cards he has played face downwards in front of him, and the player whose next turn it is, starts again exactly as before with his remaining cards. This continues until both hands are played out. Points are scored as they are made.

HOW TO COUNT THE SCORE

Pairs. If either player exposes a card which, with another card on the table, makes a pair, he scores two points.

Triplets, threes or royal pairs. If, after a pair has been claimed, another card of the same value is exposed, the player scores six points (Fig. 5). For example, take the four of diamonds, of hearts, and of clubs. The four of diamonds and the four of hearts make one pair, the four of diamonds and the four of clubs a second pair,

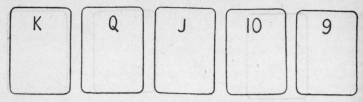

Fig. 7. A flush in Crib—from king to nine in the same suit.

and the four of hearts and the four of clubs a third pair. Two points are scored for each pair, making the six points.

Fours, double pairs or double royal pairs. If, after a royal pair has been made, the fourth card of the same value is played, the player of such fourth card scores twelve points, because he has completed six pairs (Fig. 6).

Sequences and runs. When three or more cards are played in numerical order, the player of the last card scores one point for each card in the sequence. A run of three scores three, and if a fourth card in sequence is added, the player scores four points, in addition to the three already scored, and which may have been scored by his opponent.

One for his nob. The player who holds the knave of the suit turned up on the pack, either in his hand or in his crib, scores an additional one point, i.e., " one for his nob." And the player who has the crib and turns up a knave on his opponent's cut, scores " two for his heels."

Flush. When all the cards held in the hand are of the same suit, one point is scored for each card held. A flush in crib (Fig. 7) must be of the same suit as the turn-up, and this means that the crib holder scores five points.

The points are scored as they are made on a cribbage board (Fig. 4). On the first score being made, this is immediately pegged, and when the second score is made the count is made with the second peg, and the first one used is not removed until this is done. If a player fails to peg his score correctly, his adversary on calling " muggins " may take the score to his own account.

OTHER VARIETIES OF THE GAME

Three-handed Cribbage is played in the same manner as the two-handed game, but a three-sided board is needed for scoring. Five cards are dealt to each player, one card to crib, and then each player in his turn, gives crib one card from his hand, thus making the ordinary four-card crib. The points are scored exactly as for the two-handed game.

In the game of **Four-handed Cribbage,** two players form a

partnership against the other two. One player on either side undertakes the scoring. Five cards are dealt to each, one at a time, and the deal passes to the left. The crib, of course, belongs to the dealer, and each player contributes one card to it, and a fifth card is dealt to it from the pack. The player on the left of the dealer cuts for the start, and commences the play. Sequences are scored by the player completing them. For instance, if we call the players *a*, *b*, *c*, and *d*, let *a* play a seven, *b* play an eight, *c* play a five, and *d* a six. In such a run, *d* scores. The game is for 121 points in all forms of cribbage.

A GOOD GAMBLING GAME

Vingt-et-un. This is a gambling game in which the full pack of fifty-two cards is used; any number of people can take part. The object of play is to collect cards which will either make, or nearly approach the score of twenty-one, aces counting either as eleven or one, whichever suits the player, royal cards as ten and all others at their face value.

Before starting to play, the stakes should be decided and a limit fixed. To determine the dealer and banker, the cards should be dealt round the table, the first to draw an ace becoming the banker and dealer *ipso facto*. It is usual for the same player to remain banker, until one of the others turns up a "natural" (or "Vingt-et-un"), i.e., a score of twenty-one in two cards. (A joker "natural" not counting.)

First of all, the banker deals one card face downwards to each player beginning from his left. On this card the others bet, laying their stakes before them on the table—not in a pool. The dealer does not bet. A second card on which no betting takes place is then dealt round. If the dealer or any other player has drawn the natural he must disclose it at once. If the dealer discloses one, he is paid thrice every player's stake. If another player, the banker pays him three times his stake. Beginning with player on left of the dealer, each in turn has now three alternatives :—

1. He can keep his hand as it is.
2. He can "twist" one or more cards, i.e., receive them from the dealer for nothing. In this case these cards are dealt face upwards on the table.
3. He can buy one or more cards, thus increasing his stake. In this case the cards are dealt face downwards.

No player may buy a card if he has already "twisted" one. If a player overdraws and goes over the score of twenty-one, he becomes "burst" and surrenders his stake to the bank.

If he collects five cards and his score is still twenty-one or under, he cannot be beaten by any score except a natural or another "five and under" drawn by the banker. A "five and under" is paid

Fig. 8.   A full house in Poker.   This is a strong hand.

three times his stake (if the banker, three times the stake of all other players left in the game).   A score of twenty-one is paid twice.

When play reaches the banker, he exposes his cards and draws others if he needs them.   When he decides his hand is complete, he pays the amount of their bets to all players who have *better* scores than himself.   All others surrender their stakes.   If the banker goes burst, he pays all other players left in the game.

A second deal is made from the cards left over from the first. The cards are *not* shuffled until the bank changes hands.

There are several variations of this game, but the general principles are above.

Poker is a gambling game played with fifty-two cards and a joker. Any number of players from two to eight can take part, each person playing for himself.   The ace can count high or low—whichever suits the game of the player.   The joker may represent any card but a duplicate.

POSSIBLE TYPES OF HAND

The object of the game is to collect and declare in a hand of five cards one of the combinations arranged below in order of value.

1. *A royal flush.*   The five highest cards of the same suit.   (Ace to ten.)
2. *Straight flush.*   Five cards of the same suit in sequence, e.g., ten to six of the same suit.   This would be declared a " ten high " sequence.
3. *Four of a kind.*   Any four cards of the same number.   (Say four twos.)
4. *Full house.*   Three cards of one number and two of another, e.g., three kings and two fives as in Fig. 8.   In the case of two full houses competing, the one with the highest triplet wins.
5. *Flush.*   Five cards of the same suit, not in sequence.   Flushes rank according to the highest card held.   For instance, in a flush of queen, nine, five, four and ace, a " queen high " flush would be declared.
6. *Straight.*—A sequence of five cards of mixed suits.   (The ten of diamonds, the nine and eight of spades, the seven of clubs the six of hearts.)

7. *Threes.* Any three cards of the same number. (Three tens.)

8. *Two pairs.* Any pair of the same number, with another pair of a different number, e.g., two kings and two queens. This would be called " kings up," for the higher pair gives the rank, irrespective of the value of the other pair.

9. *One pair.* Any two cards of the same number, with three cards of varied numbers.

10. *High card.* A hand which does not contain any of the combinations given, takes its rank from the highest card in it. Fig. 9 shows a bad hand of this kind; this would be called " king high."

Before play starts the following conventions must be settled: the limit to which bets can be raised, the time which is to be allowed for each game, and the ante, i.e., the bet made before the players draw any cards.

The deal is decided by cutting, the lowest dealing, aces counting low. Any player has the right to shuffle, and the dealer may make a final shuffle. The player on the dealer's right may cut if he wishes, but this is not obligatory. Five cards are then dealt, one at a time, to each player. The deal passes to the left.

Having examined his cards, the player to the left of the dealer must decide whether he is going to play that hand or not. If he thinks that his cards are not good enough, he can pass, i.e., throw in his cards face downwards on the table and take no further part in the hand. If he decides to play he must first put double the ante into the pool and then, if he wants to, raise the stake. The next player must put into the pool an equal amount to the first player, and he in his turn can raise it . . . and so on round the table. But no player can play his cards until he *has* put double the ante into the pool, plus the highest raise.

DISCARDING AND BETTING

When every player has paid the full stakes for play or dropped out, every player in turn may try to improve his hand by discarding any number of cards, and receiving an equal number in exchange from the dealer. Discarded cards must be thrown face downwards

Fig. 9. A bad Poker hand. This would be called " king high."

Fig. 10. *How a declaration in Rummy is laid out on the table.*

and must not be looked at by any one. A player, of course
need not discard, he may " stand pat," as keeping the same hand
is called.

After the discard, the player on the left of the dealer raises the
pool again if he wants to play, or drops out of the game, throwing
his cards face downwards on the table. The next player has three
alternatives, he can drop out, he can " see " the first, that is place
an amount in the pool equal to the first, with the object of making
him show his hand, or he can raise again. The third has the same
three alternatives, except that he must equal the bet of the second
if he wants to " see," and so on round the table. No player can
remain in the game unless he equals the highest bet on the table.

When a round has been completed without any further raise
being made, the player who is being seen must display his cards.
If any other player can beat him, he must show his cards in his turn.
If he is beaten he can discard without showing them.

A great object of the game is to bluff your opponents, so that they
will throw away their hand without seeing yours, but this requires a
high amount of skill, particularly in the betting. A player can
often beat a man with a superior hand by making him retire, but
it is not an advisable course for any but an expert.

A POPULAR FAVOURITE WITH CHILDREN

Rummy may be played by from two to six people. If there
are only two players only one pack of cards and one joker are used,
but when three or more are playing, two packs of cards and two jokers
are required.

Players draw for deal in the first game, the lowest card winning,
ace high. Ten cards are dealt to each player, one by one, and
the dealer then lays the next card in the pack face upwards on the
table with the rest of the cards before it, within easy reach of all
the players. The object of the game is to get rid of all the cards
in one's hand, according to the rules given here.

The player on the left of the dealer starts the game by either
drawing a card from the top of the pack, without showing it, or by
taking the exposed card. This is called the draw. The player
must now make his declaration, by laying on the table any set
of three or more cards of the same value which he may have, such
as three aces, or a sequence in suit, such as the three, four, and

five of hearts. A typical first declaration of four tens and a sequence of ace, king and queen of diamonds is shown in Fig. 10.

Next the player must make his discard, getting rid of the card which he thinks will be of the least value to him in his following play. This card he places on the top of the card exposed on the table in the actual deal, or in its place, if he has taken the exposed card.

The turns pass round the table until, by declaring sets, sequences, and by adding cards to sets already on the table—your own or other peoples—one player gets rid of all his cards. A hand in which a player has got rid of all his cards is shown in Fig. 11.

IMPORTANCE OF THE DISCARD

One card it must be remembered, must be left in the player's hand for the discard.

A set or sequence on the table may be added to, or built on to by a single card or by more, during the player's turn to play. When two packs of cards are being used, two cards of the same value and the same suit may be declared in a set. To a sequence a player may add in suit any number of cards, but a sequence ends with an ace, when the two is before it.

No player may add to his opponent's sets or sequences until he has his own first declaration on the table.

At the end of a game a player is often left with either two or three cards of no obvious use to him. As he has to discard every turn, they cannot form either a set or a sequence. His chances of getting out first lie in adding to the other sets and sequences on the table, or by buying. Buying may be undertaken when three or more are playing. If a player sees a card, that he desires, discarded and it is not his turn he may bid " one," and if the player who comes next in turn has no objection, the bidder may take it, but he must also take the top card of the pack into his hand without exposing it. He gets no declaration out of turn. When four or more are playing, it may occur that two players may wish to buy. This they may do,

Fig. 11. A player's complete hand laid out on the table, on winning the game.

if the rightful player has no objection. Bids of more than three entailing three extra cards from the pack, are not allowed. It is unwise to buy much towards the end of the game, as obviously the buyer may suffer heavily in the final score.

Once a card has been touched for drawing, it must be taken up

No further declaration or play may be made after a player has made his discard.

If the pack of cards on the table becomes exhausted before any player has got rid of all his hand, it may be turned over, without shuffling, leaving the last discard on the table face upwards as usual, thus giving the player the usual choice between the seen or the unseen card.

The joker may stand for any card in the pack, and thus can be used to complete any declaration of sets or sequences. Once the joker has been placed on the table, he becomes subject to the following rule. Supposing he has been put on the table to represent

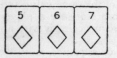   

Fig. 12. How a player lays out his hand in Long Kitty. The odd three of clubs shows his addition to another player's declaration.

the nine of hearts with the ten and the knave of the same suit. I any player becomes possessed of the nine of hearts later, he may exchange the two cards. The only restriction to the use of the joker is, that if, in a single-pack game, there is, say, one queen o clubs on the table, or two queens of clubs in a two-pack game, he cannot be put down to represent a third. Also, if there are, say eight aces on the table, the joker cannot be put down as a ninth A joker cannot be moved from one end of a sequence to the other

Very occasionally in a single-pack game it becomes impossible for either player to discard all his cards. This is because the set: and sequences so over-lap that not even the joker can be utilized

When one player has gone out the others count the cards lef in their hand. All court cards count ten, all others by their face value. The joker counts fifteen.

Long Kitty is a game like rummy played by either two, three or four people. The whole pack of fifty-two cards is used, plu two jokers (you can use the specimen card pasted on the outside o the pack as the second joker). When two or three people are playing eight cards are dealt, when four, seven cards. Players cut for the deal, the lowest card taking it, ace low. After the deal the res of the pack is put face downwards on the table as in rummy, with the top card exposed by the side of the pack. This is the kitty and the discarded cards are spread out so that they can all be seen. Each player in his turn can either take a card from the heap, or one, some, or all of the kitty. The game is played like rummy with the same order of play—draw, declare if possible, and discard, but every possible sequence must be played at once and the joker, if not utilized in your own sequence, must be played on to somebody else's. Ace always counts low in sequences', and the only sets allowed are kings and aces.

SCORING IN LONG KITTY

The object of the game is to obtain the highest score, and each player keeps before him all continuations of other people's sequences, including the joker. As in rummy the joker cannot be a duplicate.

Five points are scored for the two to the ten.

Ten points are scored for the knave, queen and king.

Twenty points are scored for the aces.

Twenty-five points are scored for the joker.

Once a player has got rid of all his cards (he need not have one to put on to the kitty) the game is over, and other players count their gains, subtracting the value of any cards not played. The top score to be aimed at is 1,000.

Coon Can (or *Coonquain*) is another rummy game played by any number of players from two to five. Two packs of cards and two jokers are used, and shuffled well together. In cutting for deal the highest wins, the king being the highest and the joker the lowest. Ten cards are dealt to each player, one at a time. The rest of the cards are then placed face downwards on the table, with the top one exposed beside them.

HOW TO GET RID OF YOUR CARDS

The object of the game is to get rid of all the cards in one's hand, by collecting threes or more of a kind, e.g., three aces, or sequences of three or more of a suit, and placing them face upwards on the table. In play, aces may either be high or low. The order of play is the same as in rummy, i.e., draw, declare if possible, and discard. A usual rule is that a player cannot declare until he can lay seven cards down on the table at once, including at least one sequence of three. Jokers may represent any card the owner wishes, including duplicates, and the appropriate card may be substituted in its place at any time, although some rules say that this can only be done once.

When one player has got rid of all the cards in his hand leaving one for discard, the game ends and all the others count their hands. Aces count eleven, jokers fifteen, court cards ten, and all others their face value. The winner of the hand adds the total number of points made by every player in the hand to his score.

H.E.—G

Racing Demon is a game which depends entirely on speed o
play; it can be very noisy, and should preferably be with
old cards.

Any number of players from two to five or six can take part
The game is played with as many packs of cards as there are players
It is important that all the packs should have backs of differen
colours or patterns.

Each player shuffles a pack, and hands it to his left-hand neighbour
Each then takes the thirteen top cards from his pack and lays them
face upwards in a pile on his right. These are the stock. To the
left of these he deals four cards also face upwards in a row paralle
to the edge of the table. The remaining thirty-five cards he keep
in his hand.

Any aces which are now visible, either among the four cards in
row or on the top of the stock, are put in the middle of the table
within reach of all the players. These are to be built on in sequence
of their correct suits (from any pack) and this is now done, as fa
as possible, from cards visible on the table. Gaps which appea
in each player's row of four are refilled from the top of the pile
which comprises his stock.

WHAT A PLAYER MUST REMEMBER

As soon as this building can be carried on no further, one playe
asks if everybody is ready, and then says "go!" Every player now
works as fast as possible with the object of building every card he ca
on the suits in the centre of the table, and of using up all his stock
As soon as any player has used up his stock, play stops.

This part of the game is played in the following manner. T
make it possible to create gaps in his row of four, a player can pac
one card on to another in his row, in descending sequence an
alternate colour, e.g., ten of clubs on knave of diamonds, nine o
hearts on that, eight of clubs on that, and so on.

With the various things he can do in mind, each player deals i
front of him from his hand. Cards thus exposed can be used t
build in the centre or to pack on his row of four. Packing on th
row of four can be very useful, but it has its disadvantages. Fo
instance, suppose that in the row of four there are a seven of spade
and a five of clubs. A six of hearts or of diamonds from the hand
can be packed on the black seven, and the black five packed or
this red six; this leaves a gap which is filled with the top card of th
stock, but it also leaves the seven and the six covered, and they canno
be built into the centre until the five has gone. A few games wil
teach you when to pack on your four and when not to.

It is surprising how often two players want to build on the same
card in the centre at the same moment : it is of course the car
which, after the collision, is underneath that is allowed to stay

Any player completing a suit by building the king on it must turn that suit upside down before playing on.

As soon as a player has exhausted his stock, he calls "stop!" and all the play ceases at once. The cards in the centre are then sorted into their packs (this is where the different backs come in) and each player counts one point for every card he has built in the centre. The player who exhausts his stock first, adds five points to his score; the other players subtract from their scores one point for each card that is left in their respective stocks. The scores are written down, the cards very well shuffled (this is important, as they will tend to be in sequences) and passed round one place to the left as before, and the next round starts.

Game can be an agreed number of points, or you can play an agreed number of rounds.

Hearts (*otherwise Dizzie Lizzie or Slippery Anne*) is a popular game for any number of players from three to six. If four are playing the full pack of fifty-two cards is used, otherwise some cards have to be subtracted to allot an equal number to each player. With three, one card is taken out—the two of diamonds. With five, two cards—the twos of diamonds and clubs, and with six, four cards—the two and three of diamonds and the twos of clubs and spades. The object of the game is to avoid taking tricks with hearts in them, as in the final count all hearts, etc., in the tricks a player has taken, count against him. Each player plays for himself. Players cut for deal, lowest dealing, ace low. The dealer deals an equal number of cards to each player, and before the actual play each player passes three cards that he dislikes, face downwards on the table, to his left-hand neighbour.

The player on the left of the dealer then leads off a card. The others must follow suit, but if they can't do so, they can discard any card they want to (a heart or the queen of spades for example).

HOW TO GET RID OF YOUR HEARTS

The highest card of the suit led wins the trick. Tactics in the game consist in unloading hearts, or the queen of spades, on to somebody else's tricks, and the usual rule is that this cannot be done until the third trick. At the end of the game each player counts the number of heart pips and the queen of spades in his tricks. The queen of spades counts fifteen, aces eleven, court cards ten, and all others at their face value. These points count against the player.

A popular variation of this game is that any player who obtains in his tricks all the hearts, plus the queen of spades, can give all other players a hundred points against them, while securing none himself. This makes the game much more complicated, for it means that every player has a double objective, either to collect

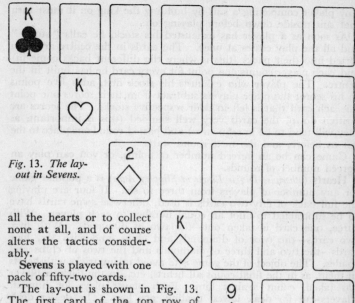

Fig. 13. The lay-out in Sevens.

all the hearts or to collect none at all, and of course alters the tactics considerably.

Sevens is played with one pack of fifty-two cards.

The lay-out is shown in Fig. 13. The first card of the top row of seven is exposed: in the second row the exposed card is left uncovered, and an exposed card is placed over the second (unexposed) one, and the row completed by unexposed cards. This method is continued for seven lines, the last one being of one exposed card only.

The object of the game is to get the four aces free and built on with the appropriate suit, and in sequence, up to the king. As the aces turn up they are placed at the top of the lay-out. The exposed cards in the lay-out may be packed low on high, and red on black, and black on red.

The first move in the example game (Fig. 13) is to place the eight of clubs on the nine of diamonds, and then to turn up the card on which the eight of clubs rested. This, say, is the three of clubs; the two of diamonds will be moved on to it, and the card under the two of diamonds being exposed will show the queen of clubs. This, in its turn will be placed on the king of hearts, and the exposed card being the ten of hearts will pack on to the king of clubs. The king of diamonds will pack on to the queen of clubs.

Fig. 14. *The lay-out in Campbell Patience.*

and so leave a vacant space. Into these vacant spaces, as they occur, only kings may be placed, together with any cards that were packed on them. Any sequence of packed cards may be added to another sequence.

The game now continues with the aid of the remaining cards in the hand. Lay out three at a time. If the top card can pack on to any of the exposed cards on the table, this can be done, or the card may go to build up the aces in suit and sequence. If an ace becomes exposed, it must be taken out at once to start the building foundation. The last three, two, or one cards of the hand are played separately.

Campbell Patience is played with two packs of fifty-two cards, well shuffled together. The lay-out is two rows of ten unexposed cards, with a third row exposed.

The preliminary moves are to place as many red cards as possible on black, and black on red, in descending sequence, removing the aces as they become exposed, and placing them at the top of the lay-out as a foundation to build on in sequence and in suit. Any vacant spaces may be filled by a king. The heaps of cards packed in sequences may be re-packed *en bloc*, so long as the colours and numbers are correct. *N.B.*—Packing is moving the cards on the lay-out; building is putting them in permanent positions on the aces, etc., as the game directs (**Fig. 14**).

In the specimen lay-out given, the nine of clubs will pack on to the ten of hearts, the eight of hearts on to the nine of clubs, the seven of spades on to the eight of hearts, the six of diamonds on to the seven of spades, the five of spades on to the six of diamonds, and the four of diamonds on to the five of spades. The cards uncovered by these moves from the second row must now be exposed, and packing continued if possible. When as much packing as is appropriate has been done, the cards in the hand have to be exposed, one by one, and used to pack or to build on to the foundation aces, or left on the table as a rubbish heap if there is no card on which it or they can be packed or built.

CHAPTER 11

AUCTION AND CONTRACT BRIDGE

In endeavouring to describe the game of auction bridge, it is presumed that the reader has at least some slight knowledge of whist, and that the value of the different cards and the meaning of the term " trump " are known.

Late in the nineteenth century there was born from the game of whist the first of its children—bridge. This game in its original form is now obsolete, but it in turn has given place to two games popular at the present time—auction bridge and contract bridge. Both these games, as in whist, are played by four players playing two against two.

As its name indicates, the game commences, after the cut and the deal, with a species of auction, the object of each bidder being to obtain the right for oneself or one's partner to play the deal in the suit (or in no trumps) that one desires and designates. This is obviously of great advantage in play.

DRAWING FOR PARTNERS

At the start of the game the pack is spread face downwards on the table, and the four intending competitors each draw one card to see who will partner whom. Those who have drawn the two highest cards will play against the two lowest cards drawn (in cutting for partners, ace ranks lowest). When one side has made two games, that is said to be rubber, and a new cut is made for partners for the next rubber.

After the cut, the pack is shuffled by the player on the left of the one who cut the highest card (the dealer), cut by the shuffler's partner and then dealt in rotation, one card at a time, by the dealer commencing on his left and continuing clockwise. The dealer then begins the auction, which proceeds in the same way round the table as the deal.

Each suit has a different value and, above the highest ranking of these, is placed no trumps. The values are as follows:—

No trump = 10, spades = 9, hearts = 8, diamonds = 7, and clubs = 6.

Every bid, according to number stated, indicates the bidder's intention to take that number of tricks over and above six, i.e., a bid of three clubs means that the declarer must, with the aid of his partner's hand, take nine tricks with clubs as the trump suit. Each subsequent bid must be of greater value than the preceding bid, whether made by partner or by an opponent. The distinction between number and value here is important to note. Suppose, for example, we designate the four players at a table by the four points

AUCTION SCORING TABLE

For	Trick score	Premium score	Undoubled	Doubled	A re-double doubles the doubled points
Each odd trick won:—					
If clubs are trumps	…		6	12	
If diamonds are trumps	…		7	14	
If hearts are trumps	…		8	16	
If spades are trumps	…		9	18	
If there are no trumps	…		10	20	
Making the contract		…	—	50	
Each overtrick		…	—	50	
Each undertrick		…	50	100	
Little slam (claimable by either side)		…	twice the trick value of the suit		
Grand slam (claimable by either side)		…	four times the trick value of the suit		
Honours (claimable by either side):—					
In a suit contract—					
three honours		…	five times the trick value of the suit		
four honours		…	eight times the trick value of the suit		
five honours		…	nine times the trick value of the suit		
four honours, all in one hand		…	nine times the trick value of the suit		
five honours, four in one hand		…	ten times the trick value of the suit		
five honours, all in one hand		…	ten times the trick value of the suit		
In a no-trump contract:—					
three aces		…	30		
four aces		…	40		
four aces in one hand		…	100		
Rubber		…	250		
one game in unfinished rubber		…	125		

By permission of Thomas De La Rue & Co., Ltd. Official Publishers to the Portland Club.

of the compass—N., E., S. and W.—the bidding might proceed as follows :—

	N.	E.	S.	W.
First round (N. dealer)	1 club	1 diamond	1 heart	1 spade
Second round ..	2 clubs	2 diamonds	3 clubs	2 no trump.

Two no trump here is a sufficient bid, as its value is 20 points against the 18 points value of three clubs.

The auction continues until three persons in succession fail to make a bid, and the deal is then played by the person who made the last bid, or by his partner if the suit finally designated was originally mentioned by him. Whichever he may be, he is called the "declarer."

Any player may double an opponent's bid and either opponent then has the right to re-double. A " double " means that points scored by the declarer are doubled in value, as are also any " penalties " he may incur. The scoring table is shown on page 199.

After the auction is closed the declarer's left-hand opponent then makes the opening lead, and immediately the declarer's partner places his hand face up on the table. As each trick is won, one of each partnership collects the four cards according to which side won the trick and stacks them on the table just as in whist. It is, of course, understood that each player must, if possible, follow suit to the lead at each trick, but if he is unable to do so he may trump the trick or " discard " any card he sees fit to play.

HOW TO SCORE

It will be seen that auction bridge is a partnership game both from the point of bidding and from the point of defence against the opponent's declaration; it is, of course, to the advantage of the defending partnership to defeat the opponent's contract by as many tricks as possible.

The score sheet is divided into two columns vertically and each column is divided into half horizontally. The two vertical columns are marked, one " WE " and the other " THEY," and one is used for your own score and the other for your opponents. Below the vertical line are scored all scores made for contracts fulfilled, and the space above the line is reserved for penalties and honours.

When either side has scored 30 points below the line, they have scored a game, and the score sheet is ruled across under the last score and the points have no effect on the next game. Scores above the line do not count towards making a game. When one side has made two games, they have won the rubber and score a bonus of 250 points.

It will be seen that it is possible for the side who win the rubber to have scored fewer points than their opponents (" THEY "), the winners having given away penalties.

Space here does not permit of any advice being given as to how the trick-taking possibilities of your hands and your partner's combined may be best assessed, but in the following article on contract bridge some valuable advice is offered and will be found applicable to auction bridge if modified. In studying this method, it must be remembered that in auction bridge it is not necessary to bid to a high level to score the maximum points available, but only necessary to bid sufficient to out-bid your opponents, or to force them into a contract which you are sure they cannot make.

POPULARITY OF CONTRACT BRIDGE

Contract bridge is the latest development of the whist family of games, and America, and in particular Ely Culbertson, must take most of the credit for making it popular.

The primary difference between contract and auction is that in the older game, it is not necessary to bid a game in order to score it, whereas at contract it is. In other words, at contract, only the value of tricks bid and made are scored below the line, the value of overtricks being credited above.

For example, playing auction if a player bids one spade and makes four by cards, i.e., ten tricks, the total trick value thereof is scored below the line. That is, he is credited with the game value although only one spade was bid. At contract, however, only the value of one spade would be scored below the line, the three overtricks being credited in the honours column above the line, and not counting towards the winning of the game.

It will be obvious therefore, that a much higher degree of skill and accuracy is required to play contract successfully.

The next point of difference to be noticed is that in contract a side which bids and makes game is said to be " vulnerable." The significance of this lies in four facts. First, a side which becomes vulnerable incurs much more severe penalties, if they fail subsequently to make the number of tricks they bid (their " contract "). Secondly, if they are doubled they score larger bonuses for any tricks they score over and above what they bid. Thirdly, they get larger bonuses from bidding and making slams; and fourthly, a side which wins the second game (and rubber) before their opponents become vulnerable are rewarded with a larger rubber bonus.

SCORING IN CONTRACT

The third distinction is to be found in the scoring, which is given herewith.

It will be noticed that the scoring at contract is simplified, in respect that the values are all in multiples of ten. The suits rank in the same order as in auction, from spades downwards, hearts being superior to diamonds, with clubs lowest of all. No trump, as in auction, ranks highest of all; but, whilst at auction three clubs (18)

CONTRACT BRIDGE SCORING TABLE

TRICK POINTS FOR DECLARER	*Odd tricks bid and won in*	UNDOUBLED	DOUBLED
	clubs or diamonds, each	20	40
	hearts or spades, each	30	60
	No trump { first	40	80
	{ each subsequent	30	60

Redoubling doubles the doubled points for odd tricks.
Vulnerability does not affect points for odd tricks.
100 trick points constitute a game.

PREMIUM POINTS FOR DEFENDERS | DECLARER		NOT VULNERABLE	VULNERABLE
	Overtricks		
	Undoubled, each	Trick value	Trick value
	Doubled, each	100	200
	Undertricks		
	Undoubled, each	50	100
	Doubled { first	100	200
	{ each subsequent	200	300

Redoubling doubles the doubled points for overtricks and
undertricks.

PREMIUM POINTS FOR DECLARER | HOLDER			
	Honours in { All honours		150
	one hand { Four trump honours		100
		Little, not vulnerable	500
	Slams bid { Little, vulnerable		750
	and won { Grand, not vulnerable		1000
		Grand, vulnerable	1500
	Rubber { Two game		700
	points { Three game		500

Unfinished rubbers.—The winners of one game score 300 points.
Doubling and redoubling do not affect points for honours,
slams, or rubber.
Vulnerability does not affect points for honours.

By permission of Thomas De La Rue & Co., Ltd. Official Publishers to the Portland Club.

is not sufficient to overcall two no trumps (20), at contract it is, although still inferior in value. In other words, in contract, majority calling prevails.

It will be observed that the first trick at no trumps is worth 40 and subsequent tricks 30 points each. This ensures that at no trumps, nine tricks (40 + 30 + 30) make game, whereas ten of a major (4 × 30) and eleven of a minor suit (5 × 20) are required.

Apart altogether from these differences, scoring in contract, whether below or above the lines, is much higher than at auction. If you play for money you are liable, at the same stakes, to win or lose three or four times as much.

The preliminaries at contract, cutting for partners, choice of seats, etc., are the same as at auction, except that the ace ranks as the highest card in drawing for partners.

THE " APPROACH FORCING " SYSTEM

With the essential differences between the games briefly explained, it is necessary to consider their influence on the bidding. Obviously, if games and slams are to be bid, to reap the full value of the cards held, some adequate method of exchanging information must be used. And to this end a common method of hand valuation must be employed and thoroughly understood.

The bidding methods advocated here are based upon the approach-forcing, or, as it is sometimes called, Culbertson system. While the general principles are similar, there is considerable divergence in matters of detail. All illustrations are from hands which have occurred in actual play.

Let us take the hand of one player, ignoring for the moment the probable holdings of the other three players as indicated by the bidding. First of all, consider the trick-taking values of the high cards, the aces, kings, etc. These and certain combinations of them are called " honour tricks," and the values thereof are as follows:—

A, K of a suit			=	2 honour tricks
A, Q of a suit			=	$1\frac{1}{2}$ honour tricks
K, Q, J of a suit			=	$1\frac{1}{2}$ honour tricks
A of a suit			=	1 honour trick
K, J, 10 of a suit			=	1 honour trick
K, Q of a suit			=	1 honour trick
K, x of a suit			=	$\frac{1}{2}$ honour trick
Q, J, x of a suit			=	$\frac{1}{2}$ honour trick

Note.—x is used to indicate a small card lower than the 10.

As distinct from honour tricks there are long card tricks and
what are known as "plus values." A plus value (half trick in
value) is made up of two honours in different suits and having no
honour trick value. These all go to make up the total "playing
trick" value of a hand, i.e., the total number of tricks which it
may be expected to take.

VALUING YOUR HAND

To count the playing trick value of the opening hand, first add up
the honour tricks, and any plus values. Then count the long card
tricks as follows: for every *trump* over three count one playing trick,
and for every card in a *side suit* over three count one half playing
trick. These examples may make the method of valuation clear:—

EXAMPLE 1.   (*Spades are trumps.*)

(S)	A, K, 9, 8, 3, 2 = 2 honour tricks +	
	3 long cards	= 5 playing tricks.
(H)	Q, 7 = plus value +	
	diamond king	= ½ playing trick.
(D)	K	already valued.
(C)	K, Q, 8, 5 = 1 honour trick	
	+ ½ long cards	= 1½ playing tricks.
	Total playing tricks	7

EXAMPLE 2.   (*With hearts as trumps.*)

(S)	A, Q = 1½ honour tricks	= 1½ playing tricks
(H)	K, 10, 8, 7, 6, 3 = ½ honour trick + 3	
	long cards	= 3½ playing tricks
(D)	K, 8, 4, 2 = ½ honour trick + ½	
	long card	= 1 playing trick
(C)	7 = nil	—
	Total playing tricks	6

REPLYING TO PARTNER'S BID

Now let us turn to the hand of a player whose partner has made a
bid. In this there will be ruffing tricks to count as well, in the
following manner. If three trumps are held, count one half ruffing
trick in respect of a doubleton in a side suit, one in respect of a
singleton and two for a void. With four or more trumps, count
one ruffing trick in respect of a doubleton, two for a singleton and
three for a void. If two short suits are held, count ruffs only in
respect of the shorter. To count both would be a duplication of
values. Count no ruffing tricks unless three trumps are held.

The long card value of trumps in the responding hand is modified
to one half trick for each trump in excess of three, and must always
be taken into the count as well as ruffing values. Trumps in the
opening hand cannot be counted as ruffing values as well as long cards.

EXAMPLE 3. (*In support of partner's one spade bid.*)

(S)	Q, 7, 2	= 1 ruff in respect of singleton	= 1 playing trick
(H)	A, 10, 6, 4	= 1 honour trick + $\frac{1}{2}$ long card	= 1$\frac{1}{2}$ playing tricks
(D)	K	= plus value + spade queen	= $\frac{1}{2}$ playing trick
(C)	9, 7, 5, 3, 2	= 1 long card	= 1 playing trick

Total playing tricks   4

EXAMPLE 4. (*In support of partner's one club bid.*)

(S)	A	= 1 honour trick	= 1 playing trick
(H)	K, 8, 6	= $\frac{1}{2}$ honour trick	= $\frac{1}{2}$ playing trick
(D)	K, 9, 7, 2	= $\frac{1}{2}$ honour trick + $\frac{1}{2}$ long card	= 1 playing trick
(C)	10, 7, 5, 4, 3	= 1 long card + 2 ruffs for singleton spade	= 3 playing tricks

Total playing tricks   5$\frac{1}{2}$

PRACTICE HAND VALUATION

Hand valuation is of vital importance, and should be practised constantly by dealing out hands and assessing their value.

An average deal contains approximately eight honour tricks distributed over the four hands. That is to say, eight tricks will be won by high cards. Therefore you should, to justify an opening bid, hold at least 2$\frac{1}{2}$ honour tricks (just *over* a quarter of the total number in the four hands). There are altogether thirteen tricks to be taken; therefore your hand, for the same purpose, should be worth four playing tricks (over a quarter of the total tricks that can be taken). For example:—

1.	2.	3.	4.
(S) A, Q, 6	(S) A, Q, 7, 4, 3	(S) 9	(S) A, K, 9, 8
(H) Q, 7, 2	(H) K, 9, 6, 3	(H) K, J, 8, 6, 3	(H) 7, 2
(D) K, J, 4	(D) K, 8	(D) K, Q, 4	(D) 9, 8, 7
(C) K, Q, 9, 3	(C) 7, 2	(C) A, 7, 6, 2	(C) A, 10, 6, 4

Hand 1 contains three honour tricks and four playing tricks, and one club should be bid. In the second hand, the honour tricks add up to a bare 2$\frac{1}{2}$, but good distribution swells the playing trick value to five, justifying a bid of one spade. The third example cited contains 2$\frac{1}{2}$ honour tricks, with a total of five playing tricks. One heart is the bid.

This brings us to the fourth hand. Here there are three good honour tricks and 4$\frac{1}{2}$ playing tricks, and an opening bid is clearly marked. But the bid should *not* be one spade, but one club, although the former suit is stronger. The reason for this is very important.

In the approach-forcing system a change of suit in response to an opening bid of one, is said to be forcing for one round of bidding. That is the opening bidder *must* bid at least once again. An example will make this clear. If N, the opening bidder, says one club, and S, his partner, responds with one heart, N *must* bid again if opponents do not intervene.

Therefore it is a rule that no player should make an opening bid, unless he has a safe rebid and further, that if there is a choice of opening bids, that chosen should be the one which is going to leave an easy and safe rebid over partner's response. With the hand above—(S) A, K, 9, 8; (H) 7, 2; (D) 9, 8, 7; (C) A, 10, 6, 4—if one spade is bid and partner responds with two diamonds or two hearts, the opener is in a difficulty. His hand is too weak and bare for two no trumps, and three clubs would be an overbid. A rebid of two spades on a four-card suit is out of the question. But if the original bid is *one club*, he can bid one spade if partner responds with either of the red suits, and if the response is in spades, very excellent support is held.

HOW TO CHOOSE THE BEST BID

Two important principles emerge from this.

(1) If a hand qualifies for an opening bid, but offers a choice of suits, choose that which will simplify the subsequent bidding.

(2) If a hand contains the strength for an opening bid, but does not offer a safe rebid to any likely response from partner, pass.

Holding (S) A, K, 3, 2; (H) A, 7, 4; (D) 9, 8, 6; (C) 7, 4, 2, the only possible bid is one spade. But where is the rebid if partner calls clubs or diamonds? There is none, and the only safe course to adopt is to pass. Nothing will be lost by doing so, because there can be no game unless partner has a good hand, and if he has, he will bid.

When discussing the problem of choosing the best bid, it is perhaps appropriate to consider when suits are strong enough, apart from the total value of your hand, to be bid and rebid. A four-card suit should not normally be bid unless it is headed by at least the jack and one higher honour, e.g., K, J, 7, 3, or Q, J, 6, 4. Occasionally, weaker four-card minor suits, such as K, 10, 9, 6, or Q, 10, 5, 4, may be bid, when there is no sound alternative. A four-card suit should never be rebid. Any five-card suit to the jack or better is biddable, but before it can be rebid it should be headed by A, K, or any three honours. A six-card suit, however weak, e.g., 9, 7, 6, 5, 4, 2, is rebiddable.

In discussing opening suit bids at the level of one, great stress has been laid on the *minimum* requirements. It must be pointed out that a bid of, say, one club may be made on a weak hand, such as: S) K, Q, 6, 2; (H) 5, 3, 2; (D) K, 5; (C) A, Q, 3, 2, or a powerful holding such as (S) A, K, 6; (H) K, Q, 6, 2; (D) A, Q; (C) A, Q, 9, 3. A bid of one, in fact, covers the whole range of hands up to a forcing two bid (which is dealt with later), with the exception of no trump bids and pre-emptive bids.

In responding to opening bids of one of a suit, it should be remembered that a bid of one may range from a minimum $2\frac{1}{2}$ honour trick to a near force, and it follows that the responding hand must keep the bidding open on very little, so as to afford his partner another opportunity of bidding.

SUPPORTING YOUR PARTNER

As already pointed out, four-card suits can be and frequently are bid. Therefore a suit should not be raised until it is rebid, unless the responding hand holds at least four small cards or three, headed by the queen or better in that suit.

The simple raise of a suit from one to two is the weakest of all responses. It shows about one honour trick and three cards in trumps. If the responding hand holds a doubleton, the honour strength can be shaded to a half honour trick, and with a singleton can be dispensed with altogether. But if there is an intervening bid, the necessity of keeping the bidding open disappears, and a simple raise shows about one honour trick plus a singleton, or $1\frac{1}{2}$ plus a doubleton or two if the hand is of even distribution.

A double raise, i.e., from one to three of a suit, forces the original bidder to bid again, and invites him to investigate the possibility of a slam. It indicates at least four trumps to the jack or five small ones. According to distribution, two or three honour tricks should be held.

Raise one spade to three with any of the following hands:—

(S) K, 7, 6, 4, 2; (H) 7, 4; (D) A, J, 2; (C) K, Q, 3
(S) K, Q, J, 2; (H) 6; (D) A, Q, J; (C) 10, 8, 7, 3, 2
(S) K, 5, 4, 2; (H) A, 10, 9; (D) K, 5, 2; (C) K, Q, 3
(S) A, K, Q, 3; (H) 5, 4; (D) 7, 4; (C) K, J, 9, 8, 3

SIGNIFICANCE OF A TRIPLE RAISE

A triple raise, i.e., from one of a suit to four, is principally intended to prevent the opponents from bidding. Only $\frac{1}{2}$—$1\frac{1}{2}$ honour tricks are required with about five playing tricks. In addition, there *must* be length in the trump suit. The following are sound raises to four over partner's bid of one spade :—

(S) 9, 8, 7, 6, 2; (H) 7; (D) A, 4; (C) J, 10, 8, 5, 3
(S) J, 10, 5, 4, 3, 2; (H) —; (D) 9, 3; (C) Q, J, 8, 4, 2
(S) Q, 10, 8, 7, 3; (H) 8; (D) 8, 7, 6, 5, 4, 2; (C) 6

In the case of a minor suit, a raise to four should not be made unless it appears certain that there can be no game at no trumps.

A change of suit in response to an opening bid is, as we have said, forcing for one round. If the suit can be bid at the level of one, only a half honour trick is necessary, provided the suit contains five cards or more. Bid one heart over partner's one diamond call on: (S) 9, 6; (H) Q, J, 9, 6, 3; (D) 8, 5, 4; (C) 10, 7, 3. If a four-card suit only is held, the hand should contain at least one honour trick. On (S) K, Q, 6, 2; (H) 5, 3, 2; (D) 4, 2; (C) 10, 6, 3, 2, bid one spade over partner's opening bid in hearts.

The examples quoted are minimum responses. A simple take-out ranges from hands of this type to anything short of a jump take-out, about 3½ honour tricks.

Where the suit has to be bid at the level of two, e.g., two clubs over one heart, the hand must be stronger. If only a four-card suit is held, two honour tricks are required; with a five-card suit, 1½ will suffice, and with very good distribution, e.g., a six-card suit or better, the honour trick strength may be shaded to one.

" FORCING TO GAME "

The jump take-out in another suit is forcing to game. Suppose the opening bid is one spade, and the response is *three* clubs (one more than is necessary for a simple take-out). The opening bidder must not now allow the bidding to die short of a game, however weak the opening bid. The jump take-out in another suit shows at least 3½ honour tricks. If the hand does not contain a good suit of its own nor good support for partner's suit, the honour strength should be higher to justify the bid.

For example, if the opening bidder bids one heart, with 1, (S) K, Q, J, 6, 2; (H) A, 4; (D) K, Q, 8; (C) K, 6; bid two spades; 2, (S) K, 8, 2; (H) A, J, 6, 3; (D) A, K, 3, 2; (C) 10, 4; bid three diamonds; 3, (S) A, K, 4; (H) 8, 6, 2; (D) A, Q, 8, 3; (C) K, 4, 2; bid two no trumps. This will be explained under no trump responses.

If the opening bidder has a second biddable suit, he should show it over partner's jump take-out. If not, he should (a) support the suit bid by partner if he has normal support, or (b) rebid his own suit if it is strong enough. If none of these courses are open to him, he should " sign off " in the minimum number of no trumps.

RESPONDER'S " ONE NO TRUMP "

Almost as weak as the simple raise of a suit is the response of one no trump, which denies either support for the opening bid or the strength to make a simple take-out into another suit. The strength necessary for this bid is one honour trick.

By comparison, a two no trump response is a strong bid, showing about 2½—3 honour tricks, including a high card in partner's suit, or 3—3½ with no honour in his suit. The distribution should be even, and usually there is no biddable suit.

The opener bidder must rebid when partner's response is two no trumps, as it guarantees sufficient strength in the combined hands to ensure a game.

A response of three no trumps shows about the same strength as a jump take-out, i.e., no biddable suit, and no particular desire to play in partner's suit, unless his hand is unbalanced, i.e., contains a singleton or void.

It is not a stop bid, as many people think, but shows the full strength of the hand, and indicates even distribution.

OPENING BIDS OF MORE THAN ONE

The bids of two in a suit are reserved for hands which, with little or no support from partner, are strong enough to produce game. Hands of such strength are, unfortunately, seldom held, but it is necessary that, when they are, a forcing bid be made to ensure that partner does not pass, or else games and slams will be missed. The two-bid is therefore forcing to game. This is called a forcing-two. To justify a bid that forces the partnership to contract for a game, no matter how weak the responding hand may be, the opening bidder must obviously be very strong indeed. Five to six honour tricks is the minimum holding which justify such a bid, unless the distribution is very freakish, e.g., two long and solid suits.

If the responder's hand is worthless, he should say two no trumps. If he holds 1½ honour tricks or more, he should show any biddable suit. With normal trump support and one honour trick he should raise the opening bid. With 1½ honour tricks with no biddable suit and no support, three no trumps should be called.

The following are examples of opening two-bids in a suit:—
(S) K, Q, J, 10, 8; (H) A, Q; (D) K, Q, 6; (C) A, K, 8. Bid two spades.

(S) 7; (H) A, K; (D) A, K, 6, 5, 2; (C) A, Q, J, 3, 2; bid two diamonds.
Opening bids of more than two in a suit are chiefly directed towards interfering with the opponents' bidding, and guarantee little or no honour strength.

A bid of three in a major suit shows about six playing tricks not vulnerable and seven when vulnerable.

A raise to game should be made on three or four playing tricks. Trump support is not necessary.

If not vulnerable, the following are sound three spade bids:—
    (S) K, Q, J, 9, 6, 4, 2; (H) 9, 3; (D) K, Q, 7; (C) 7, 3
    (S) K, J, 10, 7, 6, 4, 2; (H) 3; (D) 4, 2; (C) K, Q, J
If vulnerable, the following are good three heart bids:—
    (S) 8; (H) K, Q, J, 8, 5, 3, 2; (D) K, Q, 3, 2; (C) 7
    (S) K, 4; (H) Q, J, 10, 9, 8, 6, 4; (D) K, Q, J; (C) 6
A raise from three spades to four is justified on the following hands:—
    (S) 7; (H) A, Q, 2; (D) Q, 8, 4, 2; (C) K, 9, 7, 4, 3
    (S) 7, 4; (H) K, J, 9, 4, 3; (D) A, 10, 3, 2; (C) A, 4

A bid of three in a minor suit is an invitation to partner to bid three no trumps if he has potential stops in the other suits. It indicates a solid or near solid suit of at least six cards with a few high cards outside. Bid three clubs on:—

(S) K, 4; (H) Q, 6, 3; (D) J, 10; (C) A, K, Q, 10, 6, 4
or (S) K; (H) J, 4, 2; (D) A, 8; (C) A, K, J, 10, 7, 4, 3

The responding hand should take a bid of three clubs out into three no trumps on hands such as:—

(S) A, 8, 6, 3; (H) J, 9, 3; (D) Q, J, 4, 3; (C) 3, 2
(S) Q, J, 5, 4; (H) K, 10, 3, 2; (D) J, 9, 6, 4; (C) 3

REPLYING TO AN OPENING FOUR BID

Opening four bids in a major suit show one playing trick more than a three bid. Such openings do not call for any response from partner unless he holds a " power house " and visualizes slam.

A bid of four in a minor suit shows the same strength as in a major suit. Partner should raise to five holding about 2½ honour tricks.

Bids of five in a minor suit are one playing trick stronger than four bids, i.e., they show about eight playing tricks when not vulnerable, and nine when vulnerable.

The bid of one no trump shows from four to five honour tricks and an even distribution.

This is usually a stronger bid than an opening bid of one in a suit, and should not be made unless in every suit there is a guard or a minimum of three cards. It is a very useful bid when you have " tenaces," (A, Q or K, J) in your hand. Here is an example of an opening no trump:—

(S) A, Q, x, x; (H) K, J, x; (D) x, x, x; (C) A, K, x

To raise one no trump to two, about 1½ honour tricks should be held. If the responding hand contains a five-card suit headed by an honour, one honour trick will suffice.

To raise to three no trumps, one more honour trick is required than for a raise to two.

RESPONDING TO NO TRUMP BIDS

A take-out into two of a suit is a weak bid in response to an opening one no trump call, and is merely an attempt to find a simpler contract. Such a take-out can be made on a five-card suit headed by an honour with no other strength in the hand.

The responding hand should remember that the one no trump bid shows a very powerful hand, and should therefore make a jump take-out holding about three honour tricks or even less if a good suit is held.

Holding a long but weak suit and having little or no outside strength, the responder should jump to game in his suit, e.g., bid four hearts in reply to partner's opening one no trump call on (S) K, J, 10, 8, 7, 6, 4, 2; (H) 4; (D) 3, 4; (C) 10, 4.

An opening bid of two no trumps shows $5\frac{1}{2}$ to $6\frac{1}{2}$ honour tricks with a guard in every suit. Partner should raise to game on a half honour trick, or bid three of any biddable five-card suit.

An opening three no trump bid shows from seven to eight honour tricks with even distribution.

Any bid in response is a slam invitation and shows one honour trick and even distribution or half honour trick with a five-card suit.

Any bid made after the opponents have opened the bidding is called a defensive bid, although, in many cases, all the elements of attack are present.

A simple overcall at the level of one should not be made on less than $1\frac{1}{2}$ honour tricks and four playing tricks (five when vulnerable). If the bid suit is only of four cards, the honour strength should be slightly higher. To justify an overcall at the level of two, the playing trick strength should be one trick higher and 2 to $2\frac{1}{2}$ honour tricks should be held. A four-card suit should not be bid defensively at the two level, and a five-card suit should be as good as A, J, 4, 3, 2. On no account should overcalls be made on weaker hands than those indicated above, otherwise severe penalties will inevitably be sustained.

A bid of one no trump over an opposing bid indicates a hand of the same strength as an opening no trump, with at least one sure stopper in the opponents' suit.

THE INFORMATORY DOUBLE

The use of the informatory, or take-out double, as a reply to an opponent's opening bid is a most useful defensive weapon if carefully handled, and forces partner to bid his best suit.

A double is informatory and forces partner when (1) the double is made at the first opportunity, (2) the doubled contract is one or two of a suit, or one no trump, and (3) the doubler's partner has not previously made any bid.

The minimum strength is 3 to $3\frac{1}{2}$ honour tricks, with support for any suit partner may bid. If the doubled contract is a major suit, the doubler should hold at least four cards in the other major.

With less than 1 honour trick, the responder should bid his best suit, however weak it may be, at the cheapest possible level, e.g., partner doubles one diamond. Bid one spade with (S) 7, 5, 4, 2; (H) 10, 6, 4; (D) 9, 7, 5; (C) 10, 5, 2; or two clubs with (S) 9, 5, 2; (H) 10, 8, 2; (D) J, 4, 2; (C) 10, 8, 7, 5.

If the only four-card suit held is that bid by the opponents, bid the lowest ranking three-card suit.

A bid of one no trump over a double of, say, one diamond would not be correct on (S) 5, 4, 2; (H) 7, 6, 2; (D) K, 10, 5, 4; (C) 6, 4, 2. One no trump should indicate $1\frac{1}{2}$ to 2 honour tricks. On the hand quoted, therefore, the correct bid would be two clubs.

Holding 1½ honour tricks and a five-card suit or 2 honour tricks and a four-card suit (however weak), make a jump bid in the suit. Thus partner doubles one heart, bid two spades with (S) K, 10, 6, 2; (H) A, 4; (D) Q, 7, 4, 2; (C) Q, 6, 3.

A double should *never* be left in on the pretext that the doubler's partner was " too weak to bid." Only when the responding hand is *strong enough* to visualize a lucrative penalty may partner's take-out double be passed.

The deal set out below illustrates the use of the take-out double.

(S) Q, 6
(H) K, Q, 10, 8, 2
(D) A, Q, 3
(C) Q, 10, 7

(S) 10, 4, 2		(S) A, K, 8, 5
(H) A, J, 4	N.	(H) 7, 3
(D) 6, 4	W. E.	(D) K, J, 5, 2
(C) K, 6, 5, 4, 3	S.	(C) A, J, 8

(S) J, 9, 7, 3
(H) 9, 6, 5
(D) 10, 9, 8, 7
(C) 9, 2

North, the dealer, bids one heart, and East doubles to force his partner to bid. South is too weak to make a bid of any sort, and with a potential double guard in hearts and slightly more than 1½ honour tricks, West's best response to the double is one no trump. East's best rebid is two no trumps, since he has no five-card suit. West should now bid three no trumps on the strength of his five-card club suit, and the contract should be made without difficulty.

A jump overcall of an opposing bid is made on a hand which is too strong for a simple overcall, but unsuited on account of distribution for an informatory double. It may be (a) a hand containing a long solid or near solid suit, or (b) a strong two suiter.

Two spades should be bid over opponents' one diamond opening on:—

(S) A, K, Q, 7, 4, 3, 2; (H) K, 5; (D) 6; (C) Q, 10, 7
or (S) A, K, J, 7, 6; (H) A, Q, 10, 9, 3; (D) 8; (C) K, 4

This bid is not forcing but indicates a hand strong enough to take eight tricks with no support from partner. A raise should accordingly be given on one honour or ruffing trick.

The strongest defensive bid of all is a bid in the opponents' suit, which forces partner to keep the bidding open until game is reached.

For example, the player on your left bids one heart and your partner bids *two hearts*. This bid indicates a tremendously powerful hand, and on no account can the bidding be dropped short of a game.

To justify such a bid, therefore, the hand should be as strong as for an opening two bid. In addition, first round control (ace or void) in the opponents' suit should be held.

The responding hand should reply as if to a take-out double, but must bear in mind that a hand of tremendous power is held by his partner, and that a slam is possible if he holds as much as a five-card suit to the king, or even less.

Any double other than an informative double is a penalty double. The partner is never, as in a take-out double, compelled to answer.

Slam bidding is an intricate, fascinating but dangerous business. Many artificial bids have been invented with a view to arriving at a final bid of six or seven, but they are too complicated to be described here. It has already been said that some bids in the early stages of the auction indicate that the bidder thinks there is a possibility of a slam. If such a bid is made, subsequent bids made by both partners should be with a view to helping each other to estimate whether they have between them twelve or thirteen playing tricks. If either partner re-opens the bidding after a game call has been made, this can usually be taken as an invitation to a slam. The only occasion when this is not so, is when the suit in which the game is first called has never been supported by the partner. Here is an example of this :—

North bids one spade, South bids two diamonds, North bids two spades, South bids four diamonds, North bids four spades, South bids five diamonds.

This last bid is not an invitation to a slam. South is simply saying, " I hate your spades and I have a great many diamonds."

STRATEGY IN PLAY

Apart from one or two conventions (mostly directed towards defeating high contracts), the play of the cards has undergone little change since the days of auction. Space does not permit of an explanation of the conventions referred to, and only a few general hints on play can be given.

The ability to count is one of the greatest assets a player can have in playing the cards. As soon as the opening lead is made and the dummy exposed, the declarer should stop to count his tricks to form his plan of campaign. Playing too quickly to the first trick must cost bridge players many thousands of pounds yearly.

If the contract to be attempted is in no trumps, it will be found simplest to count the apparent winners, and if in a suit to count the *losers*.

In the former case, if the required number of tricks cannot be counted, the declarer must consider how he is to develop the necessary tricks. Similarly, in the case of a suit contract, he should plan how he is to dispose of the unwanted losers. Can they be ruffed out, or is there a side suit which can be set up to provide discards ? Is there a finesse to be taken to provide the wanted tricks, and if so, is there any safer way of playing the hand? These and many other questions should flash through the declarer's mind before he plays a card from dummy. Very often the key to the correct play can only be found in the opponents' bidding or in the first lead.

At contract, the defenders' task is simplified to a certain extent by the information regarding key cards which can be gleaned from the opponents' bidding. The most perplexing problem in defence is undoubtedly the selection of the opening lead, and a few hints may be helpful.

THE OPENING LEAD

Against a no trump contract, if the leader's partner has bid a suit, it should be led unless there is a very good reason for not doing so. If any two or three small cards are held in the suit the highest should always be led. Holding three or more cards headed by the knave or a higher honour, the smallest card is the correct lead, and with two touching honours, the higher honour should be played. For example, against opponents' three no trump contract after your partner has bid, if your holding in his suit is: 9, 6, lead the 9; 10, 8, 3, lead the 10; J, 5, 2, lead the 2; Q, J, 4, lead the Q.

If partner has not bid, the opening leader should normally open with his own longest suit, but if his hand is evenly distributed and contains tenaces, it often pays to lead the higher card of a worthless doubleton to avoid leading away from a tenace.

Against suit declarations, the highest card of any suit bid by partner is the safest lead. If partner has not bid, the lead of a trump will be found advantageous when from the bidding it appears that declarer may need ruffs in dummy to make his contract.

Here is a table, showing which card should be led from various combinations of honours, if you want to lead that particular suit.

Holding	Against no trump	Against suit contract
A, K, and small cards ..	Fourth best	King
A, Q, and small cards ..	Fourth best	Ace
A, J, 10, and small cards	Jack	Ace
K, Q, and small cards ..	Fourth best	King
K, Q, and four or more small cards	King	King
K, Q, x	King	King
Q, J, 10, and small cards	Queen	Queen
Q, J, and small cards ..	Fourth best	Queen

CHAPTER 12

BILLIARDS, SNOOKER AND BAGATELLE

ILLIARDS is no longer purely a luxury game. Modern enterprise
and industry have brought it into the home, within the reach
of people with quite modest incomes. If you cannot afford,
or if your available space does not permit, a full-size table, smaller
tables, with balls and cues of corresponding sizes can be obtained
to suit your limitations.

It is always well to strain a point to get the best table you can of
the requisite size. A slate bed, a finer cloth, rubber cushions, for
example, add enormously to the pleasure of the game, though
substitutes for these answer quite well, in spite of a lower standard
of accuracy and wearing qualities. Most sports outfitters are agents
for reputable billiard table makers, and will procure equipment for
you, if you do not see what you want in the shop; or alternatively,
you can get in touch with the makers direct.

TEMPERATURE OF THE BILLIARD ROOM

Give a thought first of all to your billiard-room. It should be
one in which the temperature is always fairly level, and as dry as
possible. A damp atmosphere affects the woollen cloth of a table,
making it " slow "—that is, the balls don't run so fast on it, since
invisible particles of water condense on the nap of the cloth, and,
being picked up by the balls, impede their normal progress and
activity. Your table should be carefully and regularly ironed.
There should be a good centre light, and the table should be centred
under this as nearly as possible, or the light adjusted. Billiards is
best played under artificial light, because the light from a window
at the end or side of a room may cause shadows around the balls.

Household tables vary slightly in height, but the ideal is from
2 feet 9½ inches to 2 feet 10½ inches from floor to top of side rail.
The light should be not more than three feet above the bed of the
table, the shade coming six inches lower. The floor should be
examined for level and for unevenness, where the legs of the table
stand, and packing applied where the unevenness is great. Most
good tables of the type for placing on top of a dining-table are
fitted underneath with adjusting screws, which will absorb quite
considerable discrepancies in level. If none is supplied with the
table, it is well worth while to get a spirit level with which to test
the adjustment periodically.

In deciding what size of table to procure, so as to get the best
out of it within the space available, due consideration should be

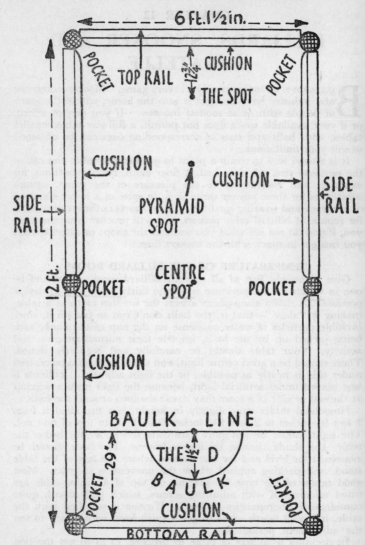

Fig. 1. *The lay-out of the billiard table in detail.*

given to " cue-room." At each side and each end of your table you must have adequate space to wield a cue in play. The length of cue varies with the size of table, and in certain awkward places a very much undersized cue is allowable, but the following standard of " cue-room " should be observed as far as possible. A full-size table, 12 feet by 6 feet, should have a space of at least 5 feet all round it to allow of comfortable cueing and the passing to and fro of people not actually engaged in play. Around an 8 feet by 4 feet table, a space of 4½ feet may be allowed, and the same limit is desirable for the 6 feet by 3 feet table, a very popular size. Less space may be allowed for smaller tables, but it is wiser to have a small table and ample cue-room than a big table with cramped cue-room, if your play is to have any pretensions to the real thing.

Such is the vogue for miniature tables that the Billiards Association and Control Council, which governs English billiards throughout the world, has standardized a 6 feet by 3 feet table which has become very popular. This is made by all the licensed manufacturers according to a set specification, so that when one miniature billiards fan visits another who has such a standardized table, he has the satisfaction of knowing that he will not have to adjust his game to a new set of angles.

STANDARD TABLE, BALLS AND CUE

The lay-out of the full standard table is given in Fig. 1; the miniature table is the same, reduced in size by one half in each direction. The balls most in use today are made of an artificial composition. There are several trade descriptions, but all are much alike. Ivory balls are now scarcely used, the composition variety having proved less vulnerable to weather changes, and they retain their shape and resilience and accuracy of angle longer, besides being considerably cheaper. Balls have also been standardized in size for full-sized and miniature tables, again a valuable consideration. Weight may differ slightly without ill effect, but whether standard balls are used or not, care should be taken that the balls of a set match one another. They can be tested for size with calipers. To have balls of varying diameters affects the angle of throw-off, and if one is at all sensitive, playing with " plain " of one diameter after previously playing with " spot " of another upsets one's judgment. One sixty-fourth of an inch variation is important, and the better player you are the more you will notice it. So have the balls carefully matched, and re-turned or replaced if necessary. This also applies to " snooker " sets (twenty-seven balls in number) which are supplied to match both full-sized and miniature tables.

A set of cues and a rest are also generally supplied with the table on purchase. These vary in length and weight according to the size of the table. For a full-size table the player should select a cue that reaches to his chin from the floor, unless he is particularly long-armed, when an inch or two more may be allowed. The choice of appropriate weight for a cue comes with experience, but for beginners a heavy cue (say seventeen ounces) is advisable, with a fairly broad tip. Most experts prefer this type of cue.

Care of the cue is very important, for obviously a warped stick will defeat your trueness of aim and manipulation. Cues should be stacked in an upright position, standing on the butt and supported a little higher up. They should not be left leaning against the wall; it makes them gradually sag at the centre. It is easy to make a proper rack for them, and cases can be procured that will adequately support their whole length in storage and protect them in transit.

A scoreboard is essential, and this again is often supplied with the table on purchase. If not, it is not difficult to construct one. Take a board two feet long and six inches deep, plane or sandpaper it smooth; stain and varnish it if you like; then, starting two inches from the left-hand side and two inches from the top, punch or prick twenty holes at intervals of an inch. An inch below this line, make five more holes, one under every fourth hole in the line above. An inch below this line, make twenty more holes as in the first line, and a further inch below punch five holes as in the second line. Paint or label these holes, from 0 to 19 on the two long lines, a figure over each hole, and 20, 40, 60, 80, and 100 for the short lines. Now your board ought to look like this :—

0	1	2	3	4	5	6	7	8	9	10	11	12	13	14	15	16	17	18	19
		20				40				60				80				100	
0	1	2	3	4	5	6	7	8	9	10	11	12	13	14	15	16	17	18	19
		20				40				60				80				100	

Now make four pegs, two with a spot on them for use on the two top rows, and two plain for use on the two bottom. Your scoreboard is then complete. As spot or plain scores his points, he pegs them on the appropriate line, pegging each twenty on the short rows and intermediate points on the long.

The chalk used on the tip of billiard cues to make them " grip " the ball, is not the ordinary blackboard quality, but a special kind. It can be obtained cheaply enough and lasts a long time. It should be applied carefully, especially around the edge of the tip. Chalk hardened on a tip after long use should be removed by tapping lightly with a fine file or some similar instrument.

Cue-tips, with ordinary care, will last many thousand points.

They should be " square " with the cue, not overlapping, when necessary, " trued," i.e., levelled up, and when shiny, gently roughened with sandpaper or the side of a matchbox. A brass ferrule is an advantage, though not essential. It saves the wood in the process of truing up or fitting a new tip, when the old wafer or cement is removed by scraping or filing.

New tips may be affixed with a good tube fixative, or by adhesive wafers which may be obtained with them. Choose a tip as near the diameter of the cue as possible, to save later dressing, clean the base and the wood with sandpaper, apply the fixative to both tip and wood, wait a couple of minutes, then join and press on. Tap several times with a file, and set the cue aside for half an hour. After trimming with sandpaper, it will be ready for use. When using the wafer, soften it by holding it flat on a knife in warm water (don't let it curl), apply to the stick-end, then press on the selected tip. When the overlap of wafer is hard, trim off, tap the tip several times with a file, sandpaper it, and set it aside for a quarter of an hour, when it will be ready for play. A special tool is obtainable which makes re-tipping much easier.

RIGHT AND WRONG STYLE

As with every other accomplishment, there are right and wrong ways of playing billiards; and though someone with a good eye and a natural aptitude for ball games may adopt a bad style and yet play well, the average man or woman stands little chance of attaining proficiency, unless he plays in accordance with the manner our best players have found most profitable. If you are reading this before you have played a stroke, let us try to put you on the right track immediately.

Stance—the way you stand at the table in making your stroke —is extremely important; it will here be described for a right-handed person, the position being in the relevant cases reversed for a left-handed player.

The aim is to produce an easy, comfortable, effective posture that will lead to a well-controlled stroke. Take your cue in your right hand, and " feel " the balance of it. You will find the point somewhere between the butt-end and the thin end of the splicing, which is often in a darker wood than the main cue. You will learn to hold your cue mid-way or perhaps rather more from that point towards the butt-end of the cue. Four to six inches from the end is a good place; some people make it eight or nine inches. This right-handed grip of the cue is no broomstick affair. You will do best, though there are fuller grips, to hold it only between your thumb and forefinger, the remaining fingers being kept clear, as you would hold a match.

Now stand up to the table at the D or baulk end, in the centre

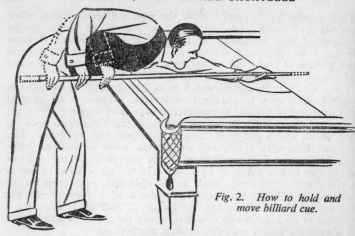

Fig. 2.   *How to hold and move billiard cue.*

your right foot at an angle of about sixty degrees from an imaginary line drawn through the spots you can see on the table, vertical to the baulk-end rail, left foot slightly forward and with the toe pointing straight up the table, in the direction of the proposed stroke.

Now bend over from the hips and place your left hand with the edge of the palm just inside the D, flat on the table. If you shuffle forward at all, be careful that your feet are in the position just described. Push your left shoulder well down to the full extent, so that your left arm is perfectly straight out, and your chin comes down in line with it (Fig. 2). Now, without moving your wrist, draw up the knuckles of the hand on the table, fingers slightly splayed, and you will find you have a sort of pyramid (Fig. 3). This is the bridge, and it is very important.

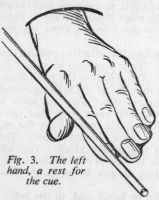

Fig. 3. *The left hand, a rest for the cue.*

Place your thumb against the side of your forefinger, making a sort of V. You should be able to slide your thumb up and down that forefinger. Bring over the thin end of the cue and place it within that V or groove created by your thumb against your forefinger. There should be eight or ten inches of full-size cue beyond the bridge. Most of your weight should be on your right leg. The upper part of

your right arm should now be
horizontal (it is of course well behind
your body), the right forearm vertical.
Now, from the right elbow and
without disturbing the upper arm,
swing the cue gently to and fro,
using the wrist, and with the light
thumb and forefinger grip. Make
your chin almost touch your cue,
keep your left shoulder well down.
Make the cue brush your top right
vest pocket (we assume you have
taken off your coat, for no good
billiard player plays in his jacket).
Practise this swing, and grip, and
firm bridge-making, adjusting your
feet until comfortable but correct,
right leg straight, left leg slightly
bent.

We are now going to put a ball
on the table. Put it on the spot in
the centre of the baulk-line, and
take up cue-position before it. Set
the tip within an inch or so of the
ball, and adjust your thumb on the
bridge, so that the cue-tip when

Fig. 4. *A good practice shot.*

taken forward would strike the ball the merest fraction above the
centre of its white spherical surface. Look at the ball while you are
doing this, having first imagined that, with your cue aligned accordingly, you are going to send it straight up the table over the line of
spots shown in Fig. 4. Automatically, you will look where you are
going to send the ball. Swing your cue backwards and forwards
several times to make sure that it maintains the line of aim for your
intended stroke, and that it will hit the ball exactly in the chosen
place.

This is called addressing the ball. All set—in taking the cue back,
raise your eyes (not your head) to the centre spot on the middle of
the table, and with a full and still gentle stroke, bring forward the
cue to the ball, letting it go through as far as your forearm will
allow over the spot on which the ball stood. The ball is on its
journey. Don't jump up! Stay put! If that ball was struck aright,
it should come back to the tip of your cue. This is the practice
stroke for straight cueing. You cannot do too much at it. And
play every stroke with the same care.

Now let us get two balls on the go in another practice stroke for
straight cueing. Place them in line opposite the middle pockets.

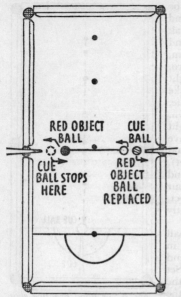

RED OBJECT BALL   CUE BALL

CUE BALL STOPS HERE   RED OBJECT BALL REPLACED

Fig. 5. Aiming at the opposite pocket.

Align your cue over the centre of the back rail of the pocket, so that it is aimed directly at the opposite pocket (Fig. 5). Strike the cue ball as before, a little above centre, causing it to go forward, make contact with the other ball, the object ball, and send it into the opposite pocket. Go round the table and repeat. When you can pocket the object ball repeatedly, without adjusting the cue ball on its straight line between the pockets, your cueing is coming on very nicely and persistence will make for perfection.

Cue practice of this sort, on these very strokes, is resorted to frequently by highly capable players before a match. When they know they are striking well, they go into the match with abundant confidence. Often they ask another player to observe them at the stroke, and say what part of the body—upper right arm, left elbow, head, foot—is at fault and not functioning correctly.

Always remember to get your chin well down to your cue and to keep your head down and keep it still. No part of your body should move except the right forearm. After addressing the cue ball, look at the object ball when making the stroke. Let the cue " go through " the ball.

SCORING STROKES IN BILLIARDS

We have gone into great detail over this initial part of billiards, because it is the secret of success or the root of all evil in the game, according as we observe or disregard all that has been described. Now we come to the scoring strokes.

The most profitable stroke for the amateur, even up to good class, is the losing hazard, or the " in-off," as it is more often called. This means causing the cue ball (the one you strike with the cue) to enter a pocket after contact with the object ball. The successful stroke counts two points when it is " in-off " the white object ball, three points when it is " in-off " the red object ball. By going " in-off " the red only twenty-five times consecutively, we can make a break of seventy-five points, which is a very good break indeed. It will be found that the losing hazard is the easiest of all the strokes to control in sequence.

Before we describe our practice losing hazard stroke, we must consider angles, or, to use a perhaps better and more ordinary term, the throw-off. This means the deviation of the cue ball after contact with another ball or cushion.

In our first practice stroke, we hit the cue ball just above its centre with our eyes on a spot directly in front of it, and if we performed the stroke correctly the ball came back to the cue-tip. There was no angle at all about that, and the throw-off from the top cushion returned the ball directly along the course it had come. Now, having put a chalk mark on the top cushion in the centre opposite the billiard spot, let us place the cue ball on the left-hand end of the D on the baulk line. We will then aim directly at the chalk mark on the top cushion, striking the ball just above the centre with moderate strength, and it should come down the table and over the right-hand end of the D.

Whatever distance you set your ball from the spot in the centre of the baulk-line, the ball, struck as instructed above, should come down the opposite side of the table at the same angle. Practise this stroke off different cushions, and at different angles, always hitting the cue ball just above the centre with moderate strength. The angle of reflection (that is, after the ball has struck the cushion) will always be equal to the angle of incidence (between the ball at rest and the point of contact). This is made clear in Fig. 6.

Now to another plain angle of billiards that we must learn. When the cue ball strikes another ball, there is a different course of events to that described above, because the second ball (the object ball) is not fixed, like the cushion. It receives an impetus from the cue ball, and the cue ball is deflected from its straight course. To grasp what happens we have to learn the half-ball angle, or natural angle, which occurs when the cue ball and object ball meet on terms described as half-ball. The

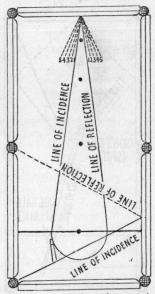

Fig. 6. *Angle of incidence and angle of reflection.*

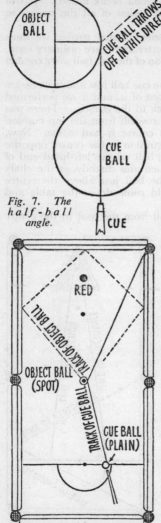

Fig. 7. The half-ball angle.

Fig. 8. Where the ball should come to rest.

half-ball angle is this: Place two balls in line a little distance apart, aim your cue on an imaginary line running through the centre of the cue ball and meeting the edge of the object ball. Fig. 7 illustrates this stroke and will help you to appreciate how it is done.

Properly played—that is at moderate strength and with the cue ball struck a little above the centre and with plenty of follow-through—this half-ball angle stroke is the strength of the amateur's game. Become really proficient at it, and you will be a very efficient player.

With experience you will find that by making a fuller contact between these two balls, you will get a wider throw-off, by making a finer contact, you will get a narrower throw-off, both very useful variations which you will learn to apply once you have learned to discern a variation from the half-ball angle.

Here are some very valuable strokes used frequently in billiards, which utilize the half-ball angle. Practise them assiduously until they are certainties every time.

Put spot ball on the centre spot, red on the billiard spot. Put plain ball on the baulk line about $3\frac{1}{2}$ inches from the right-hand end of the D. Sight the cue half-ball through the cue ball on to the spot ball, and strike with moderate strength. The cue ball should go unerringly into the top right-hand pocket. Practise this from the left-hand side of the D also, aiming at the left side of the object ball and so into the top left pocket. The object ball should be struck in such a way that it is made to pursue a course which takes it on to the side cushion, reflecting on to the top cushion, reflecting again on to the opposite side cushion, and coming to rest almost on the centre spot, or very near to it, ready for another similar stroke from hand. This is the long losing hazard, or in-off (Fig. 8).

Frequently, the object ball comes round much lower than the centre spot, and this brings us to the middle pocket losing hazard, or in-off. An important point to endeavour to achieve is to keep the object ball coming to rest within an area defined by imaginary lines running the length of the table from each end of the D (Fig. 9). An in-off with the half-ball angle is then nearly always possible from hand. Once you have learned the long loser, you will see at once when the same angle occurs on the table, and how to spot your ball in the D to create that angle for the middle pockets. When the object ball is anywhere below the centre spot, and within the area just described, a middle pocket half-ball loser is always " on," from hand.

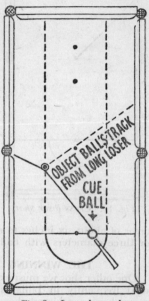

Fig. 9. Long loser shot.

There are more set half-ball strokes which the amateur should learn—one being the cross loser, at the top of the table (Fig. 10). Place the red on the billiard spot, the cue ball in the centre of the right-hand top pocket. Play half-ball at the red, gently, and the cue ball should go into the top left-hand pocket off the red. Another set half-ball cross loser is with the red on the billiard spot, and the cue ball directly over one of the middle pockets (Fig. 11).

With these strokes at your command you will be a very powerful player. They need a lot of practice. The idea is to keep the object ball running so that it comes every time within the area for a half-ball in-off.

We have mentioned " strength." That means the power of your stroke. Strength is governed by follow-through and " touch," not brute strength. Let your cue complete its course after contact with the cue ball, gracefully, smoothly, steadily. Don't push, don't poke. " Touch " we cannot describe, but it is bound up with delicacy. It is an instinct to be developed. Don't become a

H.E.—H

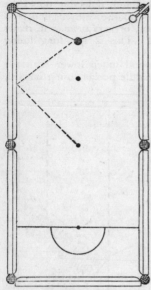

Fig. 10.   *Cross loser shot.*

slammer at billiards. It is ugly, and keeps your breaks down. " Touch " will grow upon you as you learn and love the game. It is a marvellous accomplishment.

With losing hazards mastered, we must now turn to another prolific source of points—cannons (Fig. 12). In the cannon, the cue ball proceeds from the object ball to make contact with the second object ball, and may proceed ball-to-ball, or via cushion-ball-ball (direct cannons). Each cannon counts two points. Cannons arise of course only when all three balls are on the table. When to play them in preference to an in-off, is a matter for the player's discretion, and the secret of playing them is gentleness and keeping the balls close together. Some very pretty positions arise, and many beginners find they can play cannons easily from the very start. Perhaps the reason is that, unless the balls cover one another, there is a latitude of error of about six inches to every cannon made with full-size balls, or three diameters with balls of any size.

THE WINNING HAZARD OR POT SHOT

One other shot we must explain is the winning hazard, or the pot, used frequently in billiards and exclusively in snooker. Angles as we have considered them for the losing hazard apply similarly to the winning hazard, except that instead of seeking primarily to control the throw-off of the cue ball, we now seek to control the direction the object ball shall take on impact. We endeavour to make the object ball enter a pocket (as in our second practice stroke, Fig. 5), and we can find where the object ball must be struck by the cue ball, by imagining a line from the centre of the back of the pocket running through the centre of the object ball. We must make the outside edge of the cue ball strike the object ball at that point exactly. It may be half-ball, or fuller or finer contacts. It may be a veritable "cut," a mere glancing blow, in which case, aim the centre of the cue ball about the width of a shilling in front of the object ball. You will see the idea from Fig. 13.

Now let us consider the question of " side." You may have

found it difficult to learn the half-ball stroke; if so, the reason was that you were unconsciously putting on " side."

There are at least nine special places on the cue ball which you can hit with the tip of the cue to obtain enormously different results. Just look at Fig. 14. It is not necessary to strike the ball outside the inner circle.

No. 1 is " top left side," used to keep a ball spinning over a long distance leftwards and narrowing the throw-off in that direction, after contact.

No. 2 is " top," used to give a ball rolling speed, and cause it to follow a straightforward course after contact.

No. 3 is " top right side," used to keep a ball spinning over a long distance rightwards, and narrowing the throw-off in that direction.

All the foregoing are used where the cue ball is expected to travel considerable distances.

No. 4 is " left side," used to cause a ball to turn vigorously left-wards after contact, and broaden the throw-off in that direction.

No. 5 is supposed to be neutral; the ball slides forward and will probably stop altogether very soon after impact, according to the strength used. That is why, in the half-ball stroke we have been learning, we strike the cue ball ever so little above the centre of the ball, to give it rolling pace. Why you have failed at the long in-off from the set position previously described, is that you have unconsciously applied some extraneous " side," of the sort we are now discussing.

No. 6 is " right side," used to cause a ball to turn vigorously to the right after contact, and broaden the throw-off in the same direction in which it is struck.

No. 7 is " left bottom " or " left screw," used to cause a ball to turn square to the *right* after full or nearly full contact. With this application, cue ball can be made to come back off the object ball at an angle almost equal to the half-ball angle we played off the cushion early on. It depends on the power applied, and whether just at the moment of impact

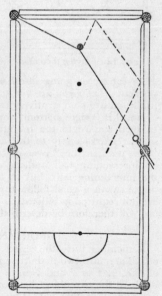

Fig. 11.   *Another cross loser, or in-off shot.*

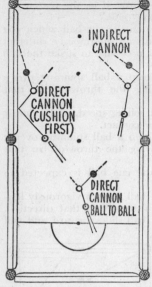

Fig. 12. *Playing a cannon*

between cue and ball, the cue is squeezed tightly between finger and thumb, halting it rather suddenly.

No. 8 has all sorts of names — " back screw," " drag," " stab," " retard," among them. It brings about all these things, according to the strength and pinch used in playing the stroke. The lower you strike from the centre of No. 5 the slower the cue ball will travel after impact with the object ball. With a sharp stroke (called " stun ") you can make it stop precisely in the place occupied by the object ball (thus laying a snooker in that game, or stopping in position for another pot). With a gentle stroke you can make it drop slowly on to the second object ball, almost in a direct line for a cannon, having first pushed the first object ball out of the way. Laying your cue flat on the table, you can bring about the " steeplechase " shot, thus evading an awkward snooker at close range, or going in-off when the object ball is close to a pocket. Then you are very clever; but it is best to leave this shot until you are comparatively expert.

No. 9 is " right bottom " or " right screw," used to cause a ball to turn square to the *left* after full or nearly full contact. The same remarks apply to this as to No. 7 in angle. This and No. 7 are used in the " swerve," when, in snooker, you seek to avoid an intervening ball and hit the ball that is marked, aiming at the intervening ball, but at the same time applying right or left bottom with a good follow-through. The swerve strokes, however, are not required in billiards as often as they are in snooker, and their use will therefore be described later in the chapter.

IMPORTANCE OF " SIDE "

Remember this—the object of side is to widen or narrow throw-off. There are two main descriptions of side: " check," a utilization of Nos. 1, 4 or 7 and Nos. 3, 6 or 9 to widen narrow angles, that is where the two object balls or the object ball and a distant pocket are almost in line with the cue ball; and " running " a similar application of the side divisions of the cue ball (1, 4, 7; 3, 6, 9) to bring down over-wide angles as compared with the natural half-ball angle, that is, narrow them. The cue ball will go after impact towards the side on which it was struck. Another description is "pocket side," where, at a narrow in-off, you play full into the object ball, aiming to reach the distant side of the pocket, and apply " side " that will cause the ball to drop into the pocket.

" Side " generally does not begin to act until impact. Cushions reverse side by friction, and the same applies to playing " against the nap." The cloth of a billiard table is laid so that the infinitesimal fibres of the nap point towards the top end. When playing down the table, towards the baulk end, use the opposite side from that you would use playing up the table. Anyway, side, charming as it is in its effects, is always dangerous — and you can have a thoroughly good game without it.

Now go and enjoy your game, but first read the rules carefully. It is strongly recommended that

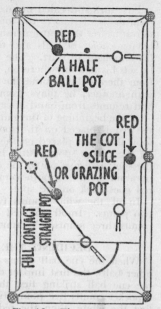

Fig. 13. *The winning hazard, or pot, from various positions.*

a copy of the Billiards Association and Control Council Handbook of Rules be obtained from the Association, 514 Cecil Chambers (West), 76 Strand, London, W.C.2. The price is 2s. net.

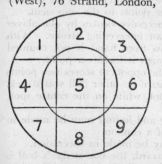

Fig. 14. *Nine divisions of the billiard ball.*

Two players are usually opposed, one taking the spot white, the other plain white. Each continues in play until he fails to score, the second player continuing the game with the balls in the position his opponent's last stroke left them in. When four players are engaged, two form a side taking spot white, the other two taking plain white, and one of each side plays alternately. The winner is he who first reaches the agreed number of points, or who, at the time limit agreed upon before the game, has scored the most points.

First turn is decided mutually or by "stringing," i.e., by playing from the baulk line to the top cushion, the player whose ball comes to rest nearer the bottom cushion after contact with the top cushion, having choice of balls and the option of starting, or of requiring his opponent to start. The first player plays from hand; that is, he sets his ball anywhere on, or within the lines of the D and plays from there. Each time the striker pockets his ball after contact with another, he plays from hand. The non-striker also begins and resumes from hand after his ball has been pocketed.

At the beginning of the game, and each time after being pocketed, the red is placed on the spot. Should there be no room on the spot, the red is placed on the pyramid spot, or, if there is no room, on the centre spot. After being potted twice in succession from the spot, red goes on to the centre spot, or if that is occupied, the pyramid spot. If both centre and pyramid spots are occupied, red goes back on the spot.

In-off the white counts two points. Potting the white counts two points. In-off the red counts three points. Potting the red counts three points. A cannon counts two points.

DECIDING THE VALUE OF A STROKE

When the cue ball enters a pocket after contact with both the other balls, the first impact decides the value of the stroke. Thus, the cue ball striking first the red, then the white, and entering a pocket counts five points (in-off the red and a cannon); striking first the white, then the red, and entering a pocket counts four points (in-off the white and a cannon). In case of simultaneous impact followed by the pocketing of the striker's ball, only two points are scored.

A miss, when the cue ball does not strike any other ball, counts one point to the opponent. If the cue ball enters a pocket without touching another ball, it counts three points to the opponent.

Two misses must not be made in successive strokes by one player unless the opponent has scored in an intervening stroke. With the two object balls in baulk, a miss from hand is not counted as one of these successive misses, though it forfeits a point.

When a ball is sent off the table, the opponent scores two points if another ball was struck, three points if no other ball was struck. The balls are spotted, red on the spot, white on the centre spot, and the striker plays from hand.

Only twenty-five hazards (winning and losing) may be made in succession without the intervention of a cannon.

Only thirty-five direct cannons may be made in succession.

If, at the twenty-fifth successive hazard, the non-striker's ball is in a pocket as a result of his and not the striker's stroke, it is brought up and placed on the spot in the middle of the D (or if that is occupied, on the D's right-hand corner) and the break continued. If the striker potted the object white, it remains in the pocket, and the break ends at the first hazard to fail or the twenty-fifth.

Once in every 200 points of a break, the cue ball must cross the baulk line.

Baulk is protection, and no ball in baulk may be played upon from hand, unless off a cushion or ball out of baulk. You may play off a cushion in baulk to hit a ball out of baulk.

One foot must remain touching the floor at each stroke.

FOUL STROKES IN BILLIARDS

Foul strokes include : playing incorrectly from hand, striking the wrong ball, touching the ball other than with the tip of the cue, striking the ball twice in the same stroke, sending a ball or balls off the table, playing with both feet off the floor.

After a foul stroke, the non-offending player, in addition to any award of points, has the option of playing the balls from the position left or of having them spotted (white on centre spot, red on the spot) and playing from hand.

When the cue ball remains in contact with another ball, the red is spotted, the white (if on the table) placed on the centre spot, and the striker plays from hand.

Balls that have become jammed in the pocket openings are spotted, red on the spot, white on the centre spot.

A ball falling into a pocket owing to vibration, after having come to rest, or moved on the table through some means beyond the control of the striker, must be replaced.

The referee is the sole judge of whether play is fair or not, awards all fouls, and on appeal decides any point of fact. He may take the evidence of a nearby spectator in helping towards a decision, and in the event of a player refusing to continue the game the referee should award the match to the other player.

FASCINATION OF SNOOKER

Snooker is a billiard-table game preferred by many, because the absolute beginner, once he has got the idea of potting the object ball, can obtain results that satisfy him, and a perfectly happy game. It is a game of winning hazards only, with the element of " snooker " (the interposition of another ball between the cue ball and the ball it is necessary to pot or pocket, that is the ball " on "), a refinement which comes very quickly as the player's expertness develops. Much of the skill in controlling the balls at snooker is shared with billiards, and we would refer the would-be snooker player to the section on billiards for information as to cue control, angles and side and its effects.

For snooker on a table 9 feet in length or over, twenty-two

balls are used, and for tables of 8 feet and under, seventeen balls (five fewer reds) of a reduced diameter are obtainable. Frames to form the pyramid with balls of any size are also made, and supplied with the balls.

To begin the game, set the table with the balls in position as shown in Fig. 15—reds (counting one point each) in a pyramid with the apex as near the pyramid spot without touching pink as possible, yellow (counting two points) on the right-hand end of the D, green (counting three points) on the left-hand end of the D, brown (counting four points) on the spot in the centre of the baulk line, blue (counting five points) on the centre spot, pink (counting six points) on the pyramid spot, and black (counting seven points) on the spot. The table is now ready for play.

POTTING AND POCKETING

The white is the cue ball, and each player in turn uses this at the conclusion of the preceding break. At the beginning of the game, and each time after it is pocketed, the white ball is played from hand from any position on or within the lines of the D.

The object of the game is to pocket as many balls as possible, in the following sequence in any one break: a red ball first and then any of the pool balls (that is, yellow, green, brown, blue, pink, or black), then a red again followed by a pool and so on until all the reds have been pocketed. When a player fails to pocket a red or the pool ball aimed at, as the case may be, his break is ended and his opponent must start by potting a red. So long as a red remains on the table, the pool balls (that is, those other than red) after they have been pocketed, are replaced on their appropriate spot. After the last red has been pocketed the player in hand may play out any pool ball, which, if pocketed, is re-spotted unless it is the yellow. After this, however, both players must start any break by potting the ball of the lowest denomination left upon the table, the ranking being yellow, green, brown, blue, pink, black. As each ball is correctly potted it is removed.

HOW TO SCORE

A " break " is the full total of points scored for every ball pocketed up to the point of failure, and the winner is he who has scored most points when all the balls have been sunk. In case of a tie on points, the black is brought up again and placed on its spot, and the players toss or otherwise decide who shall have first play at it, the first score or miss deciding the game.

It will be seen that the player can score many points by direct potting. But the fun of snooker is that almost as many points can be scored by causing the opponent to forfeit them through failing to overcome a snooker. All points forfeited are scored by the

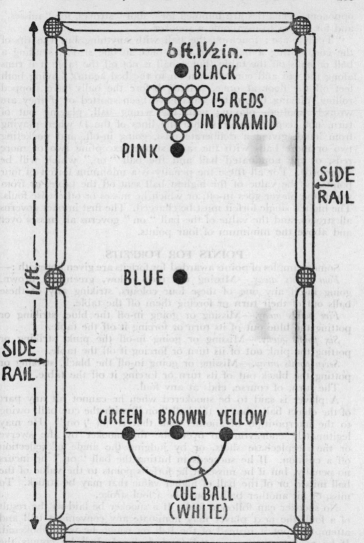

Fig. 15. *Lay-out of the billiard table for snooker.*

opponent. Penalties are imposed for " foul " strokes, for " misses," and for failing to overcome a snooker.

" Fouls " are : touching the ball with anything but the tip of the cue, hitting a ball more than once in one stroke, sending a ball or balls off the table (but a ball is not off the table if it runs along the rail and comes down on to the bed again), having both feet off the floor at once, striking before the balls have stopped rolling, playing before the balls have been spotted or if they are wrongly spotted, playing with the wrong ball, playing out of turn, not keeping on or within the lines of the D when playing from hand, giving a deliberate miss, going in-off, and pocketing two or more balls with the same stroke (excepting two or more reds, or the nominated ball and the ball " on," which will be described). For all these the penalty is a minimum forfeit of four points, or the value of the highest ball sent off the table, or from which the player goes in-off, or which he misses or otherwise fouls. The highest single forfeit must be charged. The first impact governs all strokes, and the value of the ball " on " governs all misses over and above the minimum of four points.

POINTS FOR FORFEITS

Some examples of points awarded for forfeits are given herewith :—

Four points away.—Missing the red, yellow, green, or brown, going in-off any one of these four colours, striking any of these balls out of their turn or forcing them off the table.

Five points away.—Missing or going in-off the blue, striking or potting the blue out of its turn or forcing it off the table.

Six points away.—Missing or going in-off the pink, striking or potting the pink out of its turn or forcing it off the table.

Seven points away.—Missing or going in-off the black, striking or potting the black out of its turn or forcing it off the table.

The turn, of course, ends at any foul.

A player is said to be snookered when he cannot hit any part of the object ball (that is, the ball " on ") with the cue ball, owing to the interposition of another ball that is not " on." He may legitimately endeavour to overcome the snooker by the swerve or the steeplechase shots, or by judging the angle of reflection off a cushion. If he succeeds in hitting the ball " on " he incurs no penalty, but if he misses it he forfeits points to the value of the ball missed or of the ball of higher value that may be struck. To miss, or hit another ball, would be a foul stroke.

No snooker can follow a foul. If a snooker be laid as the result of a foul, the next player may nominate any convenient ball and attempt to pot it instead of the ball on which he was snookered. If he pockets the nominated (and declared) ball he counts the value of the ball on which he was snookered, and if the nominated ball was a pool ball it is replaced on its spot. If he fails to pot it, he incurs no penalty. If during this stroke he pockets both the nominated ball *and* the ball " on," both balls are re-spotted (reds being on the table), he counts the value of the ball " on," and proceeds with his turn in the normal way. If he pots the ball " on " with the nominated ball, or off the nominated ball (by a cannon, that is), it is a fair stroke; he counts on and proceeds with his turn.

A snooker may not be laid with the nominated ball. If this happens, the layer of the snooker forfeits the value of the ball on which the snooker was laid, and the snookered player may nominate any ball convenient to him.

It should be noted that the nominated ball, whatever its colour, counts in value as if it was the ball " on."

Another peculiarity in snooker is when the cue ball is left touching another ball. If it is touching a ball that is " on," the striker plays away from it, without penalty if he misses or strikes another ball not " on," though if he disturbs the ball touched or pockets or goes in-off any other ball, he forfeits four points or the value of the ball disturbed, or pocketed, or first struck. If it is touching a ball not " on," the player must play away from it without disturbing it, and if he fails to hit the ball " on," or hits or pockets or goes in-off any other ball he pays forfeit accordingly.

Any ball pocketed by a foul stroke is re-spotted.

WHAT IS THE "SET"?

An entrancing feature of snooker is the " set," when by hitting one key red ball (or a nominated ball after a foul) a number of reds may be potted (or a snooker laid) by a stroke with the cue ball. Any two or more balls on a straight line, described from the back of a pocket create a set, and the charm is in discovering the point of contact, where the cue ball must strike the object ball farthest from the pocket in the series to send one or more into the pocket. Usually, the "set" occurs when the balls are close together.

The highest break possible at snooker is 148, and that only with the aid of penalty points at the beginning. Experts at the game close it up by keeping the cue ball at the baulk end, with the " curtain " of yellow, brown, green, blue, and pink, between it and the reds, and they make most of their big breaks by sinking the black as many times as possible with intervening reds, and then clearing the table in value-order of the balls. It is at the top of the table where most points accrue, though many points can be scored with the blue which is more get-at-able.

The origin of Bagatelle is probably an old English game called shovel-board. Methods of playing the game vary considerably, but in any form it makes a popular home game, requiring little

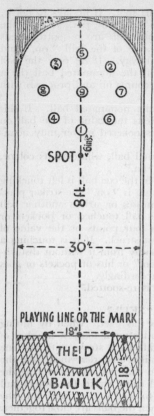

Fig. 16. *Lay-out of the bagatelle board.*

room compared to billiards, while skill in the manipulation of the balls, though affording scope for great cleverness, is not so exacting in a general sense.

In most modern forms of the game, the board is of a size from 5 feet by 20 inches to 10 feet by 3 feet, the larger sizes having a slate bed covered with green West of England cloth, the smaller sizes having wooden beds and being foldable. The table has a semicircular top end, and within this arc are eight cups completing a circle with a ninth in the centre numbered one to nine. At the bottom end of the board a fifth of the board's length from the end is a baulk line with a D as in billiards. All round the table, except in some cases at the bottom end, runs a rubber cushion. Fig. 16 shows a table which has become recognized as more or less standard, although in the absence of a representative controlling body, standard is impossible either in equipment or rules.

Skill in the game is very similar to that demanded of the billiard player as to angles and the use of side, cue action, and stance, and to that end we would recommend a perusal of the section describing billiards. The tactics of the game vary with each set of rules, and it is therefore impossible to suggest any special procedure. Here are the rules of some popular variations of bagatelle :—

Let us take first the cannon versions of the game, in which scoring cannons are made as in billiards.

In **Strict Cannon** a board without holes is used. It is played with three balls, white, red, and black, each cannon (that is, the cue ball striking the other two balls in succession) scoring two points. Each player continues his break as long as he scores, as in billiards. Game is fifty points singles, sixty-two points four-handed.

French Cannon as it is called, also uses the three balls, white, red, and black. Cannons count two points, but all balls cupped after a cannon count to the player according to the cup they enter (the red counting double). At the beginning of each turn, the red ball is placed on the spot below No. 1 cup, and the adversary's ball (which might be either white or black) between No. 1 and No. 9 cups. The striker begins from hand, and continues in play as long as he continues to score uninterrupted cannons. Balls cupped or passing the baulk line are replaced in the positions stated for the beginning of the game. To miss striking the red counts five points against the player, and the turn ends. The game is 121 points singles, or 151 points four-handed.

RULES OF BAGATELLE

A similar version to the French cannon game varies in that balls cupped count to the adversary, but are replaced so long as the striker has made a cannon. To miss the adversary's ball on playing at it means a forfeit of one point; to miss the red, five points.

Now let us consider the ordinary game of bagatelle wherein cupping the balls is the prime objective.

This game is played with nine balls, one of which is black. The black ball is placed on the spot in front of No. 1 cup at the beginning of each player's stick or break, and the player then plays from hand each of the other eight balls in turn. No score is made until one of the balls has struck the black ball. Balls which are not cupped when they are played may of course be cupped by striking them with a subsequent ball. Any ball which returns over the baulk line is " dead," and must be removed from the table.

POINTS SCORED FOR POCKETING

After the player has played all eight balls, every cupped ball scores according to the number its cup bears. The black ball counts double. Some of the older bagatelle boards have two pockets like those of a billiard table, opposite No. 8 and No. 7 cups. When these are used, three points are scored for pocketing the black, and two points for pocketing the white. This type of game is now considered obsolete, however, and when such boards are used the pockets are usually blocked up.

There are numberless other varieties of bagatelle, but the games we have given are the most generally accepted forms.

CHAPTER 13

CHESS

Tʜɪs ancient game of skill has been popular through many centuries in many countries. It is not so difficult to learn as some imagine, and once you have begun it exercises an increasing fascination.

The game is played on a board of sixty-four squares, eight rows of eight in each direction—just as a draught board. These squares are alternately light and dark in colour, and whatever their exact shades are invariably called Black and White. Similarly the " men," sixteen in each set, are termed black and white, even though the " blacks " are occasionally red. The board is so placed that each player has a white square at the right-hand corner nearest to him.

ARRANGEMENT OF THE CHESSMEN

Eight " pieces " and eight " pawns " make up the sixteen men. At the beginning of the game each player lines up his *pieces* on the back line of the board nearer to him, and his *pawns* along the second row. The arrangement is shown in Fig. 1.

There are five different pieces. The most important are the king and queen which, at the beginning of the game, stand in the two middle squares of their back row, the queen on the square of her own colour. Next to the king and queen stands a bishop; next to each bishop a knight; next to each knight a rook—or castle

Fig. 1. Arrangement of chessmen on board ready for play.

as it is often called. The pawns are all alike, but are distinguished by taking their names from the pieces in front of which they are placed. Thus: queen's bishop's pawn — generally abbreviated in writing to QBP—and so on.

In Fig. 1 the lettering makes this clear. QR stands for queen's rook; QKt for queen's knight; QB for queen's bishop; Q for queen; K for king; KB for king's bishop; KKt for king's knight; KR for king's rook. P always signifies pawn.

In draughts all men move alike, but in chess the

different "men" have different
moves. They are as follows :—

King—can move one square
in any direction, providing the
square into which it moves is not
occupied by any piece of the
same colour, nor commanded by
an enemy piece.

Queen—can move through any
number of unoccupied squares
in any direction, either straight
or diagonally.   When going
straight alternate black and
white squares are crossed; when
going diagonally the squares
passed over are all of one colour.

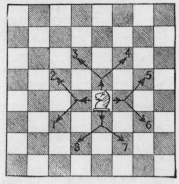

Fig. 2.   *Possible moves of a knight.*

The queen is the most powerful
piece on the board; the remaining pieces are here described in their
gradually decreasing order of values.

Rook—can move any number of unoccupied squares in a straight
line, right, left, forwards, or backwards, but not diagonally.

Bishop—can move any number of unoccupied squares, but only
diagonally. Thus each bishop stays always on the colour on which
it begins. It will be seen that each player has a bishop on each
colour.

Knight—has a peculiar " leap." It moves one square " straight "
in any direction and one square diagonally in either direction.
Thus at the conclusion of any leap it comes down into a square
of a different colour from that at which it started. It does not
matter at all if there are intervening pieces *en route* so long as
the final square is unoccupied, or occupied by an enemy. The
possible moves of a knight are shown in Fig. 2.

Pawn—moves only forward, and one square at a time, except
at its *first* move, when it can move two squares forward.

OBJECT OF THE GAME

A game of chess is a battle, the object of which is to capture
the opposing king. When that is achieved the game is won. To
achieve it opposing pieces may be captured singly and removed
from the board. The king cannot thus be removed, but every
time it is put in such direct danger of capture it is said to be "in
check," and its owner at his next move must get the king out of
check. If he cannot do this it is " checkmate "—and the game
is finished. It does not matter how many pieces each opponent
then possesses. When a king is captured the game is over. To
get the king out of check: (1) it may be moved; (2) another piece

WHITE CASTLING KING'S SIDE

Fig. 3.   *The " castling " move.*

may be interposed between the king and the attacking piece; (3) the attacking piece may be captured and removed from the board. When a position is reached in which, although a player's king is not in check, he is unable to make any move without putting it in check and has no other piece he can move, the position is a " stalemate "—and the game is a draw.

A draw may also be declared (1) when neither player has enough forces left to deliver checkmate—as king and two knights, king and bishop, etc., against a lone king; (2) when a player with an obvious check-mating force fails to deliver checkmate within fifty moves (these moves are counted from the moment the opponent signifies his intention of so doing); (3) when both players end with equal or nearly equal forces—such as king and queen against king and queen; (4) when both players persist in repeating the same moves, e.g., in perpetual check; neither being able to capture his opponent.

HOW A PIECE CAN BE CAPTURED

A chess piece is captured by the opponent occupying the square on which it stands (by one of his own men) and removing it from the board. The five important pieces—king, queen, rook, bishop, knight—make captures in accordance with the moves already described. The pawn is an exception—it moves straight forward, but it captures by going *one square diagonally to right or left*. A pawn can also be captured *en passant*. Suppose a white pawn has travelled forward to the fifth square, then if either of the black pawns on its right and left, providing they are still in the second row, attempts to move two squares—as they may at the opening of the game—they make themselves liable to capture. The capture is effected by the white pawn moving to the square which the black pawn *would* have occupied if it had moved forward only one square. The white must, therefore, move forward diagonally into a sixth square when it captures the black.

If a pawn succeeds in getting on to the back row of its opponents, it can be replaced by a queen or any other piece desired. This is called *queening a pawn* and can be effected even though the player already has one queen on the board. In theory, therefore, he could have nine queens on the board at once.

Once in the game, and once only, the king, in conjunction with a rook, may make a special move called *castling*. The king is moved two squares towards the rook, which is then lifted over him and placed on the next square to him. Castling may be performed at any stage in the game, but only (1) when the squares between the king and rook are unoccupied; (2) when neither the king nor the rook concerned have been previously moved; and (3) the king must not be in check and must not, in executing the move pass over a square commanded by an enemy piece or pawn. Castling may be performed with either rook as the player chooses. It is most usual on the king's side. The exact way in which the move is effected on either side is seen in Fig. 3.

SOME COMMON CHESS TERMS

Other terms commonly used in chess are the following: *Double check*, when a man gives check and by its move uncovers a check by another man. *Discovered check*, when the moving of a man uncovers a check by another. *Double pawns*, when two pawns of the same colour are one in front of the other on the same file. *Passed pawn*, when a pawn has no opposing pawn to stop its march to "queen."

Chess notation. It is necessary for the chess player to have a designation for each square, so that he can describe play and understand printed instructions. The squares of each player are reckoned from his own side of the board. The king's square, for instance, is the square on which the king stands at the start of the game. The king's second square, or K2, is the square in front of him on the second row, and so on right across the board—K3, K4, K5, K6, K7, K8.

The horizontal rows of squares are known as ranks and the vertical rows as files. Thus we speak of the royal rank, meaning the row upon which the pieces stand at the beginning of the game, and the pawn rank or the one on which the pawns stand. The queen's rook's file is the row of squares vertically in front of the queen's rook numbered from 1 to 8 (Fig. 1). It will be seen that the files have the same names for each player, but the numbers are different; thus white king's bishop's square, or KB1, is black king's bishop's eighth square, or KB8. It might be thought that this double numbering would lead to confusion, but this does not happen, and very little practice is needed to get used to it.

Besides the abbreviations already given in the form of initials of pieces there are a few others. A small × like the multiplication sign in arithmetic means " takes "; a plus sign + means " check "; a minus sign — means " move to." Two noughts separated by a dash (0 — 0) means " castles on the king's side." Three noughts separated by two dashes (0 — 0 — 0) means " castles on the queen's side." Thus KP — K4 means that the king's pawn moves to his king's fourth square. At the beginning of a game it would be sufficient to write P — K4 because no other than the king's pawn could legally move to that square. Kt — KB3 means that the *king's* knight moves to the king's bishop's third square. The queen's knight could not legally be moved to this square. A representative example of notation is given in the following sequence of moves:—

	White	Black
1.	P — K4	P — K4
2.	Kt — KB3	Kt — QB3
3.	B — QKt5	Kt — KB3

GENERAL ADVICE ON PLAY OF CHESS

At the beginning of a game of chess the centre pawns should be advanced first, because they enable the greatest force to be released in the fewest number of moves. After your centre pawns move your knights and bishops. The queen should be kept in the background just as artillery is used on the battlefield to cover the advance of infantry and to consolidate what has been won. The queen is too valuable to be used on raids and pawn-snatching expeditions, and if you try it against a good player you will probably lose your queen and then you might as well resign. Useless checks should be avoided, since they waste moves, and you cannot afford to waste moves any more than pawns or pieces.

Play your men so that they reinforce one another and try to have as many supports for each man as your opponent has attacking pieces ranged against it. After castling, which usually occurs soon after the bishops and knights have been moved, defend as much as possible the pawns in front of your castled king. Caution plays a great part in good chess, and while you aim at giving checkmate do not be in too much of a hurry. Try to anticipate your opponent's intentions. " Blind castling," i.e., castling for no particular reason about the seventh move, is a weak point with some otherwise good players. Castling should often be deferred until it is clearly an advantage. Once you have castled, your opponent knows where you are and where you must stay for a long period. Keep him on tenterhooks as long as it is costing you nothing. A threat of a move, especially involving an exchange, is often far more effective than the move itself. Once you have executed your threat your opponent's mind is relieved, and, as you go deeper into the game, you will sense his relief once you have done your worst. Do not be frightened by unconventional and spectacular moves. Watch for traps, and, if you are getting into difficulty, take your opponent's men how and when you can, pawn for pawn, piece for piece, taking care that he does not deceive you by offering what is apparently something for nothing.

A sound development is well illustrated in the opening known as the *French Defence*. In this opening Black is defending himself against the first onslaught of White's attack.

	White	*Black*
1.	P — K4	P — K3
2.	P — Q4	P — Q4
3.	Kt — QB3	

By this move White threatens, if Black's QP takes White's KP,

Fig. 4. *The French Defence.*   Fig. 5. *The Scholar's Mate.*

to capture the QP with his Kt. To keep on top of the situation Black replies:—

Kt — KB3

To keep up his attack White now moves his QB along its diagonal so as to pin the Black Kt and prevent its moving without exposing the Black Q to capture. Thus:—

4. B — K Kt5

Black must make it clear that he will next move his Kt without endangering his Q, so he moves:—

B — K2

This not only releases his knight but opens an attack on White's B so soon as that knight is moved. White therefore takes the Kt and is in turn taken by the Black B, effecting an equal exchange. Thus:—

5. B × Kt   B × B

The game may then continue:—

6. Kt — B3   Castles

The position will then be as shown in Fig. 4.

You will not have played many games before you come across the moves known as the *Scholar's Mate* and the *Fool's Mate*. The first (Fig. 5) is indicated by the following sequence of moves:—

	White	Black
1.	P — K4	P — K4
2.	B — Q B4	B — Q B4
3.	Q — R5	Q P — Q3
4.	Q × K B P mate	

The *Fool's Mate* is extremely simple, but it is surprising how many people, not fools, have been caught by it.

	White	Black
1.	P — K B3	P — K4
2.	P — K Kt4	Q — R5 mate

CLASSIC OPENINGS IN CHESS

The learner should try to make himself familiar with a few of the principal openings which have the sanction of master minds and long experience. It is not necessary to memorize a long sequence of moves. Frequent practice will soon fix them in the mind.

In learning these openings most people are puzzled at first when an opponent does not make the reply moves in accordance with the textbooks. What is one then to do? White, for example, begins to play the *Ruy Lopez* opening, examples of which are given below, and Black, after a few moves, perhaps even after his second move, does something quite unexpected. The answer is that White shall play as intelligently as he can off his own bat, remembering that Black's failure to give the correct reply at once puts him in an inferior position with a really skilful player. The significance of the moves and counter-moves in the text has been worked out by experts and can be relied upon. This does not mean, however, that Black should accept, say, the offer of a pawn in the opening of the *Evans Gambit* (described later in this chapter) unless he wishes to do so. He may avoid the force of a subsequent attack by refusing it, and this is very wise if he is not familiar with the later moves. In this well-known gambit the offer of the pawn is not a trap in the ordinary sense, but a bribe, and White, in offering it, places himself at a temporary

Fig. 6. Position after Black's eighth move (Ruy Lopez—III).

disadvantage, hoping that he may benefit later. (The word gambit derives from the Italian. It was originally a term used in wrestling and was applied to a trick by which the opponent was upset.)

Probably the best known of the commoner openings is the *Ruy Lopez*, of which we give three variations, using the analysis of Staunton, one of the greatest players that any country ever produced.

VARIATION 1

	White	Black
1.	P — K4	P — K4
2.	Kt — KB3	Kt — QB3
3.	B — Kt5	Kt — B3
4.	Q — K2	B — K2
5.	P — B3	P — Q3
6.	P — Q4	P × P

VARIATION 2

First three moves as in Variation 1

4.	Q — K2	P — QR3
5.	B — R4	P — QKt4
6.	B — Kt3	B — B4
7.	P — QR4	R — QKt1
8.	P × P	P × P

VARIATION 3

First three moves as in Variation 1

4.	P — Q4	QKt × P
5.	Kt × Kt	P × Kt
6.	Q × P	P — QB3
7.	B — QB4	P — Q4
8.	P × P	Kt × P

Staunton gives as many as forty-seven variations from the third and fourth moves onwards, but there is no need for the learner to go into all these combinations. The first three moves are the distinguishing feature of the opening. Fig. 6 shows the position after Black's eighth move in Variation 3.

The *Giuoco Piano* is another famous opening which varies from the *Ruy Lopez* because White, instead of moving his KB to QKt5 at the third move, plays it instead to QB4 and is therefore not so aggressive at first. This opening allows more time for development.

VARIATION 1

	White	Black
1.	P — K4	P — K4
2.	Kt — KB3	Kt — QB3
3.	B — B4	B — B4
4.	P — B3	Kt — B3
5.	P — Q4	P × P
6.	P — K5	P — Q4
7.	B — QKt5	Kt — K5

VARIATION 2

First five moves as in Variation 1
6.	P — K5	Kt — K5
7.	B — Q5	Kt × KBP
8.	K × Kt	P × P (discovered check)

VARIATION 3

First four moves as in Variation 1
5.	Castles	Kt × P
6.	Q — K2	P — Q4

A very dangerous and striking development arising from the *Giuoco Piano* opening is the *Evans Gambit*. It entails the early

Fig. 7. Position after Black's tenth move (Evans Gambit).   *Fig. 8. Position after Black's sixth move (Philidor Defence).*

sacrifice of a pawn by White if the gambit is accepted. If, however, White is not skilful and his attack fails, he is almost surely lost for the sacrifice of the pawn is serious.

VARIATION 1   *White*   *Black*

First three moves as in Variation 1 of *Giuoco Piano* opening
4.	P — QKt4	B × KtP (black accepts the gambit)
5.	P — B3	B — R4
6.	Castles	P — Q3
7.	P — Q4	P × P
8.	Q — Kt3 (!)	Q — K2
9.	P — K5	P × KP
10.	R — K1	B — Kt3

White has now a powerful attack despite his loss of pawns, but is in a vulnerable position if he loses his grip. Fig. 7 shows the position after Black's tenth move.

VARIATION 2   *White*   *Black*

First four moves as in Variation 1

5.	P — B3	B — B4
6.	P — Q4	P × P
7.	P × P	B — Kt3
8.	Castles	P — Q3

A brilliant master-game in which the *Evans Gambit* was accepted was one won by Anderssen. It is well worth studying. It has been called the *Evergreen Game*.

        White   *Black*

First five moves as in Variation 1 *Evans Gambit*

6.	P — Q4	P × P
7.	Castles	P — Q6
8.	Q — Kt3	Q — B3
9.	P — K5	Q — Kt3
10.	B — R3	K Kt — K2
11.	R — K1	P — Kt4
12.	B × KtP	R — QKt1
13.	Q — R4	B — Kt3
14.	QKt — Q2	B — Kt2
15.	Kt — K4	Q — B4
16.	B × P	Q — R4
17.	Kt — B6 (check)	P × Kt
18.	P × P	R — Kt1
19.	QR — Q1	Q × Kt
20.	R × Kt (check)	Kt × R
21.	Q × P (check)	K × Q
22.	B — KB5 (dbl.ch)	K — K1
23.	B — Q7 (check)	K — B1
24.	B × Kt mate	

The last eight moves of this game reveal a masterpiece of penetration which puts it among chess classics. It shows clearly how dangerous it can be for Black to accept the gambit by taking the pawn offered by White at his fourth move.

The *Philidor Defence* is one in which Black defends himself for the first few moves with his centre pawns without bringing out his knights or bishops as in most other openings.

VARIATION 1   *White*   *Black*

1.	P — K4	P — K4
2.	Kt — KB3	P — Q3
3.	P — Q4	P — KB4
4.	P × KP	P × KP
5.	Kt — Kt5	P — Q4
6.	P — K6	Kt — KR3

Fig. 8 shows the position after Black's sixth move.

The game may be continued:—

| 7. | P — KB3 | P × BP |
| 8. | Q × P (B6) | R — Kt1 |

(Otherwise the White Kt will fork Black Q and R by moving to B7.)
Alternatively:—

7.	P — KB3	B — K2
8.	P × P	B × Kt
9.	Q — R5 (check)	P — K Kt3
10.	Q × B	Q × Q
11.	B × Q	

Rather startling developments from what appeared to be a tame opening!

VARIATION 2

First two moves as in Variation 1

3.	B — B4	P — QB3
4.	P — Q4	P — Q4
5.	P × QP	P — K5
6.	Kt — K5	P × P

The *Allgaiere Gambit* is one of the most venturesome and amusing developments known to chess players. It involves the early sacrifice of a Kt. But if Black knows how to meet it White is in for a tough time. Allgaiere used to claim that in the hands of a good player it was invincible, but later players have proved otherwise. It certainly makes an interesting game.

VARIATION 1

	White	*Black*
1.	P — K4	P — K4
2.	P — KB4	P × P
3.	Kt — KB3	P — K Kt4
4.	P — KR4	P — Kt5
5.	Kt — Kt5	P — KR3
6.	Kt × P (!)	K × Kt
7.	Q × P	Kt — KB3
8.	Q × BP	B — Q3
9.	B — B4 (check)	K — Kt2

VARIATION 2

First six moves as in Variation 1

7.	B — B4 (check)	P — Q4
8.	B × P (check)	K — K1
9.	P — Q4	Kt — K2

A short and brilliant game illustrates the use of the *Allgaiere Gambit*:—

First six moves as in Variation 1

	White	*Black*
7.	B — B4 (check)	P — Q4
8.	B × P (check)	K — Kt2
9.	P — Q4	P — B6

10.	P × P	Kt — KB3
11.	Kt — B3	B — Kt5
12.	B — KB4	P × P
13.	Q × P	P — B3
14.	KR — Kt1 (check)	K — R2
15.	B — K5	R — B1
16.	Q — Kt3	Q — K2
17.	Q — Kt6 (check)	K — R1
18.	Q × P (check)	Q — R2
19.	B × Kt (check)	R × B
20.	R — Kt8 mate	

Traps in the Openings. A little experience will soon bring knowledge of traps in the common openings. A very usual one is the withdrawal of support from one of the pawns. In its more blatant form this sort of trap is fairly easy to see, but a trap adopted by Blackburne, and by which he was said to have won so many shillings that his friends called it " Blackburne's Shilling Game," provides a striking illustration of an effective trap.

	White	*Black* (Blackburne)
1.	P — K4	P — K4
2.	Kt — KB3	Kt — QB3
3.	B — B4	

This is the ordinary *Giuoco Piano* opening, but now Black offers a pawn by moving:—

| | | Kt — Q5 (this is the trap) |
| 4. | Kt × P | |

thinking he may be able next move to fork the Black Q and R because his B is backing up his Kt:—

| | | Q — Kt4 |
| 5. | Kt × BP | Q × KtP |

And now White is lost irretrievably. He was foolish when he took the unguarded pawn. He should have exchanged the Kt:—

| 6. | R — B1 | Q × KP (check) |
| 7. | B — K2 | Kt — B6 mate (!) |

The final position is shown in Fig. 9.

The danger, against which the learner has already been warned, of sending the queen out early on raiding expeditions, is illustrated by the following simple disaster:—

	White	*Black*
1.	P — K4	P — K4
2.	P — KB4	P — Q3
3.	Kt — KB3	Q — K2
4.	B — B4	P × P
5.	Castles (trap)	Q × P
6.	R — K1	

and the queen is lost ! The best Black can do is to take the rook.

Fig. 9. *Blackburne's " Shilling Game."*   Fig. 10. *White to mate in two moves.*

Another example, illustrating the dangers of the *Allgaiere Gambit* for an unwary exponent of it, may be given. The queen is again lost through grabbing at baits:—

	White	Black
1.	P — K4	P — K4
2.	P — KB4	P × P
3.	Kt — KB3	P — K Kt4
4.	P — KR4	P — Kt5
5.	Kt — Kt5	P — KR3
6.	Kt × BP	K × Kt
7.	Q × P	Kt — KB3
8.	Q × BP	B — Q3
9.	P — K5	B × P

and if White takes the bishop Black moves:—

R — K1 (winning the Q)

The *End Game*. Correct play in the end game is most important, and many a promising game has been lost because a player, brilliant in openings and attack, has proved weak in end play. Such weakness is common even among fairly good players. The advance of a pawn, a perpetual check or a forced stalemate has turned many an apparent defeat into a draw.

HOW TO EFFECT CHECKMATE

One of the simplest of all checkmates is king and queen against a lone king. The procedure is to force your opponent's king to the nearest side of the board by using your queen and then bring up your king. Be on your guard against forcing stalemate. Place the pieces as in Fig. 10 and practise how to mate in two moves, watching carefully not to give stalemate. If, playing White, you move K — Q6, it is clear that the Black king is not in check, but cannot move without going into check—hence stalemate. A similar situation arises if you move K — K7. The obvious solution is Q — R7, which forces the Black king to his queen's square. Checkmate is then given by moving Q — Q7. Put the pieces in other positions and bring about a similar checkmate.

King and rook against king is also an easy checkmate, but requires a little practice. The lone king must be driven to the side of the board and then your king placed in front of him with one square between them. Checkmate is given by the rook along the same row as that upon which the lone king stands.

Place the pieces as shown in Fig. 11. Black has two possible moves: K — K1 or K — B1. If he moves K — K1, then White moves R — R8 giving mate.

In Black moves K — B1, then:—

	White	Black
1.	K — Q6	K — Kt1

If not, and Black moves back to Q1 the White rook gives mate as before. By moving to Kt 1 he threatens to take the rook, hence:—

2.	R — QB7	K — R1 (forced)
3.	K — B6	K — Kt1 (forced)
4.	K — Kt6	K — R1 (forced)
5.	R — B8 mate	

King and two bishops against a king also win, but the king must be forced to one corner of the board. This is difficult, and the king must be skilfully used to assist.

King, bishop and knight against a king is more difficult still, and you would probably find it impossible to checkmate within any reasonable number of moves. The king must not only be driven into a corner, but into one commanded by your bishop.

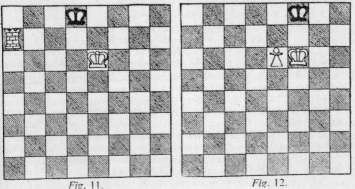

Fig. 11.   Fig. 12.

Most players, finding themselves in this situation, would be conten
with calling it a draw.

King and two knights against a lone king cannot force a check
mate.

When only king and one pawn are left on the board it is ofte
difficult to know whether or not you can queen that pawn. I
you cannot gain what is called the " opposition " you cannot d
it. That depends on whose move it is. In Fig. 12 White has th
opposition and can queen his pawn, but that is because it is Black'
turn to move. (If White had to move first the game would b
drawn.) This is how it is done:—

	White	Black
1.	......	K — K1
2.	P — K7	K — Q2 (forced)
3.	K — B7	K moves
4.	P — K8 queening	

Now suppose White must move first:—

1. P — K7 (check)   K — K1

and white must either abandon the pawn or give stalemate.

The general rule is that if you can move your pawn on to the
seventh square without giving check you can win; if this is no
possible you have no alternative but to draw.

FORCING A DRAW

Young players should remember that there are many positions
in the final stages of a game in which a weaker force can draw
against a superior one. In certain cases where a pawn has reached
the seventh square, where it is always dangerous, it may draw against
a queen. Take a simple example. Place the men on the board
as follows: White: K on QB4, Q on KB5; Black: K on K Kt7, P on
KB7. If it were Black's turn to move the pawn could be queened
next move, but suppose it is White's turn:—

1. Q — Kt4 (check)   K — R8
2. Q — R3 (check)   K — Kt8
3. Q — Kt3 (check)   K — R8

and if White takes the pawn Black is stalemated.

Queen against queen and pawn is not difficult to draw, usually
by a perpetual check, but sometimes by an exchange of queens
when your king is able to stop the pawn from queening. When
the pawn is at the seventh square the problem becomes a little
more difficult.

A single rook will often draw against a rook and pawn when
the king is in front of his pawn. The position was given as an
example by Philidor. Place the men as follows: White: K on KB5,
R on KR7, P on K4; Black: K on K1, R on Q3:—

1. P — K5   R — QKt3

If Black plays R — QR3 Philidor thought he ought to lose the game.

If a pawn at its seventh square can sometimes draw with the assistance of its king, against a queen it should be clear that the same pawn will draw more easily against a rook. It is often best, in fact, to sacrifice the rook for the pawn to prevent loss of the game. If, however, the pawn is not so far advanced and is supported by another one, cases of great difficulty occur, demanding, as Staunton says, " the utmost precision of calculation." He gives an instructive example, showing how a pawn can win against a rook, even though the rook has the move. Place the men as follows: White: K on KB4, R on K5; Black: K on Q3, P on Q7.

1.   R — K8

threatening to check and win if Black now queens his pawn. Therefore:—

	K — Q 2
2. K — K3	P — Q 8 queening

and Black wins.

It is not difficult to draw with a bishop against a rook, because checkmate can only be given with a rook when the kings are opposite each other (as has been described earlier in this chapter). It follows that if you can use your bishop to prevent your opponent's king from facing yours you can draw. The most secure position if you have the weaker force is when you can play your king to a corner square of a different colour to that on which your bishop runs. Keep king and bishop together and you have only to move them about on adjoining squares to secure a draw.

Much help in the intricacies of middle and end games may be found by studying chess problems which appear in various newspapers. These are usually problems where White has to force a mate in two or three moves. Their disadvantage, if it may be so described, is that they are artificial and it is known that a mate can be so forced, a fact which would not be so evident in actual play, nor would the excitement of the play permit such close study and experiment. They depend on a key move which is not obvious and form almost a specialized branch of chess. Practice soon brings certain facility in solving, but a good problem solver is not necessarily a winner against a good match player.

LAWS OF THE GAME

The exact laws of the game are set out at length in the British Chess Code, but for play among friends, where strict match conditions need not be insisted upon, the following rules should be sufficient:

1. To decide for colour one of the players usually takes a white pawn in one hand and a black one in the other, and shuffles them behind his back. He then presents his closed fists to his opponent,

one pawn in each hand, and the opponent chooses which he will have. Unless there are special conditions White always has first move.

2. When no odds are given the players should take White and Black in alternate games. White is usually reckoned to have a slight advantage because he has first move.

3. A piece or pawn touched must be played unless, before touching it, the player announces his intention of adjusting it. This is usually done by saying *j'adoube* (an old French word meaning *to arrange*). Usually, however, in friendly games it is sufficient to insist that if a move has been made and the mover has taken his hand away that move must stand. If it is an illegal move the opponent may insist that the " man " be moved legally. If it cannot be moved legally the offender must move his king.

4. If, after a few moves have been made, it is found that the board has been set the wrong way round, or that men have been misplaced, it is better to start afresh without quibbling. The Chess Code says, however, that either player may have the game annulled only before the second player has made his fourth move, but not afterwards.

5. A player may claim a drawn game if he can prove that the last fifty moves on each side have been made without a pawn on the board being moved or a piece taken.

CHESS DON'TS FOR BEGINNERS

Don't let your hand hover over the board until you have made up your mind which move to make. It annoys your opponent and breeds in you a bad habit of indecision.

Don't hurry yourself and don't get impatient with your opponent. Mere wood-shifting is not chess, and if he is a long time in moving it is a tribute to your skill.

Don't get used to playing constantly with one colour. Learn to play equally well with Black or White.

Don't hesitate to push your advantage, when you are sure you have one, by exchanging pieces and thus reducing your opponent's proportionate strength. The opponent who objects does not know the game. Your object should be to win, not to prevent him from losing.

Don't lose your head. Chess is very exciting, appearances notwithstanding. Good players lose games every day through excitement.

Don't refuse to accept odds from a better player. It is not much fun for him to play you on even terms. Let him state the conditions. If you beat him he will be well satisfied.

Don't move pawns carelessly or give them away lightly. Every one is a potential queen. Once you have moved them you cannot get them back, and the game is altered for good or ill.   Profligacy with pawns is a great fault with young players.

Don't, as a general rule, move your knight's pawns early in the game, and, after castling don't move those standing in front of your king till you are obliged.

Don't forget that your rooks are very powerful and should be got into play as early as convenient.   You might as well not have rooks as have them helplessly jammed in where they can do no good. Remember, however, that rooks require a fairly empty board to develop their full strength.   Don't therefore waste moves unduly in the beginning of the game for no other reason than that of developing your rooks.

Don't have doubled pawns on your rook's file if you can avoid it. In capturing with a pawn do so towards the centre of the board, unless you can see a reason to the contrary.

Don't snatch at captures.   Think hard first.   Good opponents do not give men away; therefore, watch for traps.

Don't carelessly exchange bishops for knights or knights for bishops at the beginning of a game.   Two bishops are stronger in the end game than two knights, but one knight is generally more useful than a single bishop.

CHAPTER 14

DRAUGHTS

DRAUGHTS is a game for two people, played on a chequered board, usually about fifteen inches square.   The board is divided into sixty-four squares, coloured alternately black and white (or light and dark).   Each player has twelve " men " or draughts; these are circular pieces, one inch across and three-eighths of an inch thick, coloured either black and white, black and yellow, or red and white—twelve of each colour.   Play takes place only on squares of one colour—usually on the white, and this is the colour assumed in this chapter.

The object of the game is to " take," i.e., capture by leaping over all your opponent's men, or to block them up so that they cannot be moved.

In setting the board for play, the draughtsmen are so placed that each player has a double corner on his right and a single corner on his left.   A single corner (Fig. 1) is one from which a

Fig. 1.   Single   Fig. 2.   Double
    corner.   corner.

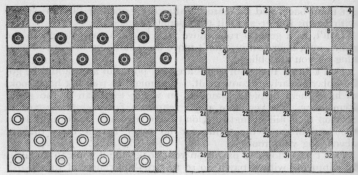

Fig. 3. *Lay-out of board.*   *Fig.* 4. *Numbering for play.*

man can only move in one direction : a double corner (Fig. 2) is one from which a man can move into either of two squares. Fig. 3 shows a board with all the men laid out in position for play.

To make explanation easier, we have given a number to each of the squares used in the play. These numbers are shown in Fig. 4 and are used throughout in referring to the squares.

Black invariably starts the game, and it is usual for players to take this colour alternately. Men can only be moved one square at a time, diagonally forward, either to the left or to the right. If a man comes next to a man of another colour it can jump over it to the adjoining square, if it is vacant, and if this puts him in a position to jump over a second man, he may do so in the same move, and so on for as long as he is in a position to jump. This is called " taking," and the draughts which are jumped over in this way are removed from the board.

PENALTY OF HUFFING

If a player neglects to take a man or men, when he is in a position to do so, his opponent can either take the man with which the capture would have been made, compel him to take the man, or ignore the omission. If he takes the first course, it is known as " huffing." Huffing does not constitute a move, but it must be done before the player makes his legitimate move.

Once the player has made the move and taken his hand off the draughtsman, that move is complete and cannot be altered. If a move is not made within five minutes, time may be called, after which one minute is allowed for the move, failing which the game is " lost " by that player for improper delay. Sometimes a special timekeeper is deputed to see that this limit is not exceeded

As soon as a man reaches the opponent's back row it becomes a " king," and is " crowned," i.e., covered with a piece of the same colour, which is not in play. Kings are of great value, for they can move either backwards or forwards.

If either player forces his opponent into such a position that he cannot move any of his men, he wins the game. If neither player can force a win, the game is drawn. When one player seems in a stronger position than the other, the weaker may require the stronger to complete his game within forty of his own moves. Failing this the game is drawn.

It is difficult to lay down any hard and fast rules for playing draughts, apart from the fact already stated that the men must be moved diagonally forward, to either side, and that in the case of kings, moves may be made in both directions.

To gain experience, various methods should be tried, and once a certain start or move appears to bring out further chances, practice should be made in seeing where such a start or move can lead. Try, for instance, playing your men to the centre of the board, so as to divide your opponent's pieces. If you find that your opponent is using the same tactics, it may be well to keep to your game and force his moves. On the other hand you can change your own game, and may thus be able to block your opponent.

TACTICS IN OPENING PLAY

If you start off by playing to the sides, the idea is to block in your opponent and prevent him getting any men crowned, for as soon as he manages to get even one king, he may well follow you up and break down all your potential side supports.

If you want to play to attack your opponent's double corner— and this is a good game—try to get your men placed on squares 14 to 19 (Fig. 4). If you try this game, always take great care never to leave your men in such a position that your opponent can take more men than you can. A certain number of wise exchanges clears the board for final action, and these come in the natural order of play—the danger lies when you take one man, and by doing so, leave open two or three, or more, " hops " for your opponent.

There are quite a number of " standard " opening moves, and if it is intended to take up this game seriously, a few of them should be learned by heart, and used systematically until the player feels that he can devise others of his own. Even when you do this and think you have invented an opening of your own, it is surprising how often it proves, on investigation, to be well known.

Amongst the well-known opening moves, there is the Alma. Here black moves 11 to 15, white 23 to 19, and then 8 to 11, 22 to 17 and 3 to 8. Another very popular, and much quoted move

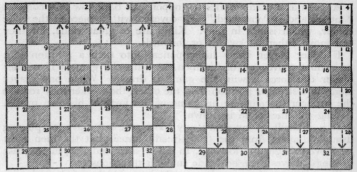

Fig. 5 (left) *Fig.* 6 (right). *Dividing board into sets for calculating " move."*

is the Ayrshire Lassie: this starts 11 to 15; 24 to 20; 8 to 11. The Old Fourteenth too is much used, and considered as a steady opening. The start is 11 to 15, 23 to 19, 8 to 11, 22 to 17, 4 to 8. We give on page 261 a played out game to illustrate this start. It is supposed to have derived its name from the fact that it was the fourteenth game given in Sturge's standard book on this subject.

There is too, the Double Corner start, when black moves off with 9 to 14; then there is the Maid of the Mill, with the start for black, as usual, with 11 to 15, followed by 22 to 17, 8 to 11, 17 to 13, 15 to 18. The Will o' the Wisp commences with 11 to 15, 23 to 19, 9 to 13. The Defiance gives the lead of 11 to 15, and then 23 to 19, 9 to 14, 27 to 23. The White Dyke starts with 11 to 15, 22 to 17, 8 to 11, 17 to 14. The Dyke makes a variation by starting with 11 to 15, 22 to 17, and then 15 to 19. The Glasgow starts with 11 to 15, 23 to 19, 8 to 11, 22 to 17, 11 to 16. The Glasgow and the Laird and the Lady openings are considered as variations of the Old Fourteenth. The latter starts off with black playing 11 to 15, white 23 to 19, and then 8 to 11, 22 to 17, 9 to 13, 17 to 14, 4 to 8, 25 to 22, 12 to 16, 24 to 20, 10 to 15, 21 to 17. Here white could have moved 27 to 24, but if the game is played out, it will be seen that white's correct move was 21 to 17. Another development of this opening is given in the game on page 262.

MATCHING SKILL AGAINST INEXPERIENCE

The object the player must bear in mind right from the initial moves is the position he is aiming for in the final stages of the game. Thus everything should lead up to these final positions. You should naturally take advantage where advantage is offered and this means, of course, using skill against inexperience or carelessness. Experts must be expected to lay traps for the unwary and you must be constantly on the look out for such. Especially must you guard against leaving your men or a man in such a position that your opponent can take more than he will lose when you retaliate.

To have the " move," or " last move " (and this is not an invariably desirable objective), means to have your men in such a position on the board that, eventually, you can block your opponent either by hemming him in to one side or the other, or by enclosing his men in the centre. Even then, if you can only do this by putting yourself in a position where you are also blocked, it is not worth doing, and maybe it will even lose you the game. The benefit in having the last move is that you can often force your opponent to make certain moves which are helpful to you, instead of those advantageous to himself. It is, however, possible for the move to be altered by clever manœuvring. Where the move is all-important is in the end game, and much should be sacrificed to achieve it.

HOW TO CALCULATE THE MOVE

There are several methods of determining who has the move. You can do it, for instance, by dividing the board into two sets of sixteen squares. The first set is made by the four vertical rows running from your own side of the board, as shown in Fig. 5. The second set runs from the opponent's side of the board as shown in Fig. 6. To find out who has the move when it is your turn to play, provided that the forces of the two sides are equal, add together all the black and white pieces left on the board in one of the sets, disregarding those in the other, and if the number is odd you have the move. In Fig. 7 it is black's turn to play, and by moving 26 to 23, as he has the move, he wins. In Fig. 8 the men on both of the sets are even in number, and as that means that

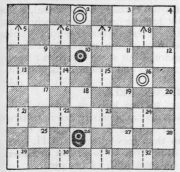

Fig. 7. Black has the " move."

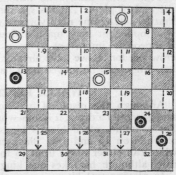

Fig. 8. Neither has the " move."

the player has not the move, he must force an exchange if he is to win the game. Whereas there is really no stage of this game which is more important than another, end play requires definite skill in sizing up opportunities and eventualities. Certainly one's chief object should be to get every piece crowned before the final stage of the game begins. Suppose you have started with a to-the-centre play, and are trying to win in the same position, one by one these men in the centre should be worked to the base to be crowned, and then manœuvred back into central positions. This is an admirable way of blocking your opponent, and especially of capturing any of his uncrowned pieces.

PLAYING TWO KINGS AGAINST ONE

The final play of two kings to one should prove a win for the two kings. There is an exception to this, however, and that is if the one king manages to get into one of the single corners.

In the case of two kings to two kings, a draw is usual, but not always inevitable. Care must be taken not to give your opponent the chance to get a king between your two kings, for here one of yours will be lost.

Three kings to two if either or both of the double corners are held by the latter means a draw, if an exchange cannot be brought about by bringing the three kings into line.

Four kings to three is a difficult position. The player with the three kings should try to avoid being made to collect his pieces together, as in separation lies the possibility of his success. The player with the four kings should, of course, try to force his opponent to one end of the board and then take up his positions in the squares facing them with only one intervening vacant space on each line.

Traps must always be watched for, from the beginning until the end of play. Always see that your exchanges are equal, and that by taking one man you are not leaving open a move whereby your opponent may make a double or even greater jump. This is especially important as soon as any of the pieces have been crowned, for, as we have already pointed out these crowned pieces, i.e., kings, can be moved both backwards and forwards diagonally.

WHERE EXPERIENCE TELLS

Although the result of two kings to two kings is, as we have said generally a draw, it is somewhat a matter of experience in tactics. For example, place black's kings on squares 3 and 8, and those of white on 15 and 16. Black can then move from 8 to 11, and white can either move from 15 to 8, or from 16 to 7; but in either case, although he takes one king he loses both of his own.

In playing two kings to one, the holder of the two kings should

win. For practice, put white's
one king on square 32. Black
should then try to work his two
up to squares 23 and 19; he
should then win in seven moves.
White, 32 to 28, black 23 to 27,
followed by 28 to 32, 19 to 23,
32 to 28, 27 to 32, 28 to 24,
32 to 28, 24 to 20, 23 to 18,
20 to 16, 18 to 15, 16 to 20,
15 to 11. The fifth move here
should be noted. 23 could have
been moved to square 19, but if
this had been done, white would
have moved to 24, and this
would leave all the previous play

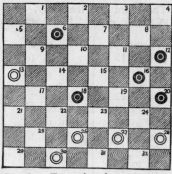

Fig. 9.   Example of middle play.

utile and black's attack would have to be started all over again.

In the illustrations of play which follow, try to think out the
reason for each move, and you will then learn a good deal more
from them.

A Game with the Old "Fourteenth Opening."
Black starts with :—

11 to 15	29 to 22	15 to 19	17 to 13
23 to 19	20 to 27	8 to 3	27 to 23
8 to 11	31 to 24	19 to 23	13 to 9
22 to 17	1 to 6	3 to 8	23 to 26
4 to 8	24 to 20	10 to 15	21 to 17
17 to 13	2 to 7	8 to 3	26 to 30
15 to 18	20 to 16	7 to 10	22 to 18
24 to 20	10 to 15	3 to 7	30 to 25
9 to 14	22 to 17	23 to 27	9 to 6
26 to 23	14 to 18	7 to 14	25 to 22
10 to 15	30 to 25	27 to 31	17 to 13
19 to 10	6 to 10	4 to 8	22 to 15
6 to 15	16 to 12	31 to 27	7 to 3
28 to 24	18 to 23	13 to 9	15 to 18
12 to 16	32 to 28	27 to 23	14 to 23
23 to 19	23 to 27	9 to 6	19 to 26
16 to 23	28 to 24	23 to 19	12 to 19
20 to 16	27 to 32	6 to 2	26 to 30
11 to 20	24 to 20	32 to 27	6 to 2
25 to 22	7 to 11	2 to 7	30 to 26
18 to 25	25 to 22	19 to 16	3 to 7
27 to 4	3 to 7	8 to 12	White must
7 to 10	12 to 8	15 to 19	win.

The Laird and the Lady.

A classic game.   Black starts and wins.

Black starts	28 to 24	12 to 3	32 to 27
11 to 15	11 to 16	2 to 7	28 to 32
23 to 19	26 to 23	3 to 10	14 to 10
8 to 11	16 to 20	6 to 31	5 to 9
22 to 17	31 to 26	29 to 25	10 to 7
9 to 13	18 to 22	31 to 24	1 to 5
17 to 14	25 to 18	25 to 21	7 to 2
10 to 17	12 to 16	17 to 22	31 to 26
21 to 14	19 to 12	21 to 17	2 to 6
15 to 18	7 to 10	22 to 26	26 to 19
19 to 15	14 to 7	17 to 14	6 to 13
4 to 8	3 to 28	26 to 31	32 to 23
24 to 19			
13 to 17			

An example of **Middle Play** (Fig. 9).

26 to 23	22 to 25	16 to 19	16 to 19
18 to 22	30 to 21	24 to 15	17 to 14
23 to 18	10 to 14	12 to 16	19 to 24
6 to 10			27 to 23
28 to 24	18 to 9	21 to 17	White must win.

An example of **End Play** (Fig. 10).

6 to 2	6 to 1	1 to 6	7 to 2
5 to 9	25 to 29	17 to 13	5 to 1
18 to 15	10 to 7	10 to 15	11 to 7
17 to 22	29 to 25	22 to 17	9 to 6
1 to 6	2 to 6	6 to 10	2 to 9
9 to 5	25 to 22	13 to 9	13 to 15
15 to 10	6 to 10	15 to 11	
22 to 25	21 to 17	17 to 13	

Besides ordinary English draughts, as already described, there are many other forms and variations of the game which are interesting.

Some need larger, some smaller boards; you may easily prepare the required size by cutting up one or more boards and pasting or gluing the pieces to a new base.

In **Spanish Draughts**, the board, of sixty-four squares, is placed so that the double corner is to the left of each player, instead of at the right as in the English game. Play follows the method already described, but there is one important difference—a crowned king can move over *any number of squares on the same diagonal*, just as a bishop moves in chess, except that it can jump over and take any opponent's pieces in its path. Also, if there are alternative moves where more men can be jumped over and thus captured, it is compulsory to take the path which allows the larger number of pieces to be captured. The king need not " come down " on the empty square immediately

Fig. 10. *Example of end play.*

beyond a captured piece. It may not, of course, jump over one of its own men—a point worth remembering in planning your defence.

Polish Draughts is the most complex form of the game, rather like a half-way game between draughts and chess.

A board of one hundred squares, ten each way, is required. Only the black squares are used, each player starting off with his twenty men placed in the four back rows—just as the twelve men of the English game fill their three rows. The board is placed with the double corner on each player's right.

RULES OF POLISH DRAUGHTS

All moves are diagonal, but men are allowed to capture backwards as well as forwards, and this greatly complicates the game. Kings are obtained in the ordinary way, but, as in the Spanish game, they can move over any number of unoccupied squares on the same diagonal and capture any intervening piece. Providing there is no other piece liable to capture in a second diagonal at right angles to the first, the king may come down where he likes after his jump, but if there is another such piece it must be taken. Similarly, a man must continue his jumps until he has taken all that are open to capture. If, during the jumps, he finds himself in his opponent's rear line and is then forced to jump back from it to take another piece, he will not pause or be made a king.

When a choice of jumps is available the highest number must always be taken. No huffing is allowed in this game; the most interesting feature of play generally proves to be the backward and forward captures of the men.

In **Italian Draughts** the sixty-four square board is used, and play resembles that of the English game, though there are four points of difference. The double square of the board must be on the left hand of each player: when more than one line of capture is available the one which holds the greater number and more valuable pieces must be taken: a king can only be taken by a king, not by a man: when a king and a man, at the same time, have the opportunity of a capture, the king is obliged to take precedence.

German Draughts is just the same as Polish, except that it is played on a sixty-four square board. French draughts is the same as German.

Russian Draughts is derived from the Polish game, but in taking, it is not necessary to make the move with the maximum number of jumps. Also, when a man gets to the back rank of the opponent he is crowned a king, even though he continues his move by jumping back from that line. In other respects the same rules are observed as for the Polish play. Russian draughts can be played on either a hundred square or a sixty-four square board.

A UNIQUE VARIETY OF DRAUGHTS

Turkish Draughts differs from all other varieties of the game. The board is of sixty-four squares, and all of them are used. Each player has sixteen pieces. At the beginning of the game they are placed across the second and third rows of the board, counting from the back.

The men are moved sideways and forwards in a straight line, instead of diagonally, across white and black squares indiscriminately. Each man can move one square at a time, either forwards or sideways. When alternative moves are possible a player must always jump and capture the highest number possible, and the men jumped over should be removed one by one as they are captured. A king, when crowned in the ordinary way, can travel over any number of squares, capturing at any distance, providing the square on the farther side of the attacked piece is vacant for alighting.

When a man has reached the crowning line and become a king the opponent must make one move before the new king can move. Kings can be taken like ordinary men.

PLAYING THE LOSING GAME

The **Losing Game** of draughts is of great interest, and gives scope for much skill. It is as difficult to play for a win as the ordinary game of draughts.

The object of the game, as the title indicates, is to lose or give away all one's men before the opponent can do the same, or to block oneself so that one cannot move. It is an exact reversal of the usual game.

Board and preliminary lay-out are as in the normal English game, and all subsequent moves and rules are similar. When there are two possible methods of capturing pieces the player is free to choose which he likes. In the opening game it is always worth while to take a few of one's opponent's pieces so as to free the board for one's own schemes.

Black always moves first. The chief chance of success lies in getting men on to such squares that they cannot be made to jump to the back or crowning row—when, of course, they would be compelled to become kings, and thus would be more capable of clearing off the opponent's pieces. The most useful squares to make for are in the third, fifth and seventh rows, counting from your own side of the board, for from none of these can you be made to jump into the crowning row.

Except at the opening of the game the pieces of your opponent should not be taken unless by such taking he will be forced to take more of yours. This is where skill and forethought are most needed. Clearing the board, in a losing game, means clearing off your own men.

Here is an example of a game of losers. Black starts:—

11 to 15	10 to 14	5 to 9	10 to 14
24 to 19	17 to 10	13 to 6	18 to 9
15 to 24	6 to 15	1 to 10	2 to 6
27 to 20	28 to 24	24 to 19	9 to 2
8 to 11	20 to 27	15 to 24	4 to 8
20 to 16	31 to 24	32 to 27	2 to 4
12 to 19	9 to 14	24 to 31	3 to 8
23 to 16	26 to 22	30 to 26	4 to 11
11 to 20	14 to 17	31 to 22	
22 to 17	22 to 13	25 to 18	Black wins.

Two players take part in the game of **Fox and Geese,** which is not really draughts at all, although it is played on an ordinary sixty-four square board. Four white pieces are used, which are the geese, and one black piece—the fox.

All the pieces move diagonally, as in draughts. But while the geese are allowed to go forwards only, like men, the fox can go diagonally in any direction, one square at a time, as a king does. There is no capturing and removing of pieces. The object of the game is for the geese to drive the fox into a corner and so pen him in that he cannot move. When this happens, the geese win. If the fox succeeds in breaking through the line of geese and reaching the far side of the board, then he wins. Since the geese can only move one way, the fox must get through the line before the geese reach his side of the board.

Play begins from opposite sides of the board, the fox being on one rear line, the four geese on the opposite back line. All should be on black squares. The geese start the game, and then the moves are alternate. The fox, by dodging from side to side, and retreating if necessary, tries to cause a gap through which he can slip. The best method of stopping the fox is for the geese to advance across the board in a straight line, making their moves always at the points farthest from the fox so that he is not near enough to take advantage of any temporary gap which a move may leave open.

A GAME PLAYED BY THE ROMANS

Latrunculi is the ancient form of draughts as played by the Romans, the earliest of which any details are known. It is played on only sixteen squares—a quarter of the ordinary draught board will serve. Each player has four men, and at the outset these are placed along his rear line. Every square of the board is used in play, and men move and take diagonally, as in the ordinary English game.

When a man reaches the back line of the opponent, he is crowned and has the power of moving backwards as well as forwards, as in the familiar modern game. Each piece, of course, because of the diagonal moving, is bound to remain on squares of one colour throughout the game.

This means that a stage may arrive in the game when each player has men left on the board, but they cannot take one another. In this case the player with more men left wins the game.

Kings is an interesting adaptation of the end game of ordinary draughts. It is in fact merely an end game without any opening or middle play preceding it.

Each player has four kings, which start from his rear line. They play the usual straightforward game, with all the customary powers and activities of kings, until one side wins.

There is considerable interest, too, in a game of kings with four players. Each person has only three kings. The players sit at the four sides of the board, with kings on the black squares of their rear lines. Then, as in four-handed draughts, each in turn makes his move, and the game proceeds along the usual lines of kings' play.

The four sets of pieces must be distinct either in colour or size.

CHAPTER 15

MUSIC FOR ALL

Iᴛ is best to study music as a child when your mind is retentive, your muscles supple, and you have plenty of time. But if you did not, or if you have forgotten much of what you learned, there is no reason why you should not start as an adult.

You may choose to take up one of the standard instruments, like the piano or violin, and, if you do, everything is straightforward, for teachers are readily available. But you must then be prepared for years of regular study and practice: there are no short cuts to good performance. On the other hand, you may decide that you cannot spare so much time and money. Well, that is no reason why you should not acquire musical ability. There are other and simpler instruments, which you may master with little or no tuition, and in quite a short time. In this chapter, therefore, the three most popular modern musical instruments are dealt with—the harmonica, the piano-accordion, and the ukulele. If you follow the instructions given here, you will learn how to play them well very quickly. To make things easier, a little elementary musical knowledge is given first of all, which will be equally necessary whichever instrument you take up. And at the end of the chapter is a section on "vamping," which will enable any one to accompany songs or tunes on the piano with ease, whether or not you can "play" the piano.

USE OF THE STAVE

Printed musical notes are placed on a sort of ladder, called a stave, so that you can see at a glance whether the note is high or low. Their positions have the names of the first seven letters of the alphabet—A, B, C, D, E, F, G. There are five lines in the stave on which notes can be written, and four spaces, and they are counted from the bottom upwards. This is shown in Fig. 1. The names of the notes on the stave depend on the clef which is marked at the beginning of the stave lines. There are two common clefs—treble and bass (Fig. 2). Long ago there was only one "grand stave"

Fig. 1   and Bass   *Fig. 2*

Fig. 3. The obsolete grand stave.

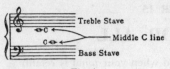

Fig. 4.

(Fig. 3) consisting of eleven lines, but it was found rather difficult to distinguish readily between some of the middle notes, so that the middle line, whose note was C, was taken out, and the top five and lower five lines pushed a little apart for convenient reading and writing of notes. Then the names treble and bass were given to the two new staves—and thus we have them today, the top stave being the treble and the bottom the bass. These are fastened together by a brace. If the missing C line is required for any note it is written in just for that note only, above the bass stave or below the treble one as

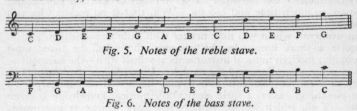

Fig. 5. *Notes of the treble stave.*

Fig. 6. *Notes of the bass stave.*

required. The two C's shown in Fig. 4 are, therefore, the same note. Fig. 5 shows the names of the notes of the treble stave. Fig. 6 shows the note of the bass stave. Of course, not all instruments require both staves. If you are learning the harmonica you need only be concerned about the treble. A violinist plays only from the treble, too, but a pianist plays the treble with the right hand and the bass with the left. When other notes are needed, outside the range of the stave, little additional lines are put in, which count just like the long stave lines. Figs. 7, 8, 9 and 10 show ledger lines. In Fig. 8 we see the lines below the treble stave. These notes, of course, could equally well be written on the bass stave, for the A would be the top line of this stave. They are only written like this for clarity. Fig. 10 shows ledger

Fig. 7.

Fig. 8.

Fig. 9.

Fig. 10.

Fig. 11. *Notes and rests.*

lines above the bass stave. These, of course, could equally well be written on the treble stave, for the E would be the bottom line of this stave. Fig. 11 shows six different kinds of notes, and six corresponding rests of equal time duration. Here they are : a dot after a note (or rest) makes it half as long again as in Fig. 12.

Upright bar lines divide music into equal time sections, rather as the inch marks on a ruler divide the ruler up equally. And as the inch may be split into any number of smaller divisions, so equal bars may contain varied numbers of notes and rests, though the total contents of the bars will be the same. Double bar lines divide music into longer sections or " movements." Both the single and the double bar lines are shown in Fig. 13.

MEANING OF THE TIME SIGNATURE

At the beginning of a piece of music, a " time signature " is written. This shows the time value of each bar. Various time signatures are shown in Figs. 14 to 19. Fig. 14 means common time, with one semibreve or its equivalent to a bar. Fig. 15 means two quarter notes, or crotchets, to a bar. Fig. 16 means three quarter notes, or crotchets, to a bar. Fig. 17 means six eighth notes, or quavers, to a bar. Fig. 18, nine quavers to a bar, and Fig. 19,

A dotted Semibreve		equals 3 Minims	
A dotted Minim		equals 3 Crotchets	
A dotted Crotchet		equals 3 Quavers	
A dotted Quaver		equals 3 Semiquavers	
A dotted Semiquaver		equals 3 Demisemiquavers	

Fig. 12.

Fig. 13.

Fig. 14.   *Fig.* 15.   *Fig.* 16.   *Fig.* 17.   *Fig.* 18.   *Fig.* 19.

twelve quavers to a bar. Before examining these it is helpful to remember that a semibreve is a whole note; a minim is a half note, so that two minims equal one semibreve; a crotchet is a quarter note; a quaver is an eighth note.

A sharp (♯) makes a note one half-tone higher; a flat (♭), one half-tone lower; a natural (♮) restores a note to its original position.

KEY SIGNATURE AND EXPRESSION

The key signature is an indication at the beginning of a piece of music telling whether notes have to be played sharp or flat throughout a piece of music. Fig. 20 shows examples of this. Two or four dots indicate that a section of music is to be repeated, as in Fig. 21.

Fig. 20.   *Examples of key signatures.*   *Fig.* 21.

The expression to be given to a piece of music is generally indicated by Italian words, or just by letters. Here are some of the commonest:

p., soft.   *pp.*, very soft.
f., loud.   *ff.*, very loud.
Cresc., or *crescendo*, gradually louder.
Dim., or *diminuendo*, gradually softer.
Allegro, lively, quick.
Andante, moderate speed.
Lento, slow.

HOW TO PLAY THE HARMONICA

After this general introduction, we come to the harmonica. This is one of the simplest instruments to learn. Certainly it has become enormously popular. The harmonica is, of course, the modern mouth organ.

The harmonica has outstanding advantages. It is cheap—just a shilling or two; it is easy to learn; pleasing results may be obtained in just an hour or two; it is easy to carry about; it is equally suitable for playing by oneself or for band work. When buying your instrument ask for a " key G."

On beginning to play, the first and chief thing to be learned is the production of single notes. In the old style mouth organ you simply pushed the instrument between your lips and blew, or drew, a mouthful of notes. But that group of four or more notes is of no use in modern playing, neither must there be, at any rate until high proficiency is gained, any of that peculiar vamping which mouth organists often did. There must be one perfectly clear note at a time.

The best way to play the modern harmonica is shown in Fig. 22. Hold the instrument between your lips, gripping it with the thumb and forefinger of the left hand. The right hand is then cupped across the back of the harmonica, lying up against the underside of the left hand. When the lips are closed over the harmonica push your tongue forward against the front edge of the instrument and so stop the three holes on the left. That will allow air to pass only through the hole on the right—which is what you want. Half an hour of practice will give you the knack quite safely, so that you can play a single clear note on any part of the instrument.

Next learn to play the scale, the ladder or series of eight sounds, which most children learn at school as *doh, ray, me, fah, soh, lah, te, doh.* As you should have a G instrument, it will be the scale of G (all the ladder or light notes beginning and ending on G). There is one important point to remember which will simplify all your playing.

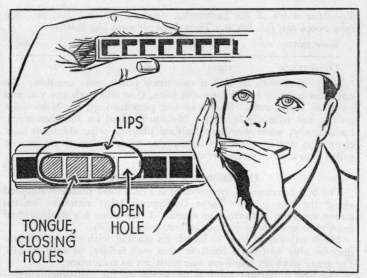

LIPS

OPEN HOLE

TONGUE, CLOSING HOLES

Fig. 22. How to play the harmonica.

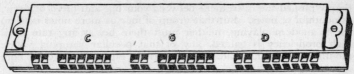

Fig. 23a.   *Outside view of the vineta.*

Key G VINETA

	KEY NOTE	MAJOR CHORD	KEY NOTE	MAJOR CHORD	KEY NOTE	MAJOR CHORD
BLOW	C	c	G	g	D	d
DRAW	G	g	D	d	A	a
	KEY NOTE	DOMINANT 7th CHORD	KEY NOTE	DOMINANT 7th CHORD	KEY NOTE	DOMINANT 7th CHORD

Key C VINETA

	KEY NOTE	MAJOR CHORD	KEY NOTE	MAJOR CHORD	KEY NOTE	MAJOR CHORD
BLOW	F	f	C	c	G	g
DRAW	C	c	G	g	D	d
	KEY NOTE	DOMINANT 7th CHORD	KEY NOTE	DOMINANT 7th CHORD	KEY NOTE	DOMINANT 7th CHORD

Fig. 23b.   *Sectional view of two types of vineta.*

The *blow* notes of the harmonica produce *doh, me, soh, doh*; the *draw* notes, *ray, fah, lah, te.* Thus the scale runs like this:—

Blow notes	*doh*		*me*		*soh*		*doh*
Draw notes		*ray*		*fah*		*lah* *te*	

Notice that with *lah* and *te* two draw notes come together. Do not blow hard or try to force the tone, that will both tire you and spoil the instrument. Breath should pass through the holes quite gently, and with the lips dry. Moisture is bad for the harmonica. Incidentally, when you have finished playing, wipe the front edge clean and dry and put the instrument away either in its case or rolled into a clean handkerchief.

CHOOSING A HARMONICA

The best harmonicas, irrespective of price, have numbers stamped along the top plate. These correspond with numbers written above the notes in harmonica music. Draw notes are distinguished from blow notes by being put in brackets, thus (8).

Much enjoyment is to be had from playing with others, and you may be able to form a band in your own family, or with friends. For more than six members one must act as conductor.

The first important thing is to decide on the instrumentation— that is, how many instruments of each sort your band shall have.

There are four types, roughly equal to the four parts of ordinary harmony—treble, alto, tenor, bass. But the names are different. A *tremolo* tuning harmonica plays the treble part; an *organ* tuning the alto; an *alto* tuning the tenor;

G g G g	D d
	D d

Fig. 24. Two bars of vineta music.

a *vineta* accompanying harmonica plays the bass. Remember that the top part, or melody, needs to be strongest, and the bass to be next strongest. The middle parts together should be about equal to the top part. Thus if you have seven players, there should be three tremolos, one organ, one alto, two vinetas. With fourteen band members, have five tremolos, three organs, two altos, four vinetas, and you may later add a fifteenth person with a set of drums.

PLAYING THE VINETA

The vineta (Fig. 23) is unlike ordinary harmonicas. The player does not need to use his tongue as do others, for the spaces on his instrument are much wider, and often he is playing full chords of four notes. Incidentally, as the vineta cannot play a tune and is consequently less interesting than the harmonica, it is a good plan to let the vineta band member learn the harmonica as well. For the vineta there is a special notation, or method of writing notes, which is quite easy. Instead of notes written on a stave, or harmonica numbers, there are capital or small letters written above or below a straight horizontal line, as in Fig. 24. Notes or chords above the line are blow notes in the top row of holes; those under the line are quadruple.

In duple, or two-time, the beating is—down; up. In triple, or three-time, it is—down; to the right; up. In quadruple, or four-time, it is—down; short stroke to the left; long stroke to the right; up. The beats for these times are all shown quite clearly in Fig. 25.

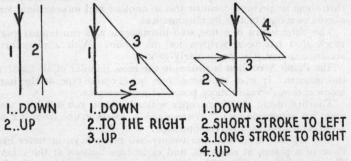

Fig. 25.   *The principles of conducting a harmonica band; for two-time (left), for three-time (middle) and for four-time (right).*

The conductor can use his right hand with outstretched fingers, or can hold a slim little stick—nowadays " batons " are not so heavy and big as they used to be. The left hand can be used for controlling expression—" lifting " out more tone, repressing, indicating particular players, and so on.

Band players must learn to see their music and the conductor's beat as well. In early stages you may be propping your books up on a table, or holding them on your knees. But it is best to have proper music stands, one between two players. You will, of course, sit for playing, usually.

Harmonicas and vinetas are ideal instruments for duets, trios, quartets.

The chromonica is a harmonica which can play in any key, that is, it can play any of the notes which are missed out of the ordinary harmonica. The ordinary harmonica is restricted to the notes of one key, or scale—G or C, whichever pitch it happens to be—and no " accidentals," that is, notes not belonging to the scale, can be played on it. This, of course, restricts the harmonica to comparatively simple music, though it makes the instrument remarkably easy.

ADVANTAGES OF THE CHROMONICA

But in the chromatic harmonica, or chromonica, all the half notes omitted from the ordinary harmonica can be played. These notes are generally marked by a sharp ($\sharp$) or flat ($\flat$). The sharp raises the note against which it is written by a half note or half tone; a flat lowers it a half tone. The tongue is used as in ordinary playing, so that single notes are sounded. If you play any single note, then press in the slide at the end of the instrument, the hole which has been sounding is closed and another is uncovered whose note is a semitone higher. In band work it is often convenient to have the main part of a piece of music taken by harmonicas, and then some single movement or trio in another and inconvenient key played as a duet or trio by chromonicas.

The chromonica is a fine solo instrument, and can readily play much that has been written for the violin. With a pianoforte accompaniment it is particularly good.

The Piano Accordion is probably the most popular of all modern instruments. It is of the same tone quality and type as the harmonica, though vastly more powerful and complex.

The first thing the shopkeeper will ask, when you tell him you want an accordion, is : " What size? " Prices range from £2 to £100, and sizes vary correspondingly.

The smallest accordion has twenty-two piano keys, or notes like those of a piano, at one end, and eight bass buttons at the other. The price is from £2 to £4. With this instrument you have, in the treble or piano end, only one complete octave—that is, the eight notes *doh* to *doh*—besides the black notes, which are sharps and flats, and a few notes above the octave. At the opposite, or bass, end there are eight buttons, in two rows of four. One set of four gives deep single notes, and the other four give chords, or harmonious groups of notes.

Naturally the instrument is restricted, though there are albums of simple music specially written for it. It is suitable for the beginner. You should, however, have some understanding of the larger accordions, even though you do not buy one at the outset.

BUYING AN ACCORDION

The next common size has twenty-five piano keys and twelve bass buttons—six single notes and six chords. Or you can get a " twenty-four bass," with the same twenty-five piano keys. These twenty-four buttons are in three rows of eight—eight single notes, eight major, or bright-sounding, chords, and eight minor, or sad-sounding, chords. This instrument gives you a really wide scope.

The bigger piano-accordions go on—the price rising with the size, of course—forty-eight bass with thirty-four piano keys; eighty bass with thirty-four keys; hundred and twenty bass with forty-one keys; hundred and forty bass with forty-one piano keys. Prices of the last go up to £100. In the large instruments there may be one or more " couplers," which " couple " additional notes or chords to those being played by the fingers.

When buying an accordion, having decided how much you can spend and so roughly what size it will have to be, do not be misled into purchasing a big instrument for little money. It is far better to get one that you have seen well advertised, and preferably one with a guarantee. The large, cheap instrument, however well it may be advertised, is always extravagant in the long run.

SIGNS OF A GOOD INSTRUMENT

Here are some of the chief points to look for when selecting an accordion :—

1. *Good air-tight bellows and treble pallets.* Pallets are the pads which cover the holes connected with the notes at the treble end of the instrument, allowing the air to pass through or checking it. Punctured bellows or badly fitting pallets result in whistling or wheezing sounds. To test, draw the bellows out and then push them together without pressing any note or button. If the resisting pressure is strong then you have a well-made instrument. While making this test you must not, of course, press the air vent (the extra button that allows all air to escape quickly without sounding any note). This vent is used when you want to pack up the instrument, with bellows tightly closed together.

2. *Easy action.* To test this run your fingers over the notes and

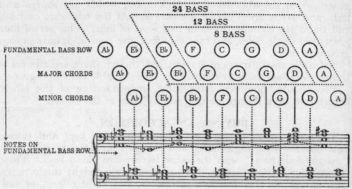

Fig. 26. *The button side of the* 8, 12, *and* 24 *bass accordion.*

buttons and make sure that none of them stick—if they do, the instrument is faulty. Sometimes a key or button will go down and stay there until you touch or jar it again. Don't buy such an instrument, or be misled into thinking it is just a trifle, caused by atmospheric conditions.

3. *Good tone.* Make sure that every note and chord is true, and does not quiver or wheeze. Buy an accordion with a clean, crisp, sweet tone, and don't think that because you have heard a brilliant player use an instrument with an unusual vibrating tone that you must get a similar special one, too. You wouldn't enjoy playing it if you did, and the sound in time would become most irritating to you. Ordinary plain, good quality tone is what you need.

4. *Finish.* Flash and glitter very often hide a multitude of faults. An accordion which is well finished within and has really first-class workmanship is usually found in a very simple case.

So take care over these four points and you will get an instrument which will give satisfaction and repay you in good performance.

KEEPING IT IN GOOD CONDITION

If you buy a second-hand accordion, remember to take even more care, and test the instrument thoroughly. Good used instruments can usually be had at about two-thirds of the original retail price.

The care of the accordion can be dealt with very briefly:—

Don't leave your accordion in a damp place; don't let it get too near a fire; don't forget to put it away in its case when you have finished playing; don't forget to lock it in the case, otherwise it may tumble out and get damaged.

Don't meddle if anything goes wrong with your instrument.

Take it straight back to the music dealer. The accordion is a very delicate instrument, and only experts are capable of dealing with it.

Don't pick the accordion up by the shoulder straps or keyboard. Always take it up by the body, or that part nearest to the bellows. The bellows, of course, is all that middle part of the instrument which closes and opens to draw air in or force it out.

It will be helpful now to explain the lay-out of the accordion— what are the various notes which can be played. In Fig. 26 the button side of the instrument is shown, not only of the eight bass but of the twelve and twenty-four bass, too.

LAY-OUT OF THE KEYBOARD

You will see that the eight buttons of the smallest instrument are also contained in the larger accordions. Even if you have the larger instrument, it will still be best for you to practise first with these simplest and most important eight buttons. So we will begin by talking only of these; all the other notes and words of the diagram will be explained later, when they are needed.

The top buttons are called the fundamental bass row—these are single notes, quite low, as will be seen on the bass stave where their positions are marked. A fundamental bass is a sort of root note above which the harmony is built up. The second row of buttons are major chords—a major chord consists of the first, third and fifth notes of the scale—*doh, me, soh*—or, if by this time you know the other names of the simplest scale, which begins on C, then the major chord notes are C, E, G. By studying the diagram closely you will soon get a fair idea of the notes which belong to the various buttons.

Now look at the treble end of the instrument, which is played by the right hand. It is just like a piano keyboard (Fig. 27), though

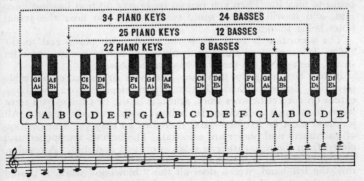

Fig. 27. The piano keyboard of the 8, 12, and 24 bass accordion.

the notes are slightly smaller. If you are already something of a pianist it will be all quite straightforward for you, and even if you are not, it can soon be understood.

You will find that if you start on the note at the extreme left of the keyboard, which is marked C in the eight-bass section of the diagram, and play up all the white notes in turn, you will be sounding the ordinary scale—*doh, ray, me, fah*, and so on. This easiest scale begins therefore on C, and has no sharps or flats in it, for it does not require any of the black notes. From C to D is said to be a full tone, or a whole tone, and the black note is half-way between them—a half tone above C and a half tone below D. This black note can therefore be called C sharp, or D flat. Every black note has two possible names like that. And as between E and F, and B and C there is only a half tone, for there is no black note separating them, you will see that in one whole octave there are always twelve half notes or semitones. Count up twelve from any letter you like, and you will find that you arrive again at the same note—one octave higher. Notice, too, that in the scale of C, as in every other scale, there are semitones between the third and fourth and the seventh and eighth notes.

Try now reckoning up a scale beginning on G, and you will find that the third and fourth come all right on the white keys—B and C, with the semitone between them. But in order to get the second semitone between the seventh and eighth notes you have to play a black note, F sharp, instead of the white F key. Therefore the scale, or key, of G is said to contain one sharp.

HOW TO HOLD AN ACCORDION

But all that has been rather a lot of theory, which you may not understand fully merely by reading. So get your accordion, and begin to play it. Then you can go back over all that has just been said, and it will become quite clear, when you hear the actual notes being sounded.

The accordion is held across the chest, with piano end to the right. It is supported and kept firmly in position by the two shoulder straps, through which the arms have to be passed.

Before beginning to play, see that you are in a comfortable position. Expressive and effective playing depends to a very large extent on correct bellows work, and one of the first things you must learn is to open and close the bellows with a steady action. All jerkiness must be avoided—and therefore an easy yet firm position of instrument and player are essential. The bellows are opened and closed from the top, rather as a fan is opened and shut. A regular, steady, motion of pulling and pushing is required. In order to get this, the left hand, which does all the " blowing " work, is passed under the strap at the bass or left end of the instrument. It must

THE 24 BASS INSTRUMENT

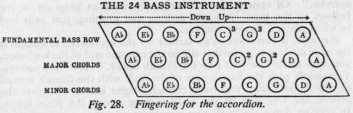

Fig. 28. *Fingering for the accordion.*

go under just far enough to enable the fingers to reach the buttons, and thus the back of the hand will be pulling against the strap when the accordion is opening, and the bottom edge of the palm will push against the end of the accordion when it is closing.

Incidentally, when referring to particular fingers playing particular notes we shall use 1, 2, 3, 4, 5. 1 will be the thumb; 2 the next, or index, finger; 3, the middle finger; 4, its neighbour farthest from the thumb; 5, the little finger.

FINGERING THE BUTTONS

When your left hand is properly placed, the 3 should be able to rest lightly on the fundamental bass buttons and 2 on the major chord buttons. You may practise playing each single bass note followed by its corresponding chord of the same name. These two are generally spoken of as being in the " oblique line "—that is easy enough to understand, especially if you look at the first diagram with its three rows of buttons, for you will then see that each lettered note has three buttons, in an oblique row. Fig. 28 shows the fingering of your two rows of buttons, with the third row put in also for future reference.

Now for a little bass practice. Count one, two, three slowly. On the one play the fundamental C; on the two, the C chord; on three, repeat the C chord. Repeat this a little quicker, emphasizing the first note, and you will have a pleasant one, two, three rhythm, known as three-four or waltz time.

Then do the same on the G oblique row—bass once; chord twice, and return to the C row. This is a very useful " vamp," or simple accompaniment, which can be utilized a great deal by those who do not aspire to high technical skill, but wish just to amuse themselves and their friends.

It is now time to begin right-hand work. You will already have found that the lowest notes of the keyboard end of your accordion are those nearest your chin. If you press down the end key, which is C, with your right thumb, which we call 1, then 2 can play D, 3 take E, 4 the F, and 5 the G. Play those notes up, and back again, with those fingers—and you will be doing a simple " five-finger exercise." Of course, the left hand will need to keep air in the bellows all the time, by gentle pulling and pushing, just as it had to when playing its own buttons.

But now, if you want to go farther up the keyboard, to complete the scale of C, or to go farther still to the extreme end of the keyboard, you must learn how to " pass the thumb under." It is easy enough. You simply play the fourth note of the scale with the thumb instead of with 4, and then you have enough fingers left to complete the octave, the top note of the scale coming under the little finger. In coming down the scale you simply reverse the process, passing the middle finger over when the thumb has played its note. Thus:

Up the scale.

Notes	C	D	E	F	G	A	B	C
Fingers	1	2	3	1	2	3	4	5

Down the scale.

Notes	C	B	A	G	F	E	D	C
Fingers	5	4	3	2	1	3	2	1

Supposing you wish to go up beyond the single octave, you merely cross under the thumb at the top, playing the top C with it, instead of with the little finger, and so you are ready to go on from the same thumb start on C that you had at the beginning of the first octave.

At this stage you will probably begin to pick out a few melodies with the right hand, playing them " by ear." That is quite a good plan, and you may do as much as you like of it, but you had better get a book of simple accordion music as well, if you are really ambitious, for playing by ear cannot take you very far. But there is still a great deal to be explained here.

KEYS AND KEY SIGNATURES

Let us retrace our steps a little, and do more work with the left hand. In addition to the C and G buttons, you should now move on similarly to the F fundamental and the F major chords. This is to the left of the C, and is said to be *below* it; just as G, on the right of C, is *above* it. If, by the way, you try a scale beginning on F, you will find it necessary to put in one flat, substituting B flat for the white note B in order to make the semitone come properly between the third and fourth notes of the key. And here is a convenient time to explain more about that.

The bass buttons C, of course, fit in chiefly with music in the key of C. When music is " in one sharp," that is " in the key of G," having a sharp written at the beginning of every line, then naturally the G buttons are most used. In the same way, some music is " in one flat," and then the F buttons are specially required.

But music can be in other keys—two sharps, three sharps, four sharps, five sharps, six sharps; and, similarly, two flats, and so on. If you refer back to Fig. 26 on page 276 you will see that on the

Fig. 29. *Button notes right and left of "C."*

right of the C button are buttons G, D, and A. These three belong to sharp keys. The scale or key of G has one sharp, as has already been explained; D has two sharps; A has three sharps. C is generally called an " open key," because it has neither sharps nor flats. On the left side of the C button are the various flat key notes, beginning with F which has one flat.

In Fig. 29, the button notes right and left of C are shown, with the proper number of sharps or flats belonging to their key (the key signature) written in.

Now for the further work at the button end. Play the F fundamental once and the chord twice, as you did with C and G. Next play these three chords and their fundamentals in the following order, listening carefully to the musical effect—C, F, G, C. Keep a good rhythm, accenting the first beat each time, thus—*one*, two, three; *one*, two, three; *one*, two, three; *one*, two, three. This succession of notes and chords is a very important and valuable musical " shape," or " form," and will be found to provide a proper accompaniment to all sorts of simple waltzes. It is a simple form of " vamping," about which you can read more at the end of this chapter.

You might like now to try a simple piece using both ends of the accordion. Fig. 30 is a straightforward waltz, which you should practice here.

It will be seen that the bass for each bar consists of a fundamental with the major chord of the same name.

Fig. 30. *A straightforward and simple waltz.*

Use the bellows smoothly. Avoid all jerkiness, at both ends of the instrument. Try to get a smooth, even tone, but with each first beat a trifle louder or more accented than the rest of the bar. You may count one, two, three to yourself at first, to keep the time regular.

If you also would like to try a piece " by ear," tackle " Way Down Upon the Swanee River," (Fig. 31), beginning on E at the treble end and with C at the bass. This is not in three-four time but in

Fig. 31. Outline of " Way Down Upon the Swanee River."

four-four. The same three bass notes and chords will serve, but the following rhythm will be necessary.

Our waltz rhythm, of course, is as follows (Fig. 32):—

Fig. 32. Simple waltz rhythm.

And here is "The Keel Row," for the twelve bass instrument, requiring the B flat button, which is the second on the flat side of the open C:—

THE KEEL ROW

In the twenty-four bass accordion, for which the next piece, " All Through the Night," is planned, there is the third row of buttons, consisting of minor chords. These are easy to understand. We have seen that the ordinary major chord is made up of the first, third and fifth notes of the scale. In the key of C it is C, E, G. But the minor chord has the third or middle note made flat. Instead of

E it would be E flat. If you play this minor chord at the treble end of your instrument, you will see how the "minor third" gives it the peculiar mournful sound. By this time you will be used to the fingering of the fundamentals and major chords—3 for the former, 2 for the latter. The third row of buttons are played also by 2, and in the printed music the letter *m* is usually placed against the name note of the chord. You will see this on the second beat of the second bar of the following piece of music, where, as the chord required is that of A minor, it is written A*m*.

HOW ACCORDION MUSIC IS WRITTEN

It will be noticed that the left-hand chords are written out in the customary musical manner, all the notes being put down. You will accordingly press the corresponding chord button, which will sound the three notes comprising the chord. The names of the chords are here written in, to make reading easy, but where chords are repeated no sign is placed until an alteration occurs. The one letter G, above the first two beats, obviously refers both to fundamental and chord. The basses are only marked where they do *not* correspond to the chord immediately following. Note, for instance, in the third bar of "Ye Banks and Braes," F and C; and also in "The Keel Row," seventh bar, F and C again.

ALL THROUGH THE NIGHT

Remember that, whatever the size of your instrument, it is important in the early stages to become thoroughly proficient first within the limited scope of smaller accordions, and you should play

YE BANKS AND BRAES

all the music you can find within the range of the eight, twelve, and twenty-four bass. There is plenty of music suitable for this type of accordion available.

But it will be well for us to consider larger accordions, too. The next move is to the forty-eight bass. This, being a larger instrument, gives a wider keyboard range, and an additional row of buttons (Fig. 33).

Compare this with that of the twenty-four bass and it will be seen that the range is not disturbed on the flat side of C, but we have now an addition of four oblique rows on the sharp side. On some makes of instruments there are only three rows on the sharp side and one extra on the flat side. The one big difference is that we have a row of counterbass.

48 BASS

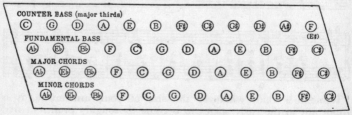

Fig. 33. *The wider keyboard in the forty-eight bass.*

These are single bass notes, like the fundamentals, and it will be seen that they are arranged in exactly the same order as the fundamental row—they are in " fifths," or at intervals of five notes apart. From C to G is a fifth, so is from G to D, and from D to A. But each counterbass is a " third " higher than the fundamental of the same oblique row. For instance, look at the C fundamental. The counterbass in the same oblique row is E, which is the third note of the C scale or a " third " above C (C, D, E). Test another. Counterbass A is the third note of the scale of F, and you will get similar evidence wherever you try.

This is a very convenient arrangement, because we do not always want to play fundamental notes with our chords. It gets monotonous.

Now the same policy can be adopted with the counterbasses, so that we can use at our discretion, for example, C fundamental or E counterbass with our C major chord. This applies to every oblique row. With D major chord can be used either the D fundamental or the F sharp counterbass. Note that the counterbass notes in the music are marked with a line below them. The A counterbass in the first bar of " The Girl I Left Behind Me " shows this quite clearly and simply.

THE GIRL I LEFT BEHIND ME

Note also that the finger which plays the fundamental button can also play the counterbass.

Play this simple tune through and you will readily see that these:

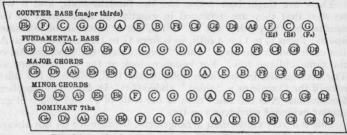

Fig. 34. The keyboard in the eighty bass instrument.

alternative basses, as they are sometimes called, add to the musical interest of the piece.

You should have gathered sufficient musical knowledge now to be able to put in a few counterbasses to your several tunes. At any rate, try to, because the effort will certainly add to your understanding and stimulate your interest, so that you will soon want to master something of even wider scope.

THE EIGHTY BASS INSTRUMENT

Next in size comes the eighty bass (Fig. 34), which you will see below has its bass extended, as well as a fifth row of buttons added.

The bass compass has added two more rows on the sharp side of C and two on the flat side, while the treble keyboard has increased from two and three-quarters to three octaves. This may not seem a great deal, but it actually means quite a lot, for much finger work is often carried out high up the keyboard while comparatively little is going on in the bass.

But the most valuable addition with this model is the inclusion of another chord—that of the dominant seventh, or seventh. To understand it in terms of treble notes, play with the right hand C, E, G and B flat, and you will find this to be the same as your C seventh on the new row of buttons.

It will help you at this stage to study the section at the end of this chapter on vamping, for there the dominant is dealt with in some detail.

The dominant seventh is a discord which always seems to need another chord to " clear up " or resolve the unsettling sound.

A good method of practising your seventh is to play the following, slowly at first:—

Fundamental C, together with the C seventh chord; then fundamental G with G seventh, and so on for four rows up from C; and similarly for four rows down from C, across the flat side buttons.

Afterwards play C fundamental, and strike the C seventh chord twice. This will give the three-four rhythm. Then play some very easy pieces, using the same bass when it seems to fit—" Swanee River," " Old Black Joe," and suchlike old favourites.

Be careful that the bass does not move about on many rows to begin with, the three illustration pieces already given can serve as your model in this respect. We will give suggestions for incorporating a few sevenths in the last piece, " All Through the Night," given on page 283.

The last chord in the third bar of this piece is D major. Make it D seventh. At its repetition in the seventh bar repeat the D seventh. In bar twelve change both D major chord to D seventh. Again in the last bar but one D seventh once more. Continually practise from row to row on this chord until you find it easy to play. The finger used will be generally the fourth finger on the fundamental row and second on the row of sevenths.

Again we can use our alternative bass with this chord, in the same way as has already been illustrated with regard to the major chords. Take C seventh as an example again—they are, by the way, marked C7. Play C fundamental with it, then, using the same fingers—namely 4, 2—play E counterbass with the same chord. Then, using the fingers 3, 2, play G fundamental with it, and you will see how interesting these varied bass buttons can make the same chord sound.

The alternative basses of the minor chord are more difficult than the major and seventh, hence they have been left till last. Now let us consider them.

Play the C minor chord (usually marked *Cm*) with the second finger and C fundamental with the third, then play E flat fundamental with the fifth finger while the second is still on the C minor chord. Next use the third finger on G, still playing the chord with

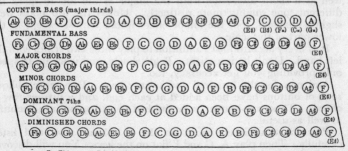

Fx This means F double sharp

Fig. 35. The elaborate keyboard of the 120 bass accordion.

the second, and here again we have the three positions of the C minor chord.

The use of the fifth finger being difficult at first, practise it well, very slowly, and in due course it will become as strong and supple as the others.

You will greatly benefit, as you proceed with your studies, by the practise of scales and *arpeggi*—an *arpeggio* is a sort of skeleton of a scale, consisting of the first, third, fifth notes of the key, and the octave at the top. It is, in fact, the notes of the major triad, plus the top octave of the keynote. Practise the scale and *arpeggio* in the key of the piece you propose to play, and the piece will " fall under the fingers " much more readily.

We now come to what is known as the " standard hundred and twenty bass " model. Fig. 35 shows how it has grown from the eighty bass.

MAJOR	{3	2	3	4	2	4	2	3
	{C	D	E	F	G	A	B	C
MINOR	{2	3	4	2	4	5	2	3
	{A	B	C	D	E	F	G♯	A

Fig. 36. *Fingering of C major and A minor scales.*

Fig. 37. *Fingering the chords.*

Before dealing with this it will be well to point out that scales can be practised with the left hand as well as the right, providing there are counterbass buttons, which means that it can be done with accordions which have at least a forty-eight bass.

Fig. 36 gives the fingering of the major and minor scale with the left hand. When practising it, have the bass chart at hand for reference. The fingering is the same wherever you commence. And the minor scale contains the distinctive " minor third " note as well as a slight alteration from the major at the top to mark the different tone quality more distinctly. Unless the top notes were slightly changed, too, the minor effect would be lost except in the lower part of the scale.

It is every accordionist's ambition to play those two scales with the left hand. Don't be impatient. Begin slowly, and work up to speed only providing you get accuracy, too.

And now for the hundred and twenty bass. Two more oblique rows of buttons have been added at each end, and a further row of chords. These are known as diminished sevenths, and are beautiful as well as useful.

Play the diminished chord on the C oblique row, and listen carefully. Then play A, C and E flat on the keys. You will discover that both these chords are the same. The interval A to E flat is a fifth. So all we have to do to make a seventh chord is to add F sharp.

This will be readily found on the counterbass row over D, the complete chord being shown in Fig. 37.

Practise these chords in various positions on the button board and you will see they are all the same in effect. The diminished chord is marked in accordion music *Cd* (in the C row), and you simply play the corresponding diminished button.

FINGERING A DIMINISHED CHORD

A well-known solo which contains this diminished chord is Rubenstein's " Melody in F," and it is not difficult to play. If you get a copy you will meet the chord in bar four. The fingering of the diminished chord is shown in Fig. 37.

Save for the diminished chords, the hundred and twenty bass is really an enlarged eighty bass, so the would-be player need have no misgivings that its size will give him any undue worries when practising on it.

The diminished seventh chord does not come very often, but you should be familiar with its use. With this chord, as with the whole of accordion playing, the more you explore them the more fascination and beauty you will discover.

The Ukulele is a pleasant little instrument, which is very popular for accompanying one's own singing and other melody instruments. It is very easily learned. In structure it is like most stringed instruments—a box-like body which gives resonance to the tone; a neck along which the strings are stretched and on which is the flat fingerboard where the notes are made by pressing down fingertips and so varying the vibrating lengths of the strings; a head in which are the pegs by which the strings can be tightened or slackened for tuning purposes. Across the fingerboard are thin metal bars or frets, behind which the fingertips have to press to make their notes.

The ukulele is tuned as shown in Fig. 38.

TUNING THE UKULELE

An unusual tuning can be obtained by setting the first string an octave lower, using a thicker string. This is shown in Fig. 39, but the former is preferable.

Quite often, however, you will see at the top of a piece of music the words " Tune to G, C, E, A," or " Tune uke to ——" some other notes, but you will see later in this chapter that this instruction does not matter if you use the shapes set out in the diagram of chord shapes (Fig. 40).

The first thing, then, is tuning the uke—the name is generally abbreviated thus. If you have not a piano available you will either have to buy a pitch pipe (which is like a panpipes and gives two sets of tunings) or else use the following method.

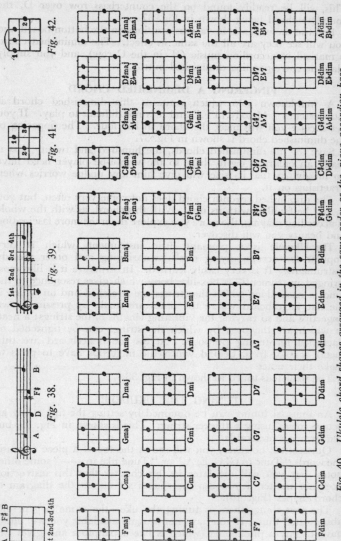

Fig. 40.   Ukulele chord shapes arranged in the same order as the piano accordion bass.

Tune the second string—that is, the second from the left as you face the instrument—until it is at about the third lowest note you can hum. Then press your finger on the same string, behind the fourth fret. Tune the third string to the resulting note. Then stop the third string on the third fret, the finger as usual just behind the metal bar, and you get the note for the first string. Lastly, stop the first string on the second fret and you will have the note for the fourth string.

Make sure that your uke is properly tuned before you start playing, or you will never get proper results. If playing with other instruments, you must tune in with them, getting them to sound their notes for your guidance.

Violin strings are better than uke strings if you want long and hard wear. You will need E strings for the first and fourth, and A strings for the second and third. If you prefer to buy the ordinary uke strings, you will find that coloured ones give best service.

HOW TO HOLD THE UKULELE

Hold the instrument right before trying to play. You should tuck the uke under the middle of your right forearm and hold it against your body, keeping the neck of the instrument between the thumb and first finger of the left hand. Get quite comfortable before you start, and make sure that when you are playing, the uke doesn't slip.

Begin by practising strumming. You should have a plectrum for this—a flat, small piece of metal or other substance which costs only a copper or two.

Take the plectrum and hold it lightly but firmly between the thumb and first finger of the right hand. Now stroke downwards across the strings, making sure that you sound all of them one after another. The whole movement should be from the wrist, not the elbow, and the hand should turn slightly away from you as you pass the plectrum across the fingerboard.

Then return the plectrum upwards, in the same manner, letting only its flat point set each string in vibration. If you push the plectrum through too far and make any up or down stroke too hard, then the movement will be clumsy and the tone bad.

You will notice that the down and up strokes give two " beats "— it is easy to count *one* for the down and *two* for the up movement. Practise this double beat. Afterwards reverse, beginning with the up stroke. Next play one up and two down beats, that gives three-four, or waltz, time. Now play one stroke up and three down, that is foxtrot, or four-four, time. Another version of this time is to make four down beats; or, alternatively, up, down, up, down. Remember to make each strum light.

But different chords are necessary before proper playing can be done, and for these you must learn the chord shapes. Fig. 40 shows a complete set of all the chords you will need.

These chords may look rather frightening at first, but actually they are easy to understand. The names of the various chords are not important, they are here merely for reference when your general musical knowledge has grown.

The four vertical lines represent the strings, the horizontal lines represent the frets (the metal strips across the neck).

The dot shows you where to put your fingers.

Let us take an easy shape and finger it (Fig. 41).

The second string is stopped with the first finger behind the second fret, the third string is stopped with the second finger behind the first fret, and the fourth string is stopped behind the second fret with the third finger.

Then there is the Barre, usually indicated as in Fig. 42.

This means that all the strings marked in this manner are stopped with *one* finger behind the same fret. Make sure that you press firmly on the string, otherwise it will not give the true note. Use only the tips of the fingers except when you use the Barre.

Now practise the chord shapes in Fig. 40.

And referring to Fig. 40, you will, of course, come across others not marked here when you are playing pieces in a different tuning to A, D, F sharp, B. But we give these shapes in order that when you find a piece not arranged for the uke but with accordion symbols, you can check up and write in your own shapes.

Now, we take it that you have more or less mastered the chord shapes and can strum in both three-four and four-four time. Let us, then, go one step further.

Fig. 43. " Swanee River " arranged for the ukulele.

Fig. 44. " The Ash Grove."

Here is the melody line of that ever-popular " Swanee River "
(Fig. 43). You know the tune. Follow the uke chords and either
hum or sing the words.

You will notice that this tune is in common or four-four time. So
you can choose any of the three ways of strumming. Practise this
until you can make the chord changes without having to stop and
think about it, thus losing time and rhythm. Now try this: " The
Ash Grove," in three-four time (Fig. 44).

That is really as much as you need to understand about the
ukulele. Just practise is required to make you proficient. And the
more you play the more enjoyment you will get.

VAMPING ON THE PIANO

Piano vamping—the fitting of a simple accompaniment to a
melody which is being played or sung—is often extremely useful.
The official accompanist has failed to put in an appearance, or an
impromptu musical evening has been decided on, and the player
who can judiciously apply his scant musical knowledge is sure of
warm appreciation.

It is not necessary to have an extensive knowledge of musical
theory and harmony in order to be able to vamp an accompaniment.
The chief asset is to be able to play the three essential chords of any
particular key with precision and facility. At first, just one or two
of the simpler keys will serve.

Incidentally, vamping comes naturally to some who have an
" ear " for harmony, without any conscious appreciation of the
nature of the chords or keys being used. But those who are not
thus gifted may cultivate it to a considerable extent by study and
practise.

Begin by playing slowly, and carefully examining, the ordinary
major scales in a few common keys—C, G and F, for example.
Notice how the general effect or character of the key is suggested
by the chord composed of the first, third, and fifth notes of it. In
the key of C this chord will consist of C, E, G. You can play this,

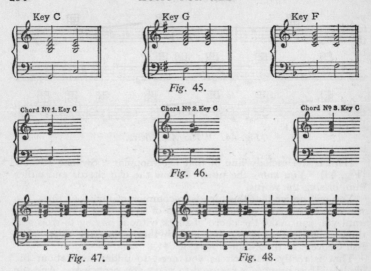

Fig. 45.

Fig. 46.

Fig. 47. Fig. 48.

right hand, with thumb, middle, and small fingers (1, 3, 5). This chord is called the common chord or major triad. Now try the dominant seventh chord. The dominant of any key is the fifth note; it is, therefore, G in the key of C. And the dominant seventh chord consists of the ordinary major triad on the dominant plus the seventh note—G, B, D, plus F, fingered 1, 2, 3, 5 in the right hand. Now, if you play this dominant seventh chord, which you remember is *in* the key of C though built *on* G, you will find that it sounds incomplete, like the first syllable of *A-men*, you simply have to sing the second syllable. So you simply have to play a finishing chord after the dominant seventh, and that final, satisfying chord will be the major triad of C.

PRACTISE THE DOMINANT SEVENTH CHORD

You should practise the dominant seventh chord followed by the major triad (common chord is its other name) in the three keys mentioned until you are quite familiar with them. These are shown in Fig. 45, with bass notes added for the left hand.

At first sight you may think that the second chord in each instance is not a major triad, but it is. The proper notes are there, although their order is slightly different. G, C, E, for instance, instead of C, E, G. But you can have the notes in any order or combination, and the effect is approximately the same. And in these instances when the dominant seventh is "resolved" into the major triad, you will notice that the top F of the dominant chord simply has to be followed by E in the next, it is so obviously right in sound. To put the G above would spoil it, that is why the G here is placed at the bottom.

Now, after this preliminary explanation and ear training, you will be ready for real vamping.

First of all, what are the chords used?

They are the chords just described, with the addition of a major triad on the fourth note of the scale; in the key of C it would be on F (F, A, C). Fig. 46 shows the chords. The chord of C; No. 2 the chord of G seventh; No. 3 the chord of F. They all belong to the key of C.

A tune in the key of C can be accompanied by those three chords. Before we give an example, it will be well to practise the chords a little first, so play slowly the exercises in Figs. 47 and 48, and get used to the sound of them.

IMPORTANCE OF INVERSIONS

You can now examine something that may have caught your attention in the illustration—the G seventh chord has its notes in a different order from that given in Fig. 45. But, as has already been explained, the order of notes does not greatly matter—these changed orders are called "inversions." This particular arrangement of the seventh chord, however, illustrates another very important point.

You will remember how in Fig. 45 the F was "resolved" on to E. Now there is an even more distinct "crying need." The B in the last chord but one simply can't help going up to C in the last chord. In fact, that B in the key of C (or the top note but one in any scale) is called the leading note because it leads so clearly to the key note. Play those final two chords over a few times and take particular notice of their top notes.

PLAYING A TUNE

For explanation of finger numbers marked in the diagrams, see the earlier section on accordion playing.

You can practise Figs. 47 and 48 also with left hand and right hand alternately, counting one, two, three, four—left, right, left, right.

If you do not want the labour of mastering the foregoing, you can purchase a vamping chart which should be fixed at the back of the piano keyboard and which indicates the notes to be played by the right hand in any key to correspond with the correct bass. But it is far better to give some study and so get genuine understanding of what has to be done.

You may try a familiar tune now: "Santa Lucia." This can

be accompanied quite satisfactorily by our three vamping chords.
Here it is:—

SANTA LUCIA

Get someone to sing or hum it, or to play the melody notes on the piano, above you.

If you have a copy of the tune, " Tramp, Tramp," try these three chords again, but this time with both hands together—a bar is given as illustration:—

Fig. 49.   Illustration bar of " Tramp, Tramp."

Of course, these chords can only accompany a tune in the key of C.   For a song in G our chords will appear thus:—

Fig. 50.   Chords for a song in G.

Practise a few pieces, like " Robin Adair," " Caller Herrin'," in G.   Returning to C again, try now to fit your own accompaniment to " Old Folks at Home."   The melody is given, and by this time your ear should tell you which chords are needed.   Notice that the left-hand bass notes always come on the accented beats of the bars—

OLD FOLKS AT HOME

the first and third beats in common or four time, and the first beat in waltz or three time. The note of the melody, which falls on the accented beat, often plainly suggests the accompanying bass and its chord, because it is a note of that chord, but the practised vamper can judge by the sound which of his three chords is required.

Continue on these lines in the keys of C, G, and F, choosing tunes with not much movement at first, and then going on to more lively ones. Careful practise will give surprising results.

When you are safe with these easiest keys, work out the corresponding " vamping phrases " in other keys, too. Vamping, by the way, can readily be done on the piano accordion, and if you happen to be an accordionist, piano vamping will help you to play your accordion very much better than you otherwise would.

CHAPTER 16

GARDEN GAMES

WHATEVER the size of your garden or lawn there are some games that will suit it. There are tennis games for courts no more than a quarter of tennis size; there are games in which you can improvise equipment and adapt rules to suit circumstances; there are even games which can be played along a garden path, or against the end of a house. Let us begin with those games which require only a few players.

Of these **Ring Tennis** is probably the most popular. Two or four players take part. A rubber ring is used instead of a ball, and as the ring does not bounce, or roll far, surrounding nets are unnecessary.

A central net is needed, however. It should be five feet high, but its bottom edge need not reach the ground; if it is just a couple of feet deep, that is adequate. The court must be marked; the lines can be chalked on to your lawn, or you may use broad white tapes held down by staples pressed into the ground. You can buy full ring tennis equipment at any sports store, or get ring, net, and tapes separately.

The standard size for the court is forty feet by eighteen feet, laid out as shown in Fig. 1; if less space is available reduce the measurements proportionately, but it is essential that the three feet strip of " dead ground " be left on either side of the net.

The game consists of tossing the ring backwards and forwards over the net, using only a single hand for catching and throwing, and a point is lost whenever the ring touches the ground. Every throw must be in an upward direction—a sort of underarm bowling

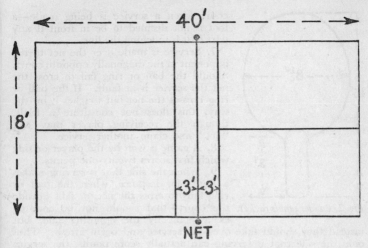

Fig. 1. Lay-out of the court for Ring Tennis.

action is used, never an overhand throw. Services are taken from the back corners of the court. As there is no bouncing of the ring all play consists of " volleying "—the ring being returned instantly from the place where it has been caught. Feinting or carrying the ring about the court is not permitted.

Ring tennis has no official rules, but the following code meets with general acceptance. These rules may also be applied to practically all of the " net games " described in this chapter, with only slight modifications.

1. A *doubles* game has two players on each side of the net; a *singles* has one on each side.

2. When you are playing doubles the court is divided down the middle by a line making right and left halves, the singles court may or may not have the same line—this will depend on the width available and on personal preference.

3. The size of a doubles court should be forty feet by eighteen feet. For singles an equal length is desirable, with width of nine feet or twelve feet. There should be a three feet " dead " strip on either side of the net.

4. The right to choose ends is decided before the beginning of play by toss; the side which wins the toss taking the first service.

5. The service is delivered alternately from behind the right and left halves of the court, beginning always from the right.

6. The server's foot must not pass in front of the rear line of the

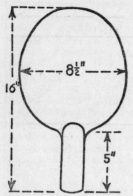

Fig. 2. Padder tennis racket.

court when a service is being made—a foot is not deemed to be in front if any part of it is touching the line.

7. Service is made over the net to the opponent in the diagonally opposite court. Should the ball or ring fail to cross the net the service is at fault. If the ball or ring crosses the net but touches it on the way, this does not constitute a fault, though the receiving player may call " let " and claim another service.

8. A game is won by the player or side which first scores twenty-one points.

9. When the side that is serving makes a fault—for instance, when the ball or ring fails to cross the net, or falls outside the court—that should not be counted as a point by the opposing side, but instead they should take over the service and begin afresh. Thus only the side that is serving can actually score points, the service simply changing over when they are at fault. To illustrate from ring tennis play: A wins the toss, and serves from the right-hand court. After some play B returns a throw which A fails to catch. B does not count a point, but instead takes the service, beginning from his own right-hand court. The play continues, and then B beats A once more with a fast ring. This time B counts one point, and continues with his service. If the next score is also his the counting will be two-love. But if after that B fails to catch a ring, letting it fall inside his court, the service goes back to A.

It will be seen that if the score is ten all, and A is serving, then B must score twice in order to reach eleven, while A need only score once.

This method eliminates the unfair advantage which one side would have if service were determined only by the toss and were retained throughout.

10. In a doubles game the same player takes all the services until the opposite side secures them, but when service comes back to the first side the other player will take it.

11. After each game the players should change ends.

12. The best of three games wins the *set*.

13. A run may be made before a service is delivered, and after the service players may take up any position they like within their court.

14. Feinting or baulking in any form is strictly forbidden in all play.

15. Stepping over the rear line when serving constitutes a fault,

and is counted as one service. Except in services the skimming of the net is of no account.

Padder Tennis is lawn tennis in miniature, played on a court half as long and half as wide as for ordinary tennis. The net's top edge must however be no more than two feet from the ground. Sponge rubber balls are used, instead of air-filled ones; and solid wood padders instead of gut-strung rackets. A padder is like a heavy table-tennis racket, sixteen inches long—it is easy to make your own from five-ply wood, with a couple of rounded pieces to thicken the handle. Fig. 2 shows the shape and proportions of the racket. Padder outfits can, of course, be bought.

The combination of solid padder, sponge rubber ball, and low net allows an ordinary tennis game to be played. Every stroke, forehand and backhand, can be played with the usual vigour—and yet the quarter-size court is adequate. The scoring, rules, and marking of lawn tennis may be used, instead of the code on page 299. The dimensions and shape of the court are shown in Fig. 3.

Singles or doubles can be played.

It often happens that net games are impracticable in a narrow garden with low fences—one cannot always be recovering balls from over the fence, and it is not always possible to put up high nets all round. Ring tennis, as already pointed out, offers a happy solution to this problem, because the rubber ring seldom goes much outside the court, and never bounces. But an even safer game is tether badminton, or **Tether Shuttle.**

In this a heavy outdoor badminton shuttlecock is used, and it is actually tethered to the net by a length of thin string, so that if it does chance to go over the side of the court, and perhaps over a fence into your next-door neighbour's garden too, it can be hauled back.

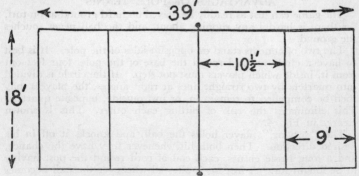

Fig. 3. How a Padder tennis court should be marked.

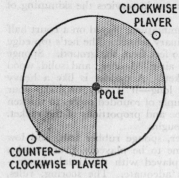

Fig. 4. Pole tennis court.

Use badminton rackets and a five feet net, and play as nearly as you can the usual badminton game. The string will be secured round the base of the shuttle and tied to the top edge of the net, at the centre. It should be long enough to reach easily to the corner of the court.

It will be found that the string does not hamper the shuttle as much as might be expected. More force is naturally needed in all strokes, and some care that the string does not become entangled with racket or player.

The excellent game of **Pole Tennis** is best played by two persons, though it is possible for four to join in. Each uses a tennis racket. The equipment can be bought—under a variety of names—or quite easily made. It consists of a pole fixed upright in the ground, and standing eight to ten feet high. From the top of this pole a cord hangs, to within two feet of the ground; and on the end of the cord is a tennis ball. This ball can be enclosed in a mesh of string, or if it is made of sponge rubber the cord can be threaded through it and knotted on the far side. A ring is painted round the post, six feet from the ground. The game consists in winding the cord round the post, above this mark, so that the ball comes to rest also above the mark. One player tries to wind the cord in a clockwise direction, and the other counter-clockwise.

ADVANTAGES OF POLE TENNIS

The game can just as readily be played on hard ground as on turf, for there is hardly any running about, and the ball never touches the ground.

The two opponents stand on opposite sides of the pole. It is best to have a circle marked round the base of the pole, four feet out from it, inside which players must not step. If the circle is divided into quarters by two straight lines at right angles, the players may then be compelled to remain in, or just outside, opposite quarters. This eliminates the risk of hitting each other. This is shown clearly in Fig. 4.

The " serving " player holds the ball, and knocks it off in his desired direction. Then both hit whenever they have the chance, and a long tussle ensues, each coil of cord round the post having to be fought for. A free hit is allowed whenever the ball becomes entangled with the racket of an opponent, or when it touches the

post below the six feet mark; otherwise there is no pause until the game is finished.

Great hitting speed is needed for this game, because once the ball is circling in your direction the racket must actually overtake it in order to augment its velocity and help to keep it going as you desire.

Another tethered ball game is **Swingball.** You will have to make your equipment for this strenuous game—but it is simple, and the game is so enjoyable that you will be well repaid. Swingball needs no courts or net, nor any boundaries. It can be played on any open piece of ground.

First get a ten feet length of strong, supple cord—a good clothes line will do. At each end of this fasten a grip—a six-inch piece of broomhandle. On the cord a strong bone or metal ring must be threaded, which will slide along freely. Fasten to this ring a two feet length of lighter cord. And at the end of this cord secure a football, or other large ball (Fig. 5).

Two players take part, one at each end of the cord. The grip is held in the right hand, and players move about quite freely. It is the aim of each to make the ball touch the opponent. When that happens a point is scored, nine points constituting a game.

A good deal of skill is needed to control the ball effectively, making it rush towards the opposing player. You will learn the quick, snaky fling of the cord which sets the ball thus in motion; and you will also learn to check an oncoming rush by throwing the cord back so that a loop hinders the ball, or grounds it before it can get to you.

There is, of course, no halt or order in the game; both players keep hard at it all through, springing about freely in their endeavours to score points.

Incidentally, look to the fastenings of your outfit occasionally, for they have to withstand a good deal of strain.

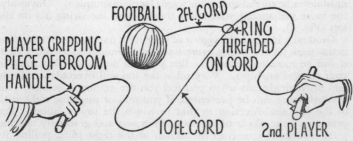

Fig. 5. Arrangement of ball and cord for Swingball.

Fig. 6. How to hold Diabolo sticks.

Diabolo is an ancient game which is always coming back into popularity, and there is never difficulty in buying the simple equipment of two sticks connected at their ends by a string, and the top, which consists of a double cone beneath the waist of which the string can pass.

First you must learn to get the top spinning, and balanced safely.

Place it on the ground, one end towards you, and pass the string under the slim waist. Hold the sticks out in front of you, horizontally, parallel with each other, and pointing away from you. They should not be more than a couple of inches apart. Keep your elbows bent and close to your sides.

Now comes the important point—only the right stick must be moved. Most learners fail because they make an up and down sawing movement with both sticks—that is wrong. Keeping the left stick motionless, whip the right sharply up and down, putting the emphasis on the up movements. This will result in a right to left spinning action being imparted to the top. Take care to make the right stick pass quite close to the left all the time—they must never be spread widely outwards for plain spinning. Obviously, the more you spread your sticks the less grip the string has on the top (Fig. 6).

Gradually increase the vigour of your right hand upward whipping action until the top begins to emit a pleasant humming sound. Then it will be spinning properly. But you will not attain that stage in your earliest attempts. Very often the top will overbalance slowly and provokingly just when you feel you are getting it going. This overbalancing can be prevented, if you pull or push the right stick in the opposite direction to that in which the top is falling. For example, if the top is tilting away from you and gradually nearing a fall you must speed up the action of the right stick, pulling its string strongly towards you; the right string thus presses against

the near face of the top and pulls it over towards you. Once this principle is understood and practised, your top will hardly ever fall, and you will get it spinning up to proper strength with very little difficulty.

That is the first part of diabolo. When you become skilled in this, try throwing your top into the air, catching it again, or tossing it backwards and forwards with a companion.

It is best to have plenty of room when you try your first throws and catches—a field is a good place. When you have gained the knack it will be all right to do it in quite a small garden, but until then it is not easy to anticipate just how far and in which direction the top is likely to fly.

Get the top spinning strongly, then, with a sudden upward spreading of the arms which will cause the string to spread taut and straight at about the level of the head, fling the top into the air. Keep your

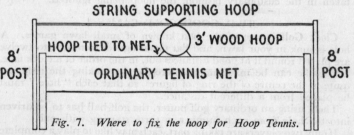

Fig. 7. Where to fix the hoop for Hoop Tennis.

sticks raised, and at full stretch until the top falls. As it descends see that the string comes under the top's waist, near the right stick. The left stick will be slightly lower, so that the top runs down towards it. Allow the string to sag as the top runs, and quickly bring the sticks into their original position so that the top is trapped and can be brought under control and whipped up to strong spinning again by rapid right-arm work.

With a friend equally skilled you will soon be able to toss the top between you. But, if you start the spinning, your friend will have to receive the top at the left-hand end of his stick, and do the whipping up with his left hand—for, of course, as he is facing you, the top will be spinning for him in the reverse direction.

An interesting variant of lawn tennis is **Hoop Tennis,** of use particularly where a lawn is not sufficiently large for the ordinary game. The hoop induces the players to hit less hard and so to keep the ball under better control and within more restricted bounds.

Have net, rackets and balls exactly as usual. But over the centre of the net suspend a wooden hoop of not more than three feet in

diameter—it can be hung from a cord running from side to side of
the court between two tall posts. In order to prevent the hoop
twisting, tie its lower edge to the net top at two places. This is
explained clearly in Fig. 7.

Play now goes on in normal tennis fashion, except that an extra
point is scored every time the ball is knocked through the hoop.
No player, however, must volley through the hoop from a distance
of closer than three yards. It is well to have a three yard mark
on the ground—otherwise a player can get close to the net and
volley back a ball just knocked through the hoop by an opponent.
Alternatively no score need be allowed for any ball volleyed through
—no line will then be necessary.

If you find, after some play, that clearing the hoop is too simple a
matter you can get a hoop of smaller size.

Singles or doubles can, of course, be played, and service will be
taken in the customary fashion, the hoop being ignored.

TWO GOOD GOLF GAMES

Clock Golf is one of the best known of small lawn games. A
hole is sunk in your lawn, and flat metal figures from one to twelve
are placed round it at good distances out, in the order of a clock face.
The game can be made more interesting by sinking the hole not
quite in the centre of the ring of figures, so that each " hole " must
be played from a different distance.

Then, using an ordinary golf putter, the golf ball has to be driven
into the hole from each number in turn, starting with one.

If only two players are taking part, each may like to play a complete
round in turn, keeping count of the number of strokes used to get
all the twelve holes. But if more than two are playing this method
involves rather a tedious wait, and it is better that each hole should
be played for in turn. Thus, instead of the player with perhaps
twenty-nine strokes winning against his opponent with thirty-four,
the winner may have won five holes against the next best player's
three.

Ladder Golf is a similar type of game, particularly suited to a
long narrow lawn. Though you can buy your clock golf equipment
at any sports store, you must make your own ladder, by marking
it on the lawn, as shown in the diagram. A good ladder should
have ten rungs, with four feet between each, and be only three feet

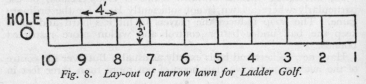

Fig. 8. Lay-out of narrow lawn for Ladder Golf.

wide. The hole—which may be a sunk tin or flowerpot, four inches across—should be beyond the farthest rung (Fig. 8).

You begin play by placing your ball on the first rung, and driving up the ladder towards the hole. The ball must be put into the hole in the fewest possible strokes. Then start from rung two, similarly. Continue until you have " holed " your ball from every rung in turn. Your opponent will then take his turn, and see if he can complete the ladder with a smaller total number of strokes than yours. If he succeeds he wins.

Every time the ball runs over the side of the ladder it must be replaced at the point where it went out, and the player adds one to his number of strokes.

As in clock golf, if more than two players are in the game it is best to let them all play each rung in turn, that person winning it who holes with fewest strokes. In the event of a tie a half-point should be counted by the equal players. Thus the final winner of the game may have scored four and a half rungs against his nearest opponent's four.

Croquet is a fascinating, though not a strenuous game. The official lawn court for the standard game is thirty-five yards by twenty-eight yards, though plenty of enjoyment may be had on quite a small lawn.

Having procured hoops, balls and mallets, lay out your court as nearly as possible on the lines shown in the diagram. The dotted lines indicate the path of the ball in making a full round. Buy the best equipment you can, and the nearest to standard size—miniature toy implements, and large hoops, are of no use.

Four balls are used, and they are coloured respectively blue, black, red and yellow. When only two players take part each plays with two balls—blue and black go together, and red and yellow. With four players the same two colours are taken by the two couples—for it will be a " doubles " game, with partners.

HOW TO PLAY CROQUET

Fig. 9 shows the two hoops down each side of the court, and one at each end of the middle avenue, with a post or stick at the centre. Each ball must finish its round by hitting this post.

Balls must be driven round so that they pass through all of the hoops twice, once in each direction. The four outside hoops are " scored " first, then hoops five and six down the middle. All the hoops are afterwards scored the reverse way, beginning from the second, which is then termed " one back." The original first hoop becomes " two back," and so on, until the original sixth which is now called the " penultimate " and the fifth which be-comes the " rover." That may all sound very complicated, but it will readily be understood by carefully following Fig. 9—whose

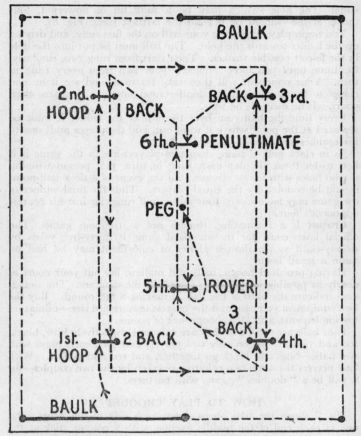

Fig. 9. Arrangement of a Croquet lawn.

dotted lines show the course of the balls through the hoops from the beginning to the end of a game.

Play is started from one of the " baulks," each ball being played in turn, according to the order of colours already given. When the ball goes through the first or any later hoop an additional stroke is gained. No player can proceed to the second hoop until he has got his ball through the first. This rule applies all round the court—every hoop must be taken in turn, and from the proper side.

Opponents, or opposing sides, play alternately, but as soon as all the balls are in play it is not necessary that the four colours shall go on in the same order, it being optional whether blue or black, or similarly whether red or yellow, is to play the " turn " of its side. The word " turn " in croquet means stroke or series of strokes. The game goes on until the winning pair of balls has been first to " score " the centre peg.

There is one important complication in the game, which gives most of its interest. A player, before " making " his hoop, or between any pair of hoops, may cause his own ball to strike either or each of the three other balls, in which case he is said to have made a " roquet." When this happens the player responsible at once picks up his ball and places it so that it is touching the ball which he " roqueted." This done he proceeds to " take croquet," by striking his own ball and causing both balls to move—little or much as he chooses. Following this he is allowed still another stroke, played in the ordinary way. The importance and value of "taking croquet " will readily be seen. It allows the player to do one of three things—to strike his own ball away, leaving the other almost undisturbed; or so to place his ball that by hitting it he drives both balls away together in the same direction; or to " split " them apart.

MAKING A BREAK

" Croquet " can be taken by a player from each ball once during his " turn," but he may not do the same a second time in the same " turn " unless he has meanwhile " run " a hoop. By a combination of taking croquet and running hoops several or all of the hoops can be " scored " by a player in one turn. This is called " making a break."

If a player roquets two balls simultaneously he may choose from which he will take croquet.

When a ball goes out of court it must be replaced in line with the spot where it went off, and one yard from the boundary. The player also loses the rest of his " turn," and play passes to his opponent. A ball is only reckoned through a hoop when no part of it protrudes on the playing side—you may test this by putting the mallet head or shaft across the hoop; if it touches the ball the ball is not through. When a player has got through every hoop and has only to " score " the post at the centre he is not compelled to do this immediately, for if he does he will be out of the game. Instead, he may prefer to stay in, helping his partner and hindering his opponents. It generally is best for both players to finish up together. A ball having only the middle peg to score is termed a " rover "—because it can rove where it likes, and generally does.

If you want to become a good croquet player you must put in plenty of practise, and study the technique of the game.

The manner in which you make your strokes is optional. You may stand with the mallet at your side, or with it between your spread feet. This latter method, with the legs wide apart, is favoured most by men. Women, because of their skirts, prefer the other. In either method you must stand squarely, facing the front.

For early practise drive your ball at another ball, or at the peg, from all sorts of distances and positions. Then go on to hoops. Make your ball run the hoop from a square position in front at first. Gradually move farther across to the side until you reach an angle when it is impossible to get through. As the angle of your stroke increases you will have to aim at the far " wire " or upright side of the hoop. In order to decide, when taking aim, if your ball can pass through from a sharp angle, divide the ball in your imagination into three equal parts. If two of these can be made to pass on the inner side of the wire, then the ball will go through—assuming that you aim correctly.

Acquire a smooth " follow through " of the mallet head.

Practise striking the ball with the upward as well as with the downward part of the swing—to get the smooth follow on or speedy stopping of your ball after it has struck the ball at which it is aimed. These shots are the equivalents of " top " and " bottom " in billiards.

Learn to make a " pilot ball " run ahead from the impact of your ball and come to rest at the far side of the hoop you are wanting to go through, your ball stopping on the near side. Thus, when with the succeeding stroke you get through, the pilot will be waiting conveniently for you to " take croquet " once more.

RULES OF GOLF CROQUET

A variant of this game is **Golf Croquet.** Ordinary croquet equipment is used for this, with the lay-out of hoops and post shown in the previous diagram. But instead of the full round being played in one continuous stretch each hoop is taken singly, like holes in golf. A point is awarded to the player or side that wins each hoop.

Begin the game in the usual way. As soon as the first hoop is scored the winner counts it to his credit and a new start is made. This start, however, does not necessitate any moving of the balls—they are played directly from wherever they happen to be.

" Roquets " are not allowed in the game, and strokes must be taken in proper rotation. One ball can, of course, knock against another, and deliberately help or hinder, but it does not as a result " take croquet." One stroke only is allowed to a player at a time.

As a matter of tactics a player may sometimes drive ahead in readiness for the next hoop when he sees he has no chance of winning the one at which he has been playing.

The games given so far have been for not more than four players. There are many garden games in which any number can take part.

In the game of **Tyre Target** ten or a dozen players can take part. The only equipment needed is an old motor tyre and half a dozen bean-bags or small balls. You are told how to make a bean-bag on page 123.

Teams should be placed as shown in Fig. 10. The bowling line down the middle is helpful, though not essential. A " bowler " from each team stands at the line ends, and the remainder of the teams form down the sides.

Suppose the A team bowler has the tyre. The rest of the team will have a bean-bag each. Their bowler then rolls the tyre down the middle of the avenue formed by all the players, and on the side of the bowling line farthest from his team. As soon as it passes in front of the players they toss their bean-bags through it—or try to. The team scores one point for each bag that goes through the tyre. If the tyre crosses the bowling line

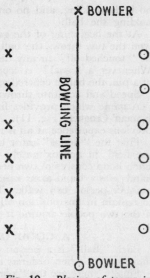

Fig. 10. *Placing of teams in Tyre Target.*

and doing so, approaches the throwers no more throws are allowed.

Then it is the other team's turn. The B bowler takes the tyre and sends it back up the middle, on the side of the line farthest from his team. They in their turn toss the bean-bags—which they will have picked up when they were thrown across by their opponents.

This is the end of one game, and that team wins which has got most bean-bags through the tyre. Then play proceeds without pause, the first bowler starting the second game. Nine games make a set.

Pin Ball is for a fairly large lawn, and for not fewer than eight players, divided into two teams. At each end of the " field " stands the pin—which may be an Indian club, a bottle, or just a stick. The object of each team is to knock over the pin of the opponents. A circle of three feet radius should, if possible, be marked round the pin, and within this ring no player is allowed to step.

Any large ball will serve. It must not be kicked or carried, but only bounced and thrown. Any player snatching up the ball can either throw it immediately to some other team member, or at the pin, or take it along himself, by bouncing it in front of him.

The ball may be snatched from an opponent, but there must be no body tackling, and no one can be touched at the instant he is holding the ball.

At the beginning of the game the leader of the team which has won the toss throws the ball into the air at the centre, and it can be " touched off " in any direction by any other player as it falls. Whenever a " goal " is scored afterwards, by the knocking over of a pin, the ball is centred afresh.

Speed and accurate throwing are the important qualities.

A game which provides little exercise, but plenty of laughter is **Human Croquet** (Fig. 11). A large number can take part, and no previous experience at all is required.

First the " hoops" must be placed in position—scattered about the field, in approximately the same fashion as for real croquet. Each hoop consists of two people who stand facing each other, with hands clasped and arms raised so as to make an arch under which another person can walk. It will not be necessary for the hoop to remain in this position all through the game; it is quite enough if the two people assume it whenever a player is wanting to pass.

A GOOD GAME FOR A PARTY

Each " ball " is a person who is blindfolded, and who does not move except when ordered to.

Finally, there are the " players," each in charge of a " ball."

As far as possible the game follows the style of ordinary croquet. Each player has one stroke in turn, and is allowed an additional one when his ball passes through a hoop or hits another ball.

To begin the play the first player gets his ball on to the starting line, standing behind him gripping his arms, and aims him at the first hoop—which of course the ball cannot see. Then the player says " Go," and the ball trots forward, until his owner calls " Stop." If the ball has passed through the hoop another " stroke " is allowed; if not, the second player makes his attempt.

Every ball must run in a straight line, and must promptly stop when ordered. When two balls collide the one that is struck stays where it is, but the other is given another " stroke," and ordered off afresh. No player may speak to his ball while it is in motion, except to stop it, nor touch or re-direct it in any way.

That player wins who first gets his ball through all the hoops, in their proper order, and back to the starting line, or to a post at the middle of the " court."

Interest and fun is added to the game if each player and his or her ball are made to wear some distinguishing colour—either ribbon or hat or rosette, so that couples are more obviously linked.

Hoops must never move from their stations, and must give no indication of their whereabouts to oncoming balls. When one game has been played the players and balls exchange roles.

Fig. 11. Playing Human Croquet, showing how two players link hands to form hoops. Other players, blindfolded, are balls.

In the game of **Robber Croquet,** played with ordinary croquet equipment, there is room for genuine croquet skill and for fun and laughable incident, too. It makes ideal amusement for a party of six or eight players. But every one needs to be quite honest.

Each player in turn is allowed one stroke, and a second when a hoop is successfully taken. Hoops should be placed in ordinary croquet fashion, as shown in Fig. 9.

All start together from the same line, but after that every player is free to go wherever he likes. When a ball is knocked through a hoop its owner counts one point, and any hoop can be taken at any time; there is even no objection to a ball being passed through the same hoop over and over again and a new point being counted each time.

The exciting novelty of the game however, lies in the fact that a player may at any time be robbed of his points, providing they have not reached a total of ten. It happens like this:—

PENALTIES FOR BAD LUCK

When a ball is made to hit another ball the attacker robs the other of whatever points he has scored, and adds them to his own score. But when any person scores ten those ten are " banked " and cannot be taken away. With the ten banked, points begin to be counted from one again—until another ten are safely collected and put away. Of course you may get your ten by robbing another person. Supposing, for example, you already have five points, won by running through five hoops, and then your ball hits that of another player who has nine points. You rob him of these nine, which added to yours give fourteen. Of these you " bank " ten, and have four remaining. If, at the next turn, some opponent, perhaps the one who has just been robbed, manages to hit your ball, he takes these four points from you.

The winner of the game is naturally he or she who collects the highest number of points.

You may find it helpful to have a scorer who writes down a record of every score made, and announces how players are faring.

For the game of **Lawn Billiards,** the " table " is a smooth piece of lawn about twelve yards by six yards. Special equipment of balls, cues, and pockets, can be procured from sports dealers— or you may improvise your own.

For lawn billiards, croquet balls are best and croquet hoops will do well for pockets. For cues you can have poles or broom-handles, to the end of each a ring or loop made of strong wire being attached. This loop must be flat, and acts as a sort of spoon on which the ball can be lifted in readiness for making a stroke.

The " pockets " should be at the centre of the table, instead of at the corners—for if they were in the more usual places the balls

would be constantly running
out of play and having to be
fetched back. But by having
them at the centre all play
is kept towards the middle
and balls rarely run out.
So, if you are using croquet
hoops, have them in square
formation, two facing the
ends of the tables and two
the sides.

The game begins, as in
real billiards, with the balls
at the bottom of the "table."
To play your ball you stand
behind it, thrusting the wire
loop forward. Do not use
too much force, and do not
lift the ball more than a
few inches above the ground,
if at all.

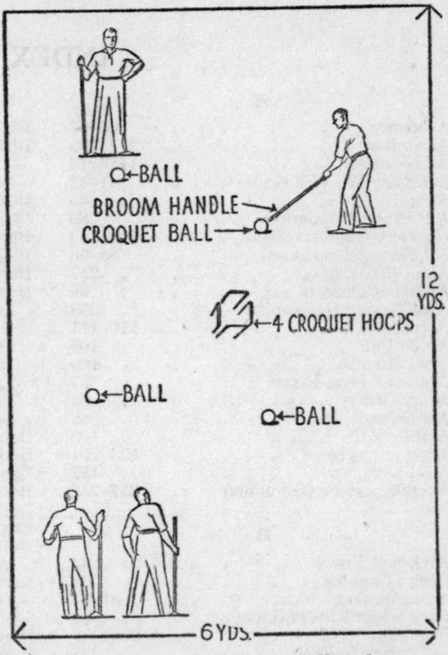

If you go into a " pocket "
you count one point, and
take another stroke. There
is one point also when you
" cannon," or hit two other

Fig. 12. Lay-out of Lawn Billiards court.

balls in succession from a single stroke. Should you " go in-off,"
by passing into a pocket after having first hit another ball, then
two points are scored.

As long as you are scoring your play continues, but when your
" break " comes to an end the next player begins his turn. Always
after a ball is " pocketed " it must be replaced at the bottom of
the " table " for the next stroke. When a ball runs off the field
of play it is replaced at the point where it ran out, and the break
is finished. No point however, is forfeited by this or any other
fault.

Two, four, or a still larger number of players can share in this
game, but most enjoyment results from keeping numbers low and
adhering as nearly as is practicable to the rules of ordinary
billiards (Fig. 12).

INDEX